The Story of Parliament

'The function of Parliament is to hold the executive to account. That is the role for which history has cast the Commons. It is the core task of Members. It is in Parliament in the first instance that Ministers must explain and justify their policies. This is the chief forum of the nation – today, tomorrow and, I hope, for ever.'

The Right Honourable Baroness Boothroyd PC
Speaker 1992 – 2000

By the same author

The King's Nurseries

THE STORY OF WESTMINSTER SCHOOL

Kingdom, Power and Glory

AN ILLUSTRATED GUIDE TO WESTMINSTER ABBEY

The Story
of
Parliament

in the
Palace of Westminster

JOHN FIELD

with new photographs by
MALCOLM CROWTHERS

James & James Publishers

First published in Great Britain 2002
by Politico's Publishing
8 Artillery Row, London, SW1P 1RZ

Telephone: 020 7931 0090
Email: publishing@politicos.co.uk
Website: http://www.politicos.co.uk/publishing

and

James & James (Publishers) Ltd
Gordon House Business Centre
6 Lissenden Gardens, London, NW5 1LX

ISBN 1-842750-31-3

Printed and bound by Butler & Tanner, Frome

Picture acknowledgements

Figures in bold type indicate colour plates.

The Art Archive / Honourable Society of the Inner Temple / Eileen Tweedy 47;
Bridgeman Art Library 37; Camera Press (IWM) 238; Malcolm Crowthers **1**, **2** (top), **3**
(bottom), **4**, **5**, **6–7**, **8**, **10**, **11**, **12**, **13**, **15** (top right, bottom left), **16**, 2, 124, 283; The
Fotomas Index (UK) 121; Hulton Archive 24, 116, 117, 136, 147, 178, 216, 229, 243, 245,
246, 260, 263, 268, 269, 273; Peter Jackson 6; Mary Evans Picture Library 51, 97, 118,
142, 144, 154, 167, 169, 203; Terry Moore **14**; National Portrait Gallery Picture Library
182; Palace of Westminster Collection **3** (top), 8, 31, 34, 36, 43, 68, 73, 83, 93, 107, 108,
129, 133, 153, 163, 183, 186, 200, 205, 213, 215, 219, 221, 225; Parliamentary Copyright,
Palace of Westminster Staff News (Deryc R. Sands, Editor) 39; Public Record Office
Image Library 161, 176, 241; The Royal Archives © HM Queen Elizabeth II / Mayall
221; Spink & Son Ltd., London, UK/Bridgeman Art Library **2** (bottom)

Foreword

For over nine hundred years the Palace of Westminster has been a centre of government. For over eight hundred of those years it has been witness to the long evolution of parliamentary democracy, as it struggled against autocratic monarchy and the power and privileges of the aristocracy. It is the focal point of the national story. Books of parliamentary history are numerous. But few combine the thorough and informative account with the lively and accessible narrative contained in this book. It is the story of Parliament and the great events of the nation as seen from inside the Lords and Commons. The reader will learn how these institutions were founded and how they have continued to evolve. In the process he or she cannot fail to be caught up in the drama, and sometimes the humour, of momentous episodes and the powerful personalities who have graced, and occasionally disgraced, the political stage. We warmly commend it, both to those who already know something about the subject, and to those who wish to acquaint themselves with the story.

Rt Hon Lord Irvine of Lairg QC
LORD CHANCELLOR

Rt Hon Michael J. Martin MP
SPEAKER OF
THE HOUSE OF COMMONS

Contents

List of Illustrations

List of Plates

Preface

'In this book I have only made up a bunch of other people's flowers, and of my own I have only provided the string that ties them together.' I am happy to enlist Montaigne both as describer and defender of the quixotic ambition of writing for the general reader an account both of the Palace of Westminster and the evolution of Parliament within it. It is an enterprise the professional historian might either shun or scorn. But the building and institution together have been central to the shaping of the national identity, and have been theatres of British political history, and it is desirable that their linked story is accessible in a narrative that strives for the highest standards of scholarly accuracy. And where that fails, as it must in a short account, I hope the reader will find some compensation in hearing the voices of history speaking for themselves.

Shortcomings are exclusively the responsibility of the author, and not of the many residents of the Palace of Westminster whose support, enthusiasm and patience have brought this project to completion. I wish to thank in particular Sir Nicolas Bevan, Speaker's Secretary, Dorian Gerhold, Clerk of the European Scrutiny Committee, Dominic Grieve MP, Malcolm Hay, Curator of Works of Art, Alan Howarth MP, Mary Morgan, Information Officer in the House of Lords, and Philip Wright, Assistant Serjeant-at-Arms, without whom there would have been no book to introduce to the reader. I am specially grateful to Pamela Carrington, Secretary to The Speaker's Chaplain, for triumphing over the old-fashioned handwriting with which I have to work. And a special debt is owed to Malcolm Crowthers, whose eye for a picture and whose patience and perfectionism in achieving it have immeasurably enhanced this narrative.

John Field
March 2002

In memory of my father and mother,
and Huw,
and for Selina, Christian and Srinivasan.

Prologue

The Palace of Westminster. Central Lobby. 2.30 p.m. – the hour for both the House of Lords and the House of Commons to sit today – is approaching. Here democracy is visible. A cross-section not only of the British electorate but of all nations of the world rubs shoulders here at this time of day. Household faces – government and opposition Front Bench spokesmen and women, world leaders, television correspondents – weave purposefully through caterpillars of wheelchairs, posses of pallid and intense research assistants, grey-haired ladies on day trips to the capital, school parties both exaggeratedly uniformed and scruffy, and confused passers-by who, seeing a moving queue on a rainy day, join it. 'Are we in a church?' The great lobby is awash with imminence: the varieties of ages, nationalities, dress, moods jostle happily together. The atmosphere is informal and unstuffy as all await the daily launch of the good ship Parliamentary Democracy.

At the Speaker's Residence at the north end of the Palace the Speaker's Procession assembles.

From 2.15 the Peers' Lobby is thronging with peers and peeresses heading for the Lords' Chamber, some pausing for a word with a friend or colleague. 2.29 p.m.: the Principal Doorkeeper of the Lords plants himself squarely in the centre of the Lobby and calls: 'My Lords, Ladies, and Gentlemen, please rise for the Lord Chancellor.' And from the Lords' Corridor a simple dignified procession of the Yeoman Usher of the Black Rod, the Purse Bearer, the Lord Chancellor and his Trainbearer passes through the Lobby and enters the Chamber. The doors are closed for Prayers.

In Central Lobby at the same time, the duty police nudge the bystanders into two sides of a square. By-sitters on the deep green leather benches are prompted to rise. A resonant call of 'Speaker!' seems to come from the depths of the earth. The senior police officer calls loudly, 'Hats off, Strangers!', and all the police, the only people in hats, remove their helmets. Echoing feet in slow march time strike the Minton tiles. Another simple procession appears from the direction of the Lower Waiting Hall: the Bar Doorkeeper, the Serjeant-at-Arms bearing the Mace, two swords, tail coats, white gloves, the Speaker and his Trainbearer, the Chaplain of the House of Commons and the Speaker's Secretary side by side behind him. The procession makes a smart right turn under the great chandelier of the lobby and vanishes into the Commons Corridor. When it enters the Chamber the door is closed for Prayers. The Union flag on the Victoria Tower flagpole signals to London that Parliament is sitting today.

The Speaker's Procession crosses Central Lobby, 2001.

CHAPTER ONE

Palace for a Thousand Years

POWER WENT with the place. An urgent tributary rolled gravel down from the northern hills, and then found its passage to the great river blocked by the barrier it had created. So it divided to form an island, low-lying and scrubby, but solid amid the shifting mud and clay of the wide tidal Thames. Later the giant ox, the narrow-nosed rhinoceros and the straight-tusked elephant roamed here. Seven thousand years ago man arrived, leaving Neolithic arrowheads and polished axes for the twentieth century to find. Flint flakes underlie New Palace Yard. A circular timber building and pottery from the late Bronze or early Iron Ages suggest that the island had become a desirable residence. It was only yesterday, on this timescale, when the Romans powered through here, probably fording the river to connect Dover Street with Watling Street: now Old Kent Road and Edgware Road. Substantial buildings reused in later structures, and a tile with a dog's pawprint indicate a settled civilisation. After them, historical silence but a gathering of legend. Lucius, a second-century native king, builds the first church from the ruins of a Temple of Apollo, destroyed by an earthquake; Sebert, a seventh-century king of Essex, is converted to Christianity by Mellitus, a friend of Augustine, and refounds the church, now itself in ruins. Monks were good at historical fantasy. What is certain is that marsh-loving Benedictines, who had settled already at Glastonbury, Ely, and Peterborough, arrived here in the tenth century, a lonely inaccessible sanctuary well removed from the city to the east, to pursue their vocation in a quiet place known disparagingly as Thorney Island, or Bramble Patch. Their little monastery gave Westminster its name.

From early days the power embodied in the place is ambivalent. A charter assigning land to the Benedictines describes their home as 'locus terribilis', but 'terribilis' might mean sacred rather than awful. The notionally unworldly monks attracted patronage from secular rulers seeking spiritual credit, or the easing of conscience. Saxon and Danish kings: Athelstan, Edgar, and Cnut, all gave relics to the monastery; Edgar joined with St Dunstan to enlarge it. The kings may have arrived on Thorney Island late in the tenth or early in the eleventh century. It was at Westminster, according to a later storyteller, that Cnut commanded the flow of the tide, intending a wise demonstration of the limits of kingly authority to his sycophantic subordinates, and instead acquired an unjust reputation in history for presumptuous folly. His spirit animated centuries of human battle with the river. Medieval river walls underpin Bridge Street, between the tube station and New Palace Yard; Sir Charles Barry's nineteenth-century rebuilding of the Palace sat on a platform bravely wrested from the muddy tide.

The Saxon king Aethelred (978–1016) was 'unraed' – not so much 'unready' as rash, unwilling to take advice – and the first ruler of the land we know for certain to have lost his throne because of a headstrong disregard for the opinions of the great men around him. Cnut seized his land, and there was a short interlude of rule by Danish kings. When Aethelred's son Edward (the Confessor) regained the crown in 1042, he took an immediate decision to build an abbey church at Westminster, as his private chapel and burial place. Thanksgiving for his return to the kingdom blended with his piety and his prudence: his first notion of a pilgrimage to Rome was discouraged by his advisers, who feared instability, and the foundation of the abbey dedicated to St Peter was substituted. This decision had momentous consequences: the turning of his predecessors' island bivouac into a full-scale palace which would become, over the next two centuries, the fixed centre of the government and administration of England, and the emergence of London as the undisputed capital. Westminster was where the theory and practice of Parliament would have to grow.

'The king's houses at Westminster', as the buildings were known until the time of Henry III, were intended not only as a royal residence, but also for the display and exercise of kingly power and government on the infrequent occasions when the king passed through. They continued to be developed for living in up to 1485. A fire in 1512 ended royal occupation, when Henry VIII decamped, eventually settling into Whitehall Palace in 1520.

Cnut, suspicious of the loyalty of London citizens, was probably the first king to reside at Westminster. We know that he loved discussion with Wulfnoth the Abbot, and his son was buried in the Abbey of which he was said to be a benefactor. Harold Harefoot and Harthacnut, his successors, were both occasional residents, and the first charter of Edward the Confessor, granted to Abbot Wulfnoth, was dated 'in regis palatio'. Edward died at Westminster in January 1066, a few days after the consecration of the great Romanesque Abbey to which he had devoted much of his reign. William of Normandy, crowned at Westminster on Christmas Day 1066, desired a finer palace than the Confessor's, and ordered shiploads of Caen stone to extend it. The surviving names of Old Palace and New Palace Yards date from the late eleventh century, and mark the transition from Saxon palace to Norman. Enlargement matched William's idea of grandeur: when in England he celebrated the year's Church festivals with sumptuous banquets, choosing Westminster for Pentecost. Magnates were summoned by royal edict, 'so that foreign legates would be impressed by the splendour of the gathering and the magnificence of the feast'. A residence was already also a place for display.

Westminster Hall

The heart of the Palace of Westminster was the Great Hall. Witness for 900 years to the making and unmaking of kings, to displays of monarchy both powerful and sacramental, to the rise of the English legal system and the great state trials, political theatre both comic and desperate, hair's-breadth escapes from destruction, no chamber in Europe has been so continuously interwoven with the history of a nation.

William of Normandy, the Conqueror, had displayed a ruthless single-mindedness in imposing his government on England; his son, William Rufus, was to apply a comparable determination to the building of Westminster Hall. William I had begun work on enlarging the Palace, and kept Whitsun there in some state, entertaining all the great men of the land. But a palace fit to embody the Norman concept of power needed a greater public hall than that left by the Confessor. Rufus provided it, an architectural marvel in eleventh-century Europe. Its ground plan has not changed in 900

An artist's impression of William Rufus's Westminster Hall, c.1100.

years: 80 yards long, and 22 yards wide, it was as vast a space enclosed under one roof as even the largest Romanesque cathedrals. Norman builders were unable to cover so great a span with a single roof, but whether the presumed double roof was supported with wood or stone columns is unknown. Ten carved stone capitals of Rufus's building were discovered as filling in the walls in 1835, but their original placing is again uncertain. The hall had twelve bays, a wall arcade and a wall passage, plastered and richly painted in red and blue, outlined in black. Glass was not used in the palace before the twelfth century, and the windows were presumably shuttered. On the long sides, the windows and buttresses are four feet out of kilter; the builders were less than competent, even if the hall was constructed around a smaller chamber which obscured their sight lines, as has been generously supposed. The exterior stonework was partly patterned like a chequerboard, with alternating pieces of stone from Caen and Reigate.

The Hall was ready for William's Whitsun feast in 1099, and it must have amazed all who saw it. Its scale made it the ceremonial centre of a dynasty which sought European pre-eminence. But the Hall was not completed without forced labour and social unrest; the chroniclers grumble that Rufus 'pilled the spiritualitie and temporalitie with unreasonable tasks and tributes', that 'men from many shires were sorely oppressed in building the wall round the Tower, and they were so worn down both there and at Westminster that many men periched of want.' The *Anglo-Saxon Chronicle* records that in many places the harvest was not gathered in because of the requisitioning of labour. An oppressed native people was predictably disposed to believe in supernatural portents: there was a great flood on the river, and the devil was seen walking in many likenesses. There were mutterings about the immorality of the court, signified by a return to the fashions of long hair and tight clothes, proof that 'there was no unnatural vice which was not practised.' William was indifferent to the discontent he provoked. When he arrived in England to view the completed hall, some of his party commented that it was rather large, even too large. William's retort, that it was only half the size it should be, may be an early instance of royal irony. Norman building was intended to endure: the Tower of London and Westminster Hall, the two grand building projects of the Conqueror and Rufus, still stand, still strong. In the core of the walls in Westminster, the original Norman masonry still supports the weight of the hammerbeam roof.

The Hall was remodelled by Richard II between 1385 and 1399. Richard's cultural sophistication, his love of magnificent display and his vision of kingship as a divine sacrament coincided in his ambitious enterprise. In 1385 he commissioned thirteen statues of all the kings of England from Edward the Confessor to his own day, carved by Thomas Canon for £2 6s. 8d. each. Their crowns were gilded and their robes painted brilliantly in emerald green and crimson by Nicholas Tyer, at a total cost of £8 13s. 4d. Six of them were set up in niches in the south wall behind the dais, in the manner of an altarpiece to convey the semi-divine status of Richard on his throne. The rest were placed on the north front above the principal doorway. The anonymities of the Norman building work are replaced by a detailed and personal schedule in the 1390s. Henry Yevele, now an old man whose death in 1400 just gave him time to see his work finished, produced the design in 1393–4, and his long-time collaborator Hugh Herland prepared the plan of the roof. In 1394 John Godmanston, Clerk of Works, received the order to 'repair the Great Hall within the Palace, to take masons, carpenters and other workmen, and set them to the said repairs . . . and to sell to the King's use the old materials of the Hall.' So the orders went out: lead from the Peak District, stone from Marr, near Doncaster, and work began. Yevele had to raise the existing walls by 2 ft.,

Artist's impression of medieval Westminster.

insert traceried perpendicular windows and build in the great cor-
bels to support Herland's 600-ton oak roof, which was prepared
at a yard called The Frame, near Farnham, using timber from
Odiham in Hampshire. More came from St Alban's Park in Hert-
fordshire. Carts carried prefabricated sections to the Thames near
Chertsey in the summer of 1395. In June alone five hundred carts
made the 16-league journey, sixteen horses to each cart. Herland's
challenge was enormous, and his design inspired: he had to span a
67-ft. space with timbers no more than 40 ft. long. A wooden scaffold inside the hall in 1395–6 eased the huge timbers precariously
into place. Herland was at work from 1394 to 1398, and was then
rightly rewarded a pension of £13 5s. for life. Richard was impatient: men were at work before dawn by candlelight in 1395. In 1397
a temporary roof was in place (above the new Purbeck stone floor)
for the coronation banquet of Richard's new queen, Isabella. But

all his attempts to affirm in architecture the divine status of kings –
the ecclesiastical north façade, the altarpiece of royal statues, the
carved and gilded angels appearing to carry the roof on their wings
(some, from Robert Brusyngdon, cost 26s. 8d. each) – were futile.
Richard's miraculous hall was still incomplete on 29 September
1399 when Henry Bolingbroke was acclaimed king. Richard was a
prisoner in William Rufus's Tower.

Between the Conqueror's death in 1087 and the accession of Henry
II in 1154 there is no news of the 'privy palace', as the domestic
quarters were known, except that in Stephen's reign it is 'neglected
and half ruined'. But an ambitious programme of building and
repairs after 1160 suggests an advance in status: a new hall in 1167, a
stone wall and quay on the river, the queen's chamber, the king's
chamber, the chapel of St John, all overseen by Ailnoth the engineer, drawing a fee of 7 pence a day as keeper of the palace. The
chronicler Roger Fitzstephen, around 1179, can boast of the king's
palace as 'an incomparable building, with a wall before it, and for-
tifications, two miles from the city'. The Pipe Rolls reveal that the
complex was divided into five: the Curia (courts), Aula (great hall),
domus (residential quarters), capella (chapel) and scaccarium (treasury). The Red Book of the Exchequer, from the end of Henry II's
reign, anatomises for us the elaborate hierarchy of the Angevin
household, 270 strong. Upper, middle and lower levels are separated by diet: 40 are allowed royal simnels, 150 common simnels,
and 120 baker's loaves only. The Chancellor, top of the pyramid, is
to receive five shillings daily, and one royal simnel, two common
simnels, one sextary of clear wine, one sextary of household wine,
one wax candle and forty candle ends. Below him are ranged a
Byzantine network of officials: the Master of the Scriptorium, Clerk
of the Household, Naperers, Usher of the Dispensary, Counter of
the Bread, Usher of the Spithouse, the King's Poulterer, the
Keeper of the Dishes, the Carter ('a double ration, and for his horse
a proper allowance'), the Porter of the King's Litter, Chamberlain
of the Candles, the Water-carrier ('and when the king goes abroad
one penny to wring out the king's clothes, and when the king
bathes, three pence, except on the three feasts of the year'), the
Keeper of the Tents, four Hornblowers, the Cat Hunters, the Bear-
ward, Keeper of the Brachs and the Wolf Catchers.

From William I to the notably restless John, kings exercised authority on the move, and their quarters were temporary encampments. But the loss of French territory under King John rooted his successors at home, though not always at Westminster; Edward I and Edward III, committed to wars in Wales, Scotland and France, often commanded the Exchequer, Chancery and the courts to follow them to Shrewsbury or York. Yet between 1218 and 1365 Henry III and the three Edwards who followed him still transformed the Palace and its state rooms (chiefly the Painted Chamber and St Stephen's Chapel) into emblems of semi-divine feudal kingship.

The Painted Chamber

Henry III loved Westminster, and turned it into the finest royal palace in Europe. His tasteful but extravagant autocratic patronage of those arts which would embody his vision of kingship and surpass the glories of France was a habitual source of political and financial friction. Keeper of the Works from 1218 was Master Odo the Goldsmith, who directed a great expansion and embellishment of the palace. By 1245, when the rebuilding of the Abbey began, £7000 had already been spent on the palace, much of it on the king's great chamber. A twelfth-century structure remodelled by Henry, 80 ft. long, 26 ft. wide and 31 ft. high, it was intended both as state bedroom and audience chamber. It was ready for decoration in 1236, and though by 1243 it was already known as the 'camera depicta', or Painted Chamber, work on the celebrated murals continued until 1297. The surviving murals in Westminster Abbey, together with the Retable preserved there, give us some idea of the style and quality of the work in the Painted Chamber, because the artist Walter of Durham, William the Painter, a monk, and the architects John of Gloucester and Robert of Beverley were employed both in the Abbey and the Palace. The paintings done for Henry III, and orientated around the state bed, displayed the same devotion to Edward the Confessor that inspired the reconstruction of the Abbey. Large scenes of Edward's Coronation and Edward's gift of a ring to St John disguised as a pilgrim were supplemented on the window splays by allegorical Virtues and Vices. To connect his reign to the 'magna historia' of Christendom, he ordered a Mappa Mundi, a Tree of Jesse above the fireplace, for which William 'the beloved painter' was paid £2 3s. 10d., and the four Evangelists. On the gable near the door was painted the aphor-

ism 'Ke Ne Dune Ke Ne Tine Ne Prent Ke Desire' – 'He Who
Does Not Give What He Has Will Not Obtain What He Desires'.
William was also commanded to depict 'the king who was rescued
by his dogs from his seditious subjects', a fit motif for Henry's
volatile reign. His state bed resembled the canopied tombs in the
Abbey: the bedposts were painted bright green, scintillated with
gold – colours the king loved – and studded with gold stars, and green
curtains enclosed it. From the bed, Henry was able to see through
a quatrefoil window the altar in his private oratory, dedicated to St
Luke. His stone bath, from France, was shaped like a peacock,
'covered all over with eyes like a real peacock, made of precious
stones called pearls, gold, silver and sapphires.' The floor was of
glazed tiles, like those in the Abbey Chapter House. A second set of
Old Testament murals, painted by Walter of Durham for Edward
I, was appropriately martial in subject: the military exploits of Judas
Maccabeus (associated at Edward's court with Arthurian legend),
and moralising images of good and bad kings and prophets. Walter
received a last payment of 54s. 7d. in 1297, and was told to stop work;
Edward was short of money, and work on St Stephen's had begun.

How this refined work survived the familiar vicissitudes of
medieval palace life is uncertain. In 1257 'the Commons of the city'
(i.e. the mob), incited by Gilbert de Clare, Earl of Gloucester,
invaded Westminster, 'and spoyled there the king's palace, and
devoured his wine, and broke the glass of the windows.' In February 1263 a great fire, 'by the negligence of a servant' damaged the
chamber, chapel and lesser hall. No sooner was restoration complete when in 1267 another mob of insurgent soldiers burst in,
drinking the wine, 'breaking with clubs and levers the doors and
windows', which they carried to Southwark and turned into barriers, and 'defacing the buildings most disorderly'. Yet in 1322 when
two Irish friars on a pilgrimage were the first recorded tourists to
the Palace, they were able to marvel at 'that famous chamber on
whose walls all the warlike scenes in the Bible are painted with wonderful skill, and explained by a complete series of texts beautifully
written in French, to the great admiration of the beholder.'

The paintings were kept in repair until the fifteenth century, and
then lost for four hundred years beneath whitewash and paper.
They were revealed in 1819 during building work, and what
remained was copied by Charles Stothard and Edward Crocker.
Their versions are the only evidence of the lost splendour of the

Chamber, which was largely destroyed in the fire of 1834 and wholly demolished during the rebuilding of the Palace by Barry.

The Parliament Chamber

To the south of the Painted Chamber was a hall from Edward the Confessor's time, reconstructed by Henry II, which became known in the fourteenth century as the Parliament Chamber. For over 500 years it was the meeting place of the House of Lords. When it was demolished in 1823, the cellars beneath were found to have been the kitchen storerooms of the Old Palace. South of that again was the Prince's Chamber, rebuilt by Henry III on the Confessor's foundations, used until the nineteenth century as the Robing Room. Nearer the Abbey, approximately where the statue of Richard I now stands, was the Court of Requests, plausibly the original hall of the Confessor's palace, and a place that came to be known, confusingly, as the White Hall. Its public function was for sittings of the Masters of Requests, law officers appointed to receive petitions to the king for justice or favour. After 1801 it became the meeting place of the House of Lords, enlarged by the Union with Ireland, until it was destroyed in the 1834 fire. From 1835 until 1850 a temporary House of Commons was rigged up within the ruins. Further west, beyond what is now Abingdon Street and abutting on the Abbey precinct, was the Private or Lesser Palace, a warren of domestic rooms of which little is known, and which was destroyed in the fire of 1512. The whole palace was encircled by a wall with many named gateways, few now placeable: Cheynegate, Chaundrygate, Sneyp Gate by the Roundhouse, the Postern towards the Mill, the Great Postern towards the Abbey. We know that the main gateway faced north, to King Street, now Whitehall, and that the Palace had a water supply delivered from Hyde Park, like the monastery's, by an arrangement of pipes and cisterns. Henry's peacock bath was not only for display.

The blend of piety and extravagance characteristic of Henry III was epitomised in the feasts he gave for the poor in the heart of his own luxury. On 29 December 1236, the Day of Circumcision, the Treasurer was commanded to feed 6000 poor people, the weak and aged in the great hall, those that were most strong in the king's chamber, the children in the queen's. In 1247 the command was to fill the King's Great Hall with the poor from Christmas Day to 1

January. There is no evidence for any other monarch doing likewise, unless we take into account royal garden parties.

St Stephen's Chapel

Louis IX of France commissioned the Sainte Chapelle, consecrated in 1248. Henry III visited it soon after, and his vision of French Gothic, translated into Westminster Abbey, haunted both the dreams and the purses of himself, and his son, grandson and great-grandson, the three Edwards. Admiration, envy and emulation made a powerful brotherhood of motives for the building of St Stephen's.

The king's chapel of St Stephen is mentioned in a charter of 1184. Henry III only beautified it: the Abbey was his prime vocation. But in 1292 Edward I began construction of a new St Stephen's modelled on the Sainte Chapelle, with two storeys, the upper for the use of the king and his family, immensely tall and light, with large windows of coloured and clear glass, a unified space without aisles. The architect-mason was Michael of Canterbury, though he was long in his grave before the building was finished: work was intermittent, and took nearly seventy years to complete. Master Thomas Houghton, engineer, sank foundation piles into the river clay; stone was gathered from Caen, Purbeck and Oxfordshire, glass from Wells, and timber from Pamber, and the building began to grow. Though only 90 ft. long, it was 100 ft. from floor to vault, as elevated as the interior of the Abbey.

Edward I's shortage of money and Edward II's turbulent reign both halted work for long periods. The failure of his predecessors weighed upon Edward III, who ordered a resumption of work in 1330. 'To John de Sene, merchant of Caen, for 400 Caen stones, called Gobetts, bought for the new chapel of St Stephen, at £4 per 100'; 'To Mich. Dissher of Wood St for 25 beams of alder tree for the scaffold at the east end of the chapel, @ 2d each'; 'Sept 26 1351 To Wm de Padryngton for making twenty Angels to stand in the tabernacles, by task work, at 6s. 8d. for each image.' In 1346, the wooden roof, vaulted to resemble stone, was complete, and Edward had earned the boast, in the Foundation Charter of that year, that 'capellam quandam speciosam per progenitoribus nostros nobiliter inchoatam nostris sumptibus regnis fecimus consummari.'*

In 1348 St Stephen's was established as a college of canons, with

*'that most beautiful chapel left unfinished by our noble forbears we will bring to completion at our own expense.'

a charter, a cloister on the north side, and a line of residences still recalled in the name Canon Row. Though the chapel was in use from that year, painting continued until 1363. The wooden roof had a blue background, and was patterned with gold and silver stars. Pigs' bristles, squirrels' tails, and goose, swan and peacocks' feathers were used for lavish decoration of every inch of the surface stone and wood. The mid-nineteenth-century embellishment of the Undercroft Chapel of St Mary by F. and G. J. Crace offers an impression of the sumptuous interior of the lost building above. In the spandrels between the windows were gilded statues of angels, some censing from thuribles suspended on wires from their hands. Eighty painted panels of Biblical scenes circled the chapel on the wall arcade of Purbeck columns covered with gold ornaments, with a carved and gilded cornice set with pieces of glass to create a jewel effect. There was an east end of great sublimity. Either side of the Purbeck marble altar were placed pictures of the Holy Family, with Edward himself, in 'armour crowned', wearing a surcoat of French lilies and English leopards, being presented by St George to the Court of Heaven. Beyond the south-east corner was the king's private chapel of Our Lady of the Pew, housing a statue of the Virgin which had a miracle-working reputation among the populace, and the sale of indulgences to pilgrims raised an income second only to Canterbury's Shrine of St Thomas Becket. The money was useful; Edward spent about £9000 on completing St Stephen's, and the problems of money supply were compounded by labour disputes. The outrage of royal authority fuels an edict of 1353, recording that labourers have withdrawn without leave, enticed away to work for others, 'in contempt of us and to the damage of our works'. No one is to employ these workmen, and they are to be brought back to the Palace. Rival employers to be sent to the Tower.

The Chapel of St Mary Undercroft

The surviving Chapel of St Mary Undercroft was intended, like the lower chapel of the Sainte Chapelle which it closely resembles, for the use of lesser members of the household. It has been brought back into use as the chapel of the Palace of Westminster after a motley, albeit somewhat apocryphal, career as Cromwellian stables, a coal store for the Commons' fireplaces, a wine cellar and the Speaker's dining room. Its structure and many details such as the fine carved bosses have survived not only all that neglect and indifference, but also the inferno of 1834 which destroyed all but the walls of the original St Stephen's. An embalmed uncoffined body, found in a window recess during nineteenth-century renovation, was identified as Tynwoode, Bishop of St Davids and Keeper of the Privy Seal to Henry VI.

St Stephen's, as finely enriched a holy building as any in Europe, was secularised in 1548 when Protector Somerset decreed it the meeting place of the House of Commons. No more radical declaration of Reformation principle could have been devised, though the nemesis of political ambition was to prove more radical still in 1552 when Somerset stood trial in adjacent Westminster Hall and was condemned to death. His peers acquitted him of treason, but found him guilty of felony. 'The people in the Hall, supposing he had been clearly quit when they saw the axe of the Tower put down, made such a shriek, casting up their caps, that their cry was heard to the Long Acre, beyond Charing Cross.' Before his death, Members of Parliament had moved in, and statues and other movables moved out; paintings disappeared behind wainscot, and were forgotten. In 1691 Wren was asked to report on the building. The ceiling, he wrote, could not be 'presumed to last many years longer, therefore a new room (should) be thought of, where the important affairs of the nation may be transacted without suspicion of this sort.' So in 1692 the first of two notable architectural vandals set about it. He demolished the clerestory and lowered the roof. His new ceiling cut across the perpendicular windows, which were blocked and replaced by sashes. Wood panelling, with galleries down the long sides, lined the walls. Worse was to follow, from every point of view, after 1801, when the Union with Ireland and the arrival of Irish members demanded more room for backsides. The architect James Wyatt decided to enlarge the chamber by stripping the walls of both Wren's panelling and the fourteenth-century wall paintings. The antiquarian John Carter, who had rediscovered the hidden paintings of St Stephen's, had also, unfortunately, organised the blackballing of Wyatt from membership of the Society of Antiquaries in 1796. Wyatt's vendetta excluded Carter from the building while he vandalised it. The antiquarian J. T. Smith was admitted, but had to be gone by 9 a.m. to give the workmen freedom to destroy the paintings Smith had been able to draw in the imperfect light of dawn. They were still a blaze of colour as they were hacked from the wall. Wren and Wyatt had taken the heart of St Stephen's, so when fire came to claim all but the bare husk in 1834, it was, perhaps, a happy consummation.

Court Life, Banquets, Political Theatre, Royal Administration

Disasters and marvels were savoured as much by medieval chroniclers as by their tabloid counterparts today. Divine providence was invoked in 1287 when a flash of lightning burst into a chamber in the Palace where Edward and his queen, Eleanor, were sitting conversing on a bed. They were unscathed, but two ladies-in-waiting standing in their presence were killed. Divine grace protected its own, however, in March 1298 when a fire lit to warm the Palace for Edward's return got out of control, and, fanned by an east wind, laid waste the lesser hall, Queen's chamber and many of the domestic rooms, besides spreading to the Abbey, damaging the living quarters but sparing Church and Chapter House. Edward abandoned the Palace, and found refuge in York House, at Charing, the London palace of the Archbishop.

So Edward II inherited a half-ruined Palace in 1307, and had to spend a large sum to prepare it for his coronation in 1308. A temporary timber hall 500 ft. long was set up along the river wall, with 40 ovens to cook the banquet, and a fountain flowing with red and white wine. Frivolity was Edward's chief contribution to palace and court. Gaveston provided 'companies of jesters, ruffians, flattering parasites, musicians, and other vile and naughtie ribalds, that the king might spend daies and nights in jesting, plaieng, blanketing, and other filthie and dishonourable exercises.' He kept Christmas at Westminster in 1311, and the royal account book speaks for itself: 'Dec 24 Delivered to the King to Play at Dice, on the Eve of the Nativity – 100s. Dec 25 Alms given in the Mass 9s. 4d.'

When Edward III succeeded his deposed father in 1327, there was much to be remedied. Between 1331 and 1365, he spent £30,000 on palace buildings which developed during his reign into the principal royal residence. A rapidly increasing volume of government and administration in the first half of the fourteenth century created a partial separation between the Great Palace to the north – Westminster Hall and its surrounding buildings, used for official purposes – and the Privy Palace, the domestic area to the south. Important works commissioned by Edward included a new chapel for the private use of the royal family and new apartments close by, in 1342–3, and the Jewel Tower, which still stands on College Green, built in 1365–6 for the king's personal plate and jewellery. The Tower encroached on monastic ground and was flanked on three sides by a moat, used as a fishpond by William de Husseborne, Keeper of the Privy Palace, whose sudden death caused delight among the aggrieved Benedictine monks, and was attributed by them to his being poisoned by a pike caught in their territorial waters. In 1360 Henry Yevele was granted the office of 'disposer of the king's works pertaining to the art of masonry' at the Palace, at the rate of 12*d*. a day, and Edward charged him to build a clock tower on the north side of New Palace Yard. By 1367 it was complete, a square tower with a low pyramid roof, housing the 4-ton bell, named Edward of Westminster, whose ringing on still days carried as far as the city. This grandfather of Big Ben, drawn by Hollar, stood until 1698, when Wren reluctantly demolished it, regretting that Parliament was not prepared to fund the relatively small sum needed for repairs. William III presented the belfry to the Vestry of St Margaret's Church, who sold the bell to the Dean and Chapter of St Paul's where, despite cracking and recasting, it still rings out as Great Tom, Big Ben's official deputy.

Edward III now had a Palace fit for the chivalric sports he loved, as did his son Edward, the Black Prince, whom he had created Duke of Cornwall, the first duke in England, in 1337. When in residence, grand tournaments, trials by battle and martial display were regular recreations. At Easter 1348 two Scottish prisoners, William, Earl Douglas, and Sir William Douglas, Knight of Liddesdale, jousted with such skill that Edward allowed them to return home. In 1356 King John of France, captured by the Black Prince at Poitiers, rode in procession from Southwark to Westminster where Edward, enthroned, surrounded by magnates and bishops, greeted him, led him to a great banquet, and lodged him in the Palace as his guest. With such strenuous physical activity and such elevated guests, it was prudent of Edward to have ordered in 1351 'two large bronze taps for the king's bath to bring hot and cold water into the baths', the first supply of hot and cold recorded in England.

The Palace, though only one of many royal residences, was to remain the centre of court life in London for another 130 years after the death of Edward III in 1377, though there was to be no major new building after Richard II's reconstruction of Westminster Hall. Ironically, the first public event in the hall he had created for his own grandeur was his deposition in 1399. The profligate and wayward autocracy of his reign was one of the factors in the destabilisation of monarchy and nobility which was to afflict England and disrupt court life for much of the fifteenth century.

At one stage his household ran, allegedly, to 10,000, with 300 in the kitchens alone. His tastes were extravagant: one cloak cost him £2000. At his Christmas festivities, after joustings and runnings at tilt, twenty oxen and 300 sheep were consumed each day. He was married to Anne of Bohemia in St Stephen's in January 1382, and her own coronation followed the ceremony. Jousts were held in her honour, English against Bohemian, as proof of manhood and valiancy, but these too were excessive, for they were 'not without damage of both parties'. Active out of the public eye, and alas, too busy to keep a diary in the 1390s was Geoffrey Chaucer, appointed in July 1389, at a wage of 2s. per day, as Clerk of the Works of the Palace, the Tower and the Mews at Charing Cross. He may have missed the Christmas jousting, for his annual bonus was a tun of wine from the royal butler every December.

The distraction of prolonged civil wars seemed to diminish the rituals of court life for the Lancastrian kings, and few of the events on record are celebrations. The reconciling interview between Henry IV and his errant son, handed down to Shakespeare by chroniclers and refashioned by him for posterity, has its historical roots in the Palace in 1412. Prince Hal urged punishment for his defamers; his father said 'he must tarrie a Parliament': it is necessary for such offenders to be judged by their peers. The prince appeared at the Parliament wearing a dog collar on his arm as a token of fidelity, and an academic gown as a mark of seriousness. A little more than four years later, as Henry V, he makes a triumphant return to England from France, riding to Westminster with his French prisoners on 23 November 1416, and, on the following day, receiving the Mayor and aldermen, with two hundred of the best commoners, who rode to Westminster and presented him with £1000 in two basins of gold.

Seven-year-old Henry VI kept Christmas at Westminster in 1428, with entertainment more appropriate than jousting for a child. 'To Jack Travel and his Companions, for performing divers plays and interludes during the festival of Christmas, before our Lord the king: £4. To others, Jews of Abingdon, performing interludes at the said festival: 20s.' But entertainment was soon displaced. The poisonous milieu of the faction-ridden court is conveyed by proceedings against Eleanor, Duchess of Gloucester, in St Stephen's in 1441, on a charge of necromantic rites to procure Henry's death. Found guilty, she was sentenced, after public penance, to banishment in the Isle of Man.

Edward IV, though insecure in possession of the throne from 1461 until the murder of Henry VI ten years later, appeared to have relished the splendour of court life at Westminster. A German visitor in 1466 witnessed the procession to church of Queen Elizabeth after child-bearing, with priests carrying relics and schoolboys singing and carrying lights. Then a great number of trumpeters, pipers and drummers. Then forty-two of the king's choristers, singing excellently. Then twenty-four heralds and pursuivants, and about sixty earls and knights. And then the queen, escorted by two dukes, with a canopy carried over her. There was luxury, too, for a Lord Gruthuse, a Dutch guest in 1472. After an evening's entertainment he was brought 'to three chambers of pleasance, all hung and decorated with white silk and linen cloth, and all the floors covered with carpets. A bed of as good down as could be imagined, sheets of Rennes, the counterpane cloth of gold furred with ermine . . . in the third chamber two baths covered with tents of white cloth . . . and when they had been in their baths as long as they pleased, they had green ginger, various syrups, comfits and hippocras, and then they went to bed.'

But golden lads and girls all must, as chimney sweepers, come to dust. Edward died in the Palace on 5 April 1483. 'The corps was lyde upon a borde all naked, saving he was covered from the navel to the knees, and so lay openly 10 or 12 hours, that all the lordes both spiritual and temporal then living in London or near thereabout, and the mayor of London with his brothers saw him so lying, and then he was seared etc. and was brought to the chapel on the morn after. Three solemn masses in the morning, dirige and commendation in the afternoon, and the psalter said, and at night watched with nobles and other his servants. This order kept for eight days, then a funeral procession to the Abbey.'

And within thirty years court life at Westminster came to its own end. After a fire in 1512, Henry VIII left the Palace, and only the Great Hall and adjacent offices used for royal administration were kept in good repair. Parliaments and law courts were left in possession of much of the rest of the Palace, together with a hotch-potch of trades which moved into the warren of smaller rooms and cellars. The royal household had gone, but the royal presence and royal authority remained in both the rituals and practice of government, ceremony, administration and law which continued to be closely identified with Westminster Hall and its adjacent buildings.

The Hall was built above all to display power to awed spectators. Opulence, status and patronage were united in the spectacle of a banquet. From Richard I in 1189 to George IV in 1821, a lavish, often vulgar and disorderly banquet after the coronation service in the Abbey was a recurrent ritual which the room had to endure. For over 600 years many features were unchanging, in the manner of most establishments. Citizens of London acted as butlers, the Earl Marshal rode about on horseback to keep order. Feudal services were ritualised: the lord of the Manor of Heydon, for example, was appointed to hold the towel when the monarch washed his hands, and from this feudal duty derived half his acreage. Queens consort had their separate coronations and banquets; Matthew Paris's description of the festivities for Eleanor of Provence, Henry III's queen, in 1236 sounds the unvarying sycophantic tone of many chroniclers: 'What need is there to recount the lavish provision of food and wine at the banquet, the abundance of game, the variety of fish, the pleasure given by the jesters and the comeliness of the servants? Whatever delight and splendour the world could provide was abundantly displayed there.' The consecration of the rebuilt Westminster Abbey and the translation of the Confessor's coffin to its new shrine was celebrated by a royal feast in 1269. A meticulous steward counted 22,460 capons served at the feast for Edward I in 1274. King Alexander of Scotland was there, with a hundred knights who, 'as soon as they had dismounted, turned their steeds loose for any one to catch and keep that thought proper.' They had no intention to drink and ride. Ambitious men were easily discountenanced at so public a ritual: only three days after Gaveston flaunted himself immediately behind Edward II in the procession to the banquet in 1308, the barons met and petitioned the king to 'banish' him. Ten-year-old Richard II had to be carried into the

Hall in the arms of his tutor after the exhausting ceremony in the Abbey in 1377. He was allowed to rest before taking his place at table, where he began the banquet by ennobling four new earls. The Hall was so thronged that lords on horseback had to make pathways for the servants bearing dishes for the guests. The chronicler Thomas Walsingham was particularly impressed by a huge golden eagle standing on a marble column, beneath whose claws all kinds of wine flowed throughout the whole day. Nobody was refused a drink, not even the poorest man.

The fifteenth-century chroniclers seem to have eased their way closer to the tables, and take a much fuller interest in gastronomy. The coronation feast for Catherine de Valois in 1419 is described in absorbing detail. 'Menu. 3rd course. Dates in compost. Creme motley. Coupe. Dorey. Turbot. Tench. Perch with gogyns. Sturgeon fresshe. Welkes. Porpes rostid. Creves de ewe douce. Shrympes goosee. Elis with laumprons rostid. A lessh called the White Lessh, with hawthorne leves grene and redd hawes. A mete in paste with iiii aungels in fourme of Seint Katerine whele in the myddes with a Reason:

> Il est escrite   Par mariage pure
> Par voir et dit   Ce guerre ne dure.'

Such edible allegorical tributes were called 'subtleties', and each of the three courses at 8-year-old Henry VI's feast in 1429 culminated in one. At the end of a spread which included 'Custard royal with a leopard of gold sitting therein, Fritter like a sun, with a fleur-de-lis therein, Jelly divided by the writing and musical notation, *Te Deum Laudamus*, and Pig gilded, a subtlety is displayed by Our Lady sitting and her child on her lap, and she holding in her hand a crown and St George kneeling on one side and St Denis on the other, presenting the king, kneeling to Our Lady, with this reason following:

> O blessed Lady, Christ's own mother dear,
> And then St George, that called art her knight,
> Holy St Denis, O martyr most entire,
> The sixth Henry here present in your sight
> Shed, of your grace, on him your heavenly light,
> His tender youth with virtue does advance,
> Born by descent and by title of right,
> Justly to reign in England and in France.'

Spectacular and costly entertainments called 'disguisings' were held outside the Hall in early Tudor times to celebrate royal events. When Catherine of Aragon arrived in England in 1501 to marry Prince Arthur, wheeled pageant-cars carried castles, mountains and ships around the courtyards, and for the tournaments and jousting in New Palace Yard, the rival parties processed through the hall with extravagant visual allegories. A great green mountain was borne above the Earl of Essex, 'with trees, stones and marvellous beasts upon the sides, and a beautiful maiden seated on the summit.' But the greater the striving for chivalric effect in these Tudor festivities, the closer nemesis appeared to shadow them. Prince Arthur died soon after the marriage, but the dispute about its consummation was to shake the fabric of Church and State in Henry VIII's quest for a legitimate male heir. At his Coronation banquet in 1509 Catherine, now his wife, sat 'apparelled in white satyn embroidered, her hieire handing downe to her back of very great length, bewtefull to behold'. A fair vision, but at the feast Lady Margaret Beaufort, patroness of learning, mother of Henry VII, who had outlived her son, took sick, allegedly after eating a poisoned cygnet, and shortly died. There was a last flourish of pageantry in the hall before the fire of 1512 turned royalty into refugees to celebrate the birth of a son to Catherine. Forests, hills and dales, ornamented with flowers made of velvet, damask, silk and satin, filled the hall with gorgeous illusion. But the young prince died nine days later. 'Novel triumphs and pastimes, with a sea fight and radiant fireworks' flourished again a hundred years later when James I created his eldest son Henry Prince of Wales in the White Hall in June 1610. But the curse on the first-born was reawakened by the stir: Henry was soon to die of typhoid. His death stripped Walter Raleigh of patronage and exposed him to the rigours of the law. He was beheaded in Old Palace Yard, outside the White Hall, in October 1618.

The traditional Coronation banquet was resumed for Charles II in 1661, but over the next hundred years its character gradually altered. The number of guests was reduced, but, in specially built temporary galleries, the number of spectators increased. It becomes rather like a zoo of exotic animals which opens its gates only once every generation. The eyewitness accounts are less automatically reverential, and the scenes described are mixtures of magnificence and muddle, the latter more pronounced in a context of attempted grandeur. Samuel Pepys was in the Hall for Charles II's feast on St George's Day in 1661. He had been in the Abbey earlier for the Coronation, but 'had so great a list to pisse' that he had to leave before the end. Much relieved, he was ready to enjoy himself in a scene full of 'brave ladies'. The king entered, wearing his crown, under a canopy with little bells at each corner borne up by six silver staves carried by the Barons of the Cinque Ports. Immediately there was an unseemly scuffle for possession of the canopy between the barons and royal footmen. The king's first course was carried up by Knights of the Bath; there were many fine ceremonies, with heralds leading up people before him and bowing. Feeling much at home, Pepys wandered from table to table to see the bishops and lords, and was 'infinite pleased with it'. But all that food. 'At the Lords' table I met with Will Horne and he spoke to my Lord for me and he did give him four rabbits and a pullet; and so I got it, and I got Mr Michell to give us some bread and so we at a stall eat it, as everybody else did what they could get.' He took a great deal of pleasure to go up and down and look upon the ladies – and to hear the music of all sorts – and his evening ended just as he wished, with a pretty lady.

The Lord of Misrule was in charge of George III's feast in 1761. Guests and spectators had been waiting in the Hall for six hours before king and queen arrived because of mismanagement in the Abbey. To create a visual sensation, 3000 candles in chandeliers were lit in half a minute by fuses of flax. But strands of burning flax dropped down on the guests and singed their finery. The starving spectators in the galleries, mostly ladies, lowered baskets to their gormandising husbands and hauled up chickens and wine. Their majesties left at 10 p.m., and by convention the doors were thrown open, and 'the people immediately cleared it of all the moveables, such as the victuals, cloths, plates, dishes – in short, of everything that could stick to their fingers.'

But the prize for the greatest comic debacle in Westminster Hall's history was won by the last such event, the coronation banquet for George IV in 1821. It was like an end-of-term celebration which got so desperately out of hand that the beleaguered headmaster at the final assembly could announce sepulchrally that it was cancelled for ever. George had spared no expense: the cost of his Coronation day was nearly £250,000. Prizefighters had been appointed to help keep order, but even they failed to prevent a mob

George IV's Coronation banquet, 1821.

of gatecrashers from attacking the tables beforehand. Once they had been ejected, George could make the appearance in glory he had so long dreamed about. 'Something rustles', noted Benjamin Hayden the artist, 'and a being buried in satin, feathers and diamonds rolls gracefully to his seat. The room rises with a sort of feathered silken thunder. Plumes wave, eyes sparkle, glasses are out, mouths smile and one man becomes the prime object of attention to thousands . . . he showed like some gorgeous bird of the East.' For a time, all was well. Trumpets brayed, drumrolls sounded, and cheering shook the hall and raised the dust. But there was too much food: 7742 pounds of beef; 7133 pounds of veal; 2472 pounds of mutton; 100 dozen of champagne, 20 dozen of burgundy, 200 of claret, 50 of hock, 50 of Mosel, 50 of Madeira, 350 port and sherry, 100 gallons of iced punch, 100 barrels of ale and porter. And it was too hot for guests swathed in finery. Everyone was sweating, ladies fainting, and melting candle grease dripped on them all and ruined their clothes and their complexions. The king's staggering off home was the signal for the guests to ransack the Hall and drink themselves to a stupor. 'Arms were everywhere being stretched for breaking and destroying the table ornaments, which were of themselves too cumbrous to remove, for the purpose of obtaining some trophy commemorative of the occasion. The pewter plate and dishes, engraved with the Royal arms and the letters "Geo IV" were greatly coveted.' And when all lay in ruins, the guests did the same: 'Peers and peeresses, judges and privy councillors, knights of all orders, and commoners of all degree, lay promiscuous, some on sofas, some on chairs, and a still greater number on the matted floors of the rooms and passages in which they happen to have sought refuge.' One by one, in the middle of the night, they were carried to their coaches and driven home unconscious. Ten years later, the thrifty William IV refused to countenance such an event, and that was the end of them. But the story of Coronation banquets cannot be complete without a mention of the Dymocks, the family holding the hereditary right to ride as King's champion into the feast, and issue a challenge to any present who dared contest the monarch's right to his throne and his beef. On most occasions, the Dymock performed his office irreproachably, but only the failures are chronicled. The first Dymock claiming the right, in 1377, turned up at the door of the Abbey instead of the Hall, and had to be sent away to take off his armour until the evening. Charles Dymock in 1685 fell from his horse as he bent to kiss the hand of James II. So heavy was his armour that he was unable even to rise to his feet without the leverage of servants. In 1689 and 1727 popular romance had it that the champion was challenged by Jacobites disguised as ladies, who melted away in the crowd as the Dymock prepared for action. The last active champion, in 1821, is said to have hired a horse from Astley's Circus, but when the guests applauded, it began its repertoire of tricks. The family was present, though not in the saddle, at the banquet to mark the Hall's 900th birthday in 1999. It is reassuring to know that out in the shires a Dymock is still ready for the call to arms, and perhaps keeping in practice.

The Hall was for hundreds of years, as William Rufus intended, a natural theatre for power as well as indulgence. At times when relations between king and people were strained, or when dynasties were locked in competing ambition, it was also a cockpit for political conflict. Henry III's exactions from the citizens of London had brought them close to rebellion in 1250. He summoned them with their families so that the Hall and courtyard outside were crammed. Then in a theatrical act of contrition, he tearfully begged them generously to set aside their feelings of anger, hostility and rancour towards him. The next threatened group of subjects were the lords and bishops, who believed that Henry's rule threatened the rights established in Magna Carta. They gathered round him with lighted tapers in an intimidating circle in the Hall and the liberties underwritten by the charter were recited. Henry held his hand to his breast with a serene and willing countenance. The Archbishop of Canterbury invoked a curse. The tapers were thrown, 'stinking and smoking, to the ground, and a dire malediction uttered that the souls of those who infringed the Charters might thus be extinguished to stink and smoke in hell.' Henry used such rituals to buy time, but rashly provoked further trouble. For a stormy Council meeting in 1258 the barons assembled in the Hall in full armour. Henry entered, and quailed. 'Am I then a prisoner?' 'Not so,' replied Roger Bigod, the Earl Marshall, 'but as you, Sir, by your partiality to foreigners and your own prodigality have involved the realm in misery, we demand that the authority of the state be delegated to commissioners.' The threat had its effect: Henry shortly after accepted the Provisions of Oxford, where the next sitting of Parliament was convened (Chapter 2). In the even more turbulent times of Edward II, the barons, who had triumphantly secured the execution of the loathed favourite Gaveston, knelt before the enthroned king to express ritual regret for offending him and acknowledging his clemency. But this slice of humble pie was soon digested, for in 1321 the Council filled the Hall with armed men to force Edward to banish his next favourites, the Despenser family.

It was in Henry III's reign, when both Great Council and assemblies of the early Parliaments met in the Hall, that the throne at the south end of the room acquired ritual significance as the 'throne of England'. Until a king had been seated in this throne and publicly acclaimed there, he was no true possessor; any man seeking to claim the crown de facto attempted to gain the magic of the royal seat – the equivalent, in Arthurian legend, of pulling the sword from the stone. Henry had shown a most particular concern when he ordered the flanking decoration for his throne from Edward of Westminster in 1245. 'We remember that you said to us that it would be little more costly to have two brass leopards made and placed on each side of our seat, than to have them made of sculptured marble, so we command you to make them of metal, and to make the steps before the seat of carved stone.'

This throne, and the dais on which it stood, became the scene for the making and unmaking of kings. Edward I, absent abroad on Henry's death in 1272, was proclaimed here, and until 1625 the monarch was enthroned here, when the succession was unchallenged, after riding in state from the Tower through the city, before processing to the Abbey for the anointing. After hearing mass on 16 July 1377, 10-year-old Richard II sat in the royal seat while the prelates arranged the procession on the red-striped cloths with which the stone pavement was laid. Another boy-king, Henry VI, came in state to the Hall before his Coronation in 1429. 'And so the kynge was ladde through the palys yn to the halle, and alle the newe knyghtys before hym in hyr araye of scharlette . . . thenne came the Chaunceler with hys crosse bare heddyd, and after hym came cardenelle with hys crosse . . . and thenne folowyde the kynge, and he was ladde by-wyne the Byschoppe of Dyrham and the Byschoppe of Bathe, and my goode Lorde of Warwyke bare uppe hys trayne.' Thirty-one years later, the Duke of York made his bid here for Henry's faltering throne with swaggering arrogance. Bourchier, Archbishop of Canterbury, asked him if he would come and see the king. 'I remember not that I know any within this realm, but that it beseemeth him rather to come and see my person, than I to go and see his.' He then broke open the locks and doors of the best guest rooms, and occupied them. Within months York was dead, killed in a skirmish at Boroughbridge. Henry was deposed, and York's son Edward Earl of March was conducted to the royal seat in 1461 and acclaimed as king, carrying St Edward's sceptre in his hand as proof of his right to take possession. Richard III had no need to be reinvented by Shakespeare. He gave a star performance in 1483 from the royal seat 'in the Court of the King's Bench', telling his audience that he would take upon him the crown in that place because 'the chiefest duty of a king is to sit there and minister the law.' His eloquence aimed to disarm his listeners: he issued a general pardon, and invoked unity and concord. He sent for one Fog, whom he had long hated, from sanctuary and took him by the hand in sight of the people. But not every critic was fooled, for 'Wise men tooke it for a vanitie'.

Even after the abolition of the monarchy and the destruction of the regalia (and, probably, the marble seat) in the 1640s, Oliver Cromwell, no-nonsense country squire and hard-headed republican, was seduced by the genius loci. In 1653 he was invested as Lord Protector in the Hall, receiving the Great Seal and the sword and Cap of State. In 1657 only the crown was missing when he was invested with a purple robe, the Sword of State and a sceptre, and seated in the Coronation Chair, brought across the road from the Abbey, while heralds and trumpets proclaimed him. Just above this spot, after the Restoration, his disinterred head was fixed to a pole on the roof above the south end of the Hall, from where it surveyed the reign of Charles II for about 20 years before a gale dislodged it. A month after Charles's Coronation, the most hated acts of the Long and Rump Parliaments were ritually burned in the middle of the hall where Cromwell's triumphs were sealed.

Kings were unmade here too, though their prudent displacers made sure that they were out of the way. Edward II, abandoned in despair at Kenilworth, was compelled to renounce the throne there. On the feast of St Hilary, 13 January 1327, came to the Great Hall at Westminster the archbishops, bishops, earls and barons, abbots and priors, and all the others from cities and boroughs alike together with the whole community of the land. The case against the king was presented: the loss of Gascony and Scotland, bad counsel, dishonour and loss to his realm, his people, himself. He should no longer reign. The king's renunciation was received and read, together with his request to ask in full Parliament for them to pardon his trespasses against them. 'The whole commune of the kingdom shouted praises to God and most willingly accepted Prince Edward as king.'

Richard II, in the Tower, 'clearly willingly and cheerfully', if Walsingham is to be credited, read out his formal abdication to a group of magnates at Michaelmas 1399. Next day his declaration was read to a gathering of the estates of the realm in Westminster Hall. The Archbishop of Canterbury asked if they were in agreement, and they cried out, 'Yes, yes, yes'. Henry Bolingbroke, Duke of Lancaster, rose in his place, and standing erect so that he might be seen by the people, and humbly making the sign of the cross on his forehead and breast and invoking the name of Christ, made his claim. 'I, Henry of Lancaster, challenge this realm of England and the Crown, as I am descended by right line of the blood coming from the good lord King Henry III, and

Plan of the buildings, c.1400.

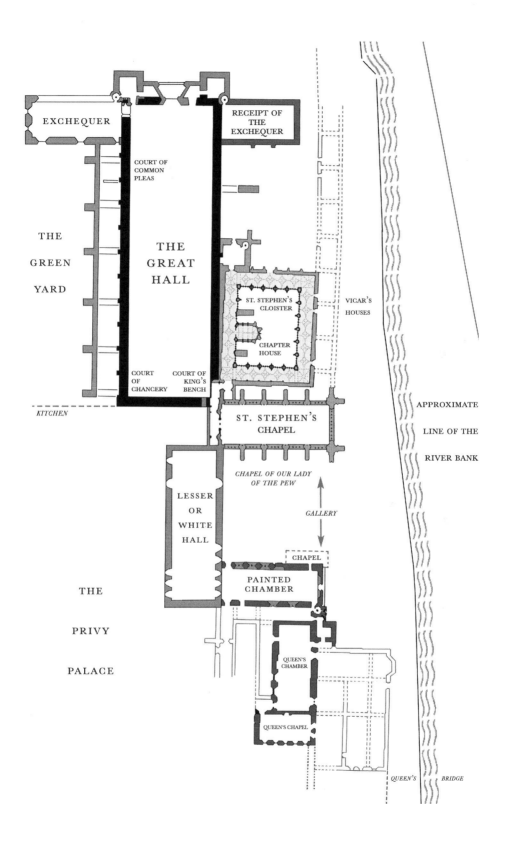

EXCHEQUER

RECEIPT OF THE EXCHEQUER

COURT OF COMMON PLEAS

THE GREEN YARD

THE GREAT HALL

ST. STEPHEN'S CLOISTER

VICAR'S HOUSES

CHAPTER HOUSE

COURT OF CHANCERY

COURT OF KING'S BENCH

KITCHEN

ST. STEPHEN'S CHAPEL

APPROXIMATE

LINE OF THE

RIVER BANK

CHAPEL OF OUR LADY OF THE PEW

LESSER OR WHITE HALL

GALLERY

CHAPEL

PAINTED CHAMBER

THE

PRIVY

PALACE

QUEEN'S CHAMBER

QUEEN'S CHAPEL

QUEEN'S   *BRIDGE*

through that right that God of his grace has sent me, with the help
of my kindred and my friends to recover it, the which realm was
on the point of being undone for default of governance and undo-
ing of good laws.' An apologia heard year after year in every new
military coup. Each of the Lords spiritual and temporal was asked
to give his assent to Lancaster's becoming king, and each did so.
Lancaster then said: 'My lords, we beg you not simply to speak
these words with your mouths if they do not come from your
hearts . . . nevertheless, should it happen that some of you do not
in your hearts assent to this, that would be no great surprise to
me.' But they all shouted, 'Yes, yes, yes'. So the Archbishops of
Canterbury and York rose from their seats, kissed his hands, and
led him to the throne. He went down on his knees and said a
prayer, and made the sign of the cross at the front and the back
of the throne, and then, 'to the great joy of all the people crying
out loudly both inside the hall and outside', they sat him down on
the throne as king. The Archbishop of Canterbury then preached
a sermon, presumably not extempore, on the text 'This is the
man who shall rule over my people.' It was very smooth, as *coups
d'état* go.

Equally inexorable, but spread over 150 years, was a revolution in
government which meant that Parliament would grow at Westminster, if anywhere. Saxon and Norman kings had been condemned
to be nomads, and the idea of a capital city was anachronistic; the
centre of government was wherever the king happened to be. Their
territories spanned the Channel, and they were always on the
move. The only rooted institution was the treasury at Winchester
Castle, secure, and well sited for the movement of valuables
between England and France. But under the Angevin kings the
administration of government and the machinery of law became
centralised at Westminster, which in consequence was the only
royal residence to be styled a palace.

Henry I, in whose reign the court of audit known as the Exchequer was established, held his first council for 'all the chief men
of England both clergy and laity' in the newly built Westminster
Hall in 1102. By the middle of the twelfth century the Exchequer
met biennially at Westminster, and a second treasury was set up
there by Henry II. Finance was effectively centralised. In King
John's reign it became the principal treasury, and Winchester just a

The Hall, c.1730. The Court of Common Pleas is on the right.

staging post. The development of government at Westminster involved an expansion of the functions of Westminster Hall and of
the buildings surrounding it. The Exchequer's first building was at
the north-east corner of the Hall, on two floors, the lower for
receipt, the upper for the making up of accounts on a chequered
cloth which gave the department its name. There was a smelter and
furnace, and an assayer who authenticated the coinage (a process
known as the trial of the pyx). Even when the king and court were
absent, a permanent official, the Usher of the Receipt, was empowered to conduct business. The Exchequer was to retain its
functions in buildings adjacent to the Hall until the early nineteenth

century. Next to it were a group of storerooms called Heaven, Para-dise, Purgatory and Hell, which evolved over the centuries into taverns and coffee-houses.

The Law Courts

Until the middle of the twelfth century, justice as well as government had to follow the king. An ordinance of Henry II in 1178 decreed that five judges should sit in a fixed place, for the convenience of those seeking redress. Justices began to hear pleas in the Hall: 'For a man drawn to the gallows who ought to have been hanged'; 'For royal fish (concealed)'; 'For wines sold contrary to the Assize'; 'Because he took a wife in the king's gift without licence'; 'In the King's mercy, for a watermill'. When John suspended the practice, Magna Carta in 1215 not only ordained that common pleas were to be heard in a fixed place next to the Exchequer, but also created two courts, one for civil litigation, the other for cases in which the king had an interest, which became known as Common Pleas and King's Bench. In 1224 Henry III confirmed fixed places for the courts: Common Pleas in the north-west corner of the Hall, near the draughty entrance; King's Bench at the south end, around the marble throne. For a time this territory was shared with Chancery, originally the Crown secretariat, the heart of the administrative machine, which had also made the Hall its permanent base by 1310. Through the fourteenth century, the royal seat was also occupied by Chancellors when they affixed the great seal to royal documents. In the fifteenth century Chancery also became a court in which the Lord Chancellor provided justice for any unable to obtain it under common law. It occupied the south-east corner of the Hall, nudging King's Bench along into the south-west corner. Star Chamber, an upstairs room near the Watergate, at the north-east corner of the Hall was built for the King's Council to hear cases of riots, routs and other misdemeanours. Its decorated ceiling of gilded stars survived successive rebuildings, but forfeited its innocence. The evolution of Star Chamber under the Tudors and Stuarts as an instrument of tyranny has perpetuated it as a metaphor for terror down the years since its abolition by the Long Parliament in the seventeenth century.

And – improbable as it now seems – it was under these makeshift conditions, cramped, crowded, noisy and cold, that the public face

The Law Courts,
Westminster Hall, 1809.

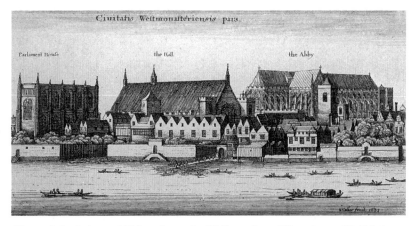

View of the Palace of Westminster by Hollar, 1647. Westminster Hall is in the centre. St Stephen's Chapel, then the House of Commons, is on the left, Westminster Abbey on the right.

of the entire English judicial system functioned until 1826. The courts were separated only by partitions which had to be removed for state occasions; all available floor space bustled with lawyers and litigants, market stalls, pretty girls selling ribbons and trinkets, and 'men of straw' who displayed a straw in their shoes as a badge of their readiness to take a fee for false testimony.

Sometimes public penances were ordered to be performed in and about the Hall: Perkin Warbeck, pretender to Henry Tudor's crown, was fettered in the stocks at the door of the Hall and stood a whole day, 'not without innumerable reproaches, mocks and scornings'; Titus Oates, after the exposure of the false Popish Plot, was dragged around the Hall with a placard declaring his perjury, and was then set in the pillory by the door and whipped until he bellowed hideously and then swooned. Peter the Great was appalled when he viewed the scenes in the Hall in 1697, particularly by so many busy lawyers: 'Why, I have but two in my whole dominion, and I believe I shall hang one of them the moment I get home.' Justice in Russia has taken its time to recover.

Apart from the conservatism of the legal profession, the reason why men put up with so much inefficiency and inconvenience for so long was probably the throne, its physical presence legitimising the authority of the courts, and in which Edward IV had sat with King's Bench for three days in 1462 in order to find out how his laws were executed. In addition, Magna Carta's provision of a fixed place for justice continued to be accorded a disproportionate reverence.

The Hall, thronging with prosperous lawyers, was a magnet for commerce. Shops and trades were flourishing by 1340, when the Keeper of the Palace was entitled to rents from those setting up booths or carrying their wares. Pepys was a keen customer in the seventeenth century, for books, gloves and caps, and was on friendly terms with many of the shopkeepers. Betty Martin, a linen-draper in the Hall, was one of his many mistresses. In 1666 there were forty-eight shops, each with a frontage of about 8 ft. All, of course, had to be removed for Coronations. They may not have been replaced after the 1761 Coronation, and had completely disappeared by 1780.

In this confused space, ebbing and flowing with all sorts and conditions of humanity, the great state trials have been conducted. Those of Guy Fawkes and Charles I belong to the history of Parliament, and will be heard in due order. Down the years the dignity of many of the victims, oppressed by the savagery of vengeful state justice, outlived their desperate punishment. Sir Thomas Turbervile, traitor, spy for the French in 1295, was brought to Westminster on a poor hack, feet tied beneath the horse's belly, around him riding six torturers dressed like the devil, the hangman holding the halter. On the dais in the Great Hall he was condemned to be drawn and hanged, and to hang so long as anything should be left whole of him. William Wallace, who had allegedly boasted that he should wear a crown in Westminster Hall, is tried at the south bench in 1305 wearing a mock crown of laurel. He denies the charge of treachery because he owes no allegiance to the King of England. He is sentenced to a traitor's death nonetheless, and is dragged on a hurdle from Westminster to Smithfield, hanged on a high gallows for indignity, cut down before he is dead, disembowelled and mutilated. His body is cut up and distributed in London and the North to bring good cheer to the English. His was the first head to be displayed on London Bridge. Thomas More, recently Chancellor of England, convicted of treason in the King's Bench Court in 1535 on the perjury of Richard Rich, Solicitor-General, addresses parting words to his judges: 'Though your Lordships have now here in earth been judges to my condemnation, we may yet hereafter in Heaven merrily all meet together, to our everlasting satisfaction.' While Strafford, on trial for high treason in 1641, was making ready for answers, the Lords and Commons walked and clattered; 'after ten hours much public eating, not only of confections but of flesh and bread – bottles of beer and wine going thick from mouth to

The trial of Lord Lovat, 1747.

mouth without cups; and all this in the King's eye.' The end of the
Jacobite cause is signalled by the trial of Simon Lord Lovat for high
treason after the 1745 Rising and the catastrophe at Culloden; his
beheading at the Tower in 1747 a foregone conclusion. Warren
Hastings, in 1788, is charged with oppression in ruling India. It is as
fashionable as Ascot, with 2000 seats for spectators, and special
tickets printed. After more than seven years, and 142 sitting days, he
is acquitted, but broken, like the reputation of Edmund Burke, his
chief accuser. As Burke fell, Sheridan rose; his rhetoric gripped
fashionable London and, despite its theatricality, still points at
tyrants from Stalin to Pinochet: 'It is true, he did not direct the
guards, the famine; and the bludgeons; he did not weigh the fetters,
nor number the lashes to be inflicted on his victims, but yet he is
just as guilty as if he had borne an active and personal share in each
transaction. It is as if he had commanded that the heart should be
torn from the bosom, and enjoined that no blood should follow. He
is in the same degree accountable to the law, to his country, to his
conscience, and to his God.'

Westminster Hall: Survival into Our Time

The clutter of the courts disfigured the Hall until it was rescued by
Lord Liverpool. The Prime Minister, on his way to the Lords
through a hall cleared for George IV's Coronation, was 'much
struck with the grand effect of that unique edifice', and consider-
ations of good taste prompted the building of a new block of seven

Sketch of the trial of Warren Hastings (far left), 1788. On the right of the witness box, back row, are Sheridan, Fox, and Burke.

courts by Sir John Soane adjacent to the west side of the Hall, accessible by new doorways cut through the old masonry. But almost at once the facilities were found to be inadequate, and in 1882 the lawyers departed for the new courts in the Strand, returning once a year, for the Lord Chancellor's breakfast at the beginning of the law term in October, when the slumbering echoes of legal chatter in the roof beams are briefly stirred.

Fire has caught hold of the Hall twice and threatened total ruin, in 1834 and 1941. Only heroic human effort when it seemed lost secured its survival. Those stories belong to the history of Parliament in subsequent chapters. The lesser misadventures it has endured are easily classified: floods and bombs. In 1236, and again in 1242, after exceeding rain, the Thames drowned all the country for the space of 6 miles about Lambeth. It was possible to sail boats in the hall, and people had to cross to the rooms of the Palace on horseback.

Terrorist explosions are not an invention of the twentieth century. In 1736 Thames boatmen protesting at the threat to their livelihoods posed by the planned bridge at Westminster left a packet of gunpowder in the Hall. It exploded harmlessly (perhaps damp). After two earthquakes in 1750, for which no one could be blamed, it was the turn of the Irish. A bag of Fenian dynamite was removed from the Chapel of St Mary Undercroft by PC William Cole in January 1885, but it exploded on the stairs, blowing a hole in the paving and shattering the south window. Almost at once a second explosion in the Commons Chamber caused more extensive damage. A third, almost simultaneously, at the Tower, confirmed a propaganda coup for the Irish nationalists, and marked the start of more than a hundred years of security precautions. A further Irish bomb exploded in the cafeteria at the north-west corner of the Hall in 1974; the scorch marks in the masonry remain. Yet Parliament was unprepared for the shock of the assassination of Airey Neave, Conservative spokesman on Northern Ireland, on 30 March 1979, when he was blown up as he was driving out of the Commons car park. The outrage transformed security policy in the Palace, and created barriers and tensions, physical and psychological, that will not easily be removed.

Lawyers and death-watch beetles throve together. Anxieties in the eighteenth century about the state of Herland's wondrous roof had a practical solution: strip off and sell the lead with which the roof had been covered since 1400, and use the proceeds for repairs. But the removal of the lead merely revealed even greater decay than was feared. The structure was patched up, and re-roofed in slate. When John Soane built the new law courts, he too had a go at repairs, with oak from old ships broken up at Portsmouth. But when the lawyers departed for the Strand in 1882, they left the beetle behind. Infestation was massive, and major repair was essential in 1914, but the right man, Frank Baines, was on hand. His painstaking work over ten years preserved 90 per cent of the original timber, and installed a discreet structure of steel to give heart to the old oak. The very last beetle, it is believed, was the victim of advanced chemical warfare in the 1970s.

For centuries the Hall had been one of London's favourite fashionable meeting places, but during the nineteenth century it lost its appeal. The departure of the lawyers, however desirable for the dignity of the place, seemed to strip away the centuries' accreted life, and leave it purposeless. Charles Barry's rebuilding of the rest of the Palace after the 1834 fire intended it as the grand entrance to Parliament, but the removal of the south wall to link it with St Stephen's entrance turned it into Europe's noblest corridor, and now, because of security jitters, a largely unused one. It was the venue in 1843 for a successful exhibition of designs for the internal decoration of the new Palace, and it remained the antechamber to the law courts until 1882, but for over fifty years from 1860 it also lapsed into a part-time drill hall for militias. It acquired a new lease of death in 1898 with the lying-in-state of Gladstone, the first commoner to be accorded such panoply in Westminster Hall. Edward

Nelson Mandela, President of South Africa, on 11 July 1996, when he addressed both Houses of Parliament – only the third head of state to do so in the Hall.

VII, George V, George VI, Queen Mary and Churchill have followed Gladstone to the catafalque there. Anniversary commemorations: for the United Nations, Parliament itself, VE day, the Glorious Revolution; even addresses to both Houses of Parliament by General de Gaulle and Nelson Mandela as distinguished heads of state, seem temporary violations of a somnolence it seems to have earned. Now and again it is stirred into festivity: the great banquet for its own 900th anniversary, and a staff party at which, for the first time in 500 years, there was dancing, but for long tracts of time it is as if the Hall itself is lying-in-state, and its scatters of visitors creep about in whispers, dwarfed alike by the building, its ghosts, and the weight of history it bears.

CHAPTER TWO

The Development of
Parliament to 1529

I F ENGLAND IS, in John Bright's phrase, 'the Mother of Parliaments', the gestation period was the longest and the parent–child relationship the stormiest ever recorded. To follow the process is like wandering in a maze. But there are four guiding threads. First, Parliament evolved not by design, but pragmatically, and slowly, in response to shifting political, social and economic needs. Secondly, it was the king's Parliament. Until 1689 it was in his power alone to summon it, prorogue it, dissolve it, and consent to or reject its proposals. Thirdly, it was not democratic. The only constitutional balance that mattered was the relation of monarch to nobles; participation by other social ranks was not a necessary part of the political process. Even after the House of Commons had established a separate identity, its functions were limited to giving advice, receiving and presenting petitions and clinging to the leverage on power given by its long-established right of consenting to royal requests for taxation. Not until 1489, when a judicial decision was made that no legislation was valid unless it had received the assent of the Commons was there any claim to parity between Lords and Commons. For much of the period the Commons simply accepted the supremacy of the Lords as a shield against tyrannical power. And lastly, at no point in this period did Parliament have a coherent identity or agenda. It met far too intermittently for that. It did not seek to usurp royal power, but settled for bargaining and a quest for consensus to advance the interests of the powerful subjects who composed it. It gained authority chiefly in times of war, when the king required taxation, and at times of misgovernment when relations between king and nobles soured into mistrust.

It was axiomatic for Saxon kings to take wise counsel from the witan, the powerful men of the kingdom. The witan – 'the knowing ones' – were convened at meetings, called Witenagemots, when kings went on progress through southern England. At the end of the ninth century, Alfred required the witan to assent to legislation, appraising it, as in all conservative, essentially feudal societies, by the criterion of precedent. Edgar, Aethelred and the Danish Cnut followed this practice when issues of moment needed broader advice than the king's immediate household could supply. Edward the Confessor presided over a royal council of churchmen and lay representatives of the king in the shires – earls (earldormen) and thegns – at the crown wearings held in Winchester, Gloucester and Westminster at the year's great religious festivals.

After the Conquest, meetings linked with crown wearings continued, but were altered in character by the structure of Norman society. The great men were barons, the chief tenants of their royal landlord, bound to William in contract to provide services in return for land. Their assembly was called Curia Regis, the King's Council, and its support of and advice to the Norman kings was central to the dynasty's hold on power. Within three days of the killing of William Rufus in 1100, Henry I was crowned 'by the mercy of God and by the Common counsel of the barons of the kingdom'. His immediate proclamation promising reforms was also backed by baronial consent. During the twelfth century the Council grew in political stature. It claimed the right to be consulted about the king's decisions; its reciprocal obligation was to assent to royal proposals for raising money. The Constitutions of Clarendon in 1164 accorded baronial status to archbishops and bishops, and defined an additional role for the baronage as judges in the king's court. Under Henry II, therefore, the Council began to prefigure Parliaments: it discussed political matters placed before it by the king, assisted him in financial management, adjudicated the customs of the law and, as when it sentenced Thomas Becket, acted as the highest court in the land. This regular assembly of magnates both clerical and lay can clearly be seen as the source of three different components of subsequent government: the House of Lords, the Privy Council and the Courts of Law.

Painting in the Palace of Westminster depicting King John signing Magna Carta.

At court, the Saxon Witenagemot developed into the King's Council; in the provinces the Saxon shire courts, for the purpose of local administration and presided over by sheriffs, were retained after the Conquest. The two structures were sometimes linked. The Council could, if it wished, command the attendance of representatives from the shires for the purposes of sounding out opinion and of communication. In 1213 the Council issued a summons to all sheriffs to cause 'four discreet men of your country' to attend a Council at Oxford. The precedent for the summoning of knights to Parliament was thus set.

Councils continued to meet long after the functions of Parliament had been established. Edward III built a room called Star Chamber in which Council meetings were held. Between 1400 and 1460, the council met nearly fifty times and Parliament only twenty-two. Henry VII preferred to rule without Parliament for most of his reign, summoning Councils instead. But from the mid-fourteenth century they are clearly distinguished from Parliaments: a group of nobles, able, if it wishes, to summon knights as representatives, but meeting only to debate and advise. The last Council with representatives present was held in 1353, after which the Commons, ever alert to loss of status, asked that the legislative and financial decisions taken at the Council should be referred to the next Parliament. So the oligarchy of the Council found itself questioned by a Commons beginning to grasp its role, just as in 1215 the Council, newly confident in its own powers, had mounted the challenge to despotic royal authority which led to the signing of Magna Carta. The altered political circumstances created by that agreement made the development of Parliament both possible and necessary, as the statues of the Runnymede barons around the chamber of the present House of Lords bear witness. Those barons would no doubt be surprised that the mythologisation of history has credited them with the founding of Parliament.

In the twelfth century, each baron secured from the king an individual charter granting him land and rights. Court life was diffuse; the kingdom of Normandy, divided by the Channel, required the Angevin kings to spend much time out of England, and to delegate administration to deputies. But the loss of Normandy and Anjou in 1204 transformed the conditions of government, quickening interest in the processes of power. The king was now based in England, and the council gathered around him was enabled to acquire a collective identity. Ministers and judges were permanent members, joined from time to time by bishops and barons present in the court. In John's reign the collective action of a group of nobles, soon to develop into the core of Parliament, secured a foundation of rights for society in general. A charter of liberties issued by Henry I was used as a precedent for the struggle with John. Signed at Runnymede in 1215, Magna Carta is the first articulation of the concept of a contract between the king and all his free subjects. It marks the cusp of social change between a feudalism in decline and the consequent search for a more comprehensive community of the nation. The rise of Parliament is one manifestation of that quest.

Magna Carta ended the primitive assumption that subjects owed their ruler absolute and unconditional obedience, and replaced it with two principles: that the king's government is itself subject to the law and that the king's law-making and tax-raising required the consent of 'the community of the realm'. Clause 14 defined the process for summoning men to secure 'the common counsel of the nation': the peerage, lay and clerical by letter; others to be selected by sheriffs; the machinery that would send knights and burgesses in due course to the Commons. As well as a list of specific liberties exacted from the king, chiefly financial, the Charter also set out a definition of the general liberties of the citizens and freemen. 'No freeman to be deprived of his property, outlawed, exiled, imprisoned, or in any way ruined except by the judgement of his peers, or by the law of the land.'

Henry III reaffirmed the charter of liberties within a month of John's death, hoping to establish his reign on a happier footing than his father's. It is unlikely that either he or the barons at Runnymede foresaw that the ideas of government expressed in Magna Carta made the development of a regular political and legal authority independent of the king a practical consequence. But it was money, not principles, that brought it into existence.

Henry loved Westminster. He enhanced the Palace, began rebuilding the Abbey, and centred court life there, which is why Parliament took root where it now is. During his 56-year reign, Parliament acquired both a name and prescribed functions, as a court of justice, as a legislative body – though only in alliance with the king – as a forum for debating matters of state, and exercising the power to grant or refuse taxation. It was dominated throughout the thirteenth century by the nobility; others had only the most peripheral part in a process which the signing of Magna Carta had initiated.

The word 'Parliament' was first used of a court assembly in England in November 1236, when Henry adjourned a legal case to the 'Parliament' due to meet at Westminster in January 1237. 'Parleys' had been used in France in 1234 for a formal discussion between the king and his principal subjects. The term is in regular use in the 1240s, less as a formal title than a description of a distinctive kind of court meeting, attended by lay and clerical magnates. Its purpose was to vote taxation, pass laws, hear legal cases, and to confirm Magna Carta. Sometimes it was called a 'colloquium'. The chronicler Matthew Paris provides the first account of a debate, in 1242, about the cost and expediency of the French War, and in 1246 he uses the term 'parlamentum generalissimum' for a gathering of the nobility of the whole kingdom summoned by royal edict to discuss, as a matter of urgency, the critical state of the realm.

Taxation was, then as now, disliked, but, then as now, the obligation to pay it was not seriously questioned. The power to raise money belonged to the royal prerogative, for the land had to be administered and defended. Tax grants, once discussed in regional assemblies, became a matter for court meetings, where royal authority had fullest weight. The thirteenth century was the first in which kings needed regular tax revenues: the loss of French territories and the dispersal of Crown lands as rewards for supporters reduced Crown income. The success of Magna Carta in limiting royal extortions left Henry III needing to make regular tax requests. Meetings of the Great Council in the 1220s agreed that taxation was binding on all those liable to pay, and the Roman law phrase, 'what affects all shall be dealt with by all', was invoked then and throughout the century as the rationale of the common council of the realm. But as early as 1237 the opportunity was seized to use taxation as a lever for bargaining: Henry was granted a tax on movable goods (a subsidy which soon came to be known as tenths and fifteenths) in return for confirming Magna Carta and the charter of the Forests. This taste of power was pleasing. When Henry requested a subsidy in 1248, he was only handed a list of grievances, including the complaint that he had no chancellor or treasurer 'by the common counsel of the realm, as would be right and proper'. Bitter wrangles for centuries to come about the royal choice of ministers are already foreshadowed.

The Emergence of the Commons

The Council had continued to ask the shires for representative opinions in Henry's early years: in 1227 'knights and honest men are to elect in the county court four knights to appear before the king on behalf of all the county.' In 1254 the king's financial plight made desperate by his war in Gascony intersected with the increasing prosperity of knights in the shires who were summoned for the first time to a Parliament 'to represent all and single in the counties, to determine what aid they will afford us in our necessity'. This was the point at which the Commons began to speak for their communities and gain a taste of power, not by either political principle or popular pressure, but by the royal need to spread the tax net and to secure the appearance of general consent to the topping up of Henry's purse. For the next 200 years, as expensive foreign wars were the fashion, this was to be the one undisputed lever of power wielded by men below the rank of the nobility.

Parliament as Court of Law

One piece more of the historical jigsaw and then Parliament can at last be opened. The House of Lords is still the highest court in the land. The empty throne shows that the ruler is always symbolically present, as in Westminster Hall where the marble chair of kingship attracted to it the court of King's Bench. The judicial function of Parliament was also created in Henry III's time. In 1234 the Council

The Court of King's Bench, c.1450.

of Gloucester, consolidating the central principle of Magna Carta that the king was himself subject to his law, defined three courts of common law, the King's Bench, the Common Bench, and the Exchequer, which kept records, were professionally staffed and whose functions laid the foundations of the modern state. In authority over them was the Great Council, called within two years, 'Parliament', to which problems arising from the lesser courts were passed. After Gloucester, the next council, with ten bishops, ten earls and twenty-two barons present, was devoted entirely to clarifying legal issues: it was presumed to embody the highest judicial wisdom in the land.

Parliament Established: 1258–65

The barons institutionalised Parliament by collective action in 1258 as they had done to bring the king within the law in 1215. The politically and financially capricious Henry was intimidated into accepting the Provisions of Oxford. 'Let it be remembered that there are to be three Parliaments a year: the first at the Octave of Michaelmas, the second in the morrow of Candlemas, and the third on the first day of June, to review the state of the realm and to deal with the common business of realm and king together.' By the Provisions, the barons claimed control of executive and legislature, and affirmed that Parliament was an indispensable arm of government. Henry bitterly resented being bullied, and repudiated the Provisions in successive Parliaments, but his disapproval failed to prevent them from meeting: eleven were held in the next four years. But what were called 'Parliaments' were in essence specialised court meetings, consultations on policy and resolutions of administrative and legal problems, conducted by an exclusive group of twelve barons chosen by their peers to represent 'the whole community of the land'. But arising from the civil turbulence of the 1260s, which saw even the king briefly a prisoner of Simon de Montfort, Parliament acquired a new dimension which was to evolve within 50 years into a permanent House of Commons. De Montfort, briefly in command of government, issued, in the king's name, writs to each county to select four 'prudent and law-worthy knights' to come to Parliament 'to discuss the affairs of the King and the kingdom'. By the time his second Parliament met in Westminster Hall in January 1265, two burgesses from each major town had also been summoned. Though de Montfort only needed them for a specific purpose, to help in mediating the peace of the realm, he had nonetheless extended the idea of Parliament. Though knights and burgesses were to be summoned to very few Parliaments for the next 50 years, it is notable that after 1265, no tax was levied without the consent of a Parliament which had to include representatives of the shires and the towns.

By the end of Henry's reign in 1272, the status of Parliament and a pattern for its proceedings were clear. The royal need for money was the opening for barons, knights and burgesses to force the king to remedy discontents. The assembly had claimed the right to meet even in the face of royal disapproval, and it is a mark of the growing status of the term that the signing of Magna Carta at Runnymede began to be known retrospectively as a Parliament. Its function was understood: a meeting of king and subjects to settle disputes about power, law and money.

Edward I had learned from his father's blunders, and accepted that Parliament was a means of consolidating royal authority. He summoned forty-six Parliaments in 35 years, and was usually present himself. Regular meetings as a law-making body gave it momentum and effectively committed his successors to working with it. The need for money compelled him to deal with representatives of all classes who could supply it. In the 1290s, when his costly wars in France and Scotland made him a beggar, Parliament relished its growing capacity to frustrate the royal will by demanding the redress of grievances. What has passed into history as the Model Parliament of 1295 was more likely to have been regarded by Edward as a kind of Frankenstein's monster. Relations between king and Parliament became soured towards the end of the reign, but it was too late for the parliamentary experiment to be aborted, because the king's continual need of money had rooted it at the heart of government. Other procedures were also established: there was recourse to a well-tried emollient for political distemper. The chamberlain of London is required to stock up 'one hundred tuns of wine . . . because the king is to hold the forthcoming Parliament at Westminster, so that he will require many wines there.'

Under Henry III Parliament had been a closed world. Only ministers and judges referred business to it, and no one else had access. But at his first Parliament in 1275, Edward I opened it to his subjects by means of petitions. So popular was this initiative that Parliament began to be held in widespread esteem, and many believed that its only function was as a complaints office. The volume of work was soon enormous: by the early fourteenth century, four-fifths of the Parliament Roll is occupied by the hearing of petitions. By 1305 the procedure was defined. Proclamations in advance of a meeting required written petitions to be handed to clerks who were 'receivers of petitions' by a specified date. Ordering and recording now became essential: John Kirkly is the first clerk to Parliament, and the oldest surviving Parliament Rolls date from 1290, when the lawyer Gilbert Rothbury was clerk. The hearing of many petitions was delegated to committees: the tradition that the spadework of Parliament is done in committee is over 700 years old. By the mid-fourteenth century, petitions are being heard by committees about twenty strong: English petitions in the Chamberlain's Room, foreign ones in Marcolf's Chamber. Though the king, of course, retained the prerogatives both of discussing state business and dispensing justice, if he pleased, independently of Parliament, it was only in Parliament that officials were appointed to receive petitions, and where there was a certainty that they would be addressed. The early-fourteenth-century handbook *Modus Tenendi Parliamentum* asserted that Parliament could not be dissolved until the last petition had been answered, in fulfilment of the king's Coronation oath to dispense justice to all. Its function as a court of law open to all bestowed upon it a special status from which the first parliamentary privilege grew: immunity from arrest and distraint, exemption from appearing in lower courts when Parliament was meeting, and special protection for those travelling to and from 'the king's service at his palace at Westminster'. With these rights went obligations – no brawling, no bearing of arms – which, together, won for Westminster the accolade of 'the freest place in England'.

Though the king enjoyed, in theory, an unlimited discretion to modify measures agreed by Parliament, the hearing of petitions rapidly circumscribed his freedom. Parliament was in practice modifying statute law by adjudicating petitions, and was seen to be doing so by the population. So by the end of Edward II's reign in 1327, Parliament had stolen from the king the initiative for making laws, just as it had stolen the financial initiative from Edward I at the end of the previous reign. In the modern House of Commons, a

The Parliament of Edward I.

green baize bag hangs on a hook behind the Speaker's chair. It too is for the receipt of petitions, in proper form, and a daily reminder that the popularity of Parliament in its infancy was fuelled by its readiness to dispense justice to all who sought it.

The thirteenth century had seen the Anglo-Norman feudal barons transform themselves into a constitutional force. Magna Carta, the Provisions of Oxford and the holding of regular Parliaments enhanced the authority, confidence and responsibility of a group of about seventy barons forming a settled core of parliamentary membership. The character of the nobility was fashioned by politics under Henry III and Edward I, and by the foreign conquests under Edward I and Edward III through which England grew into nationhood. But the nobility were also stepping into more perilous waters. From 1135 to 1307, there had been no capital punishment for a member of the nobility; not even after civil war conflicts such as the battle of Evesham. The influence of chivalry and the diffuseness of the Norman kingdom may both take some credit for a period of comparative mercy. But the execution of Gaveston in 1312 and the factional rivalries of the rest of Edward II's reign marked the start of a long period when torture followed by execution became the expected price to pay for political failure. The savage sport of blood-letting persisted as late as the 1680s.

Where the Lords had trod in the thirteenth century, the Commons were to follow in the fourteenth. In 1300 the idea that representatives should participate in the process of law-making was entirely alien: knights and burgesses were only required in Parliament when the king wished to dip into the pockets of the classes they represented. But between 1311 and 1325, knights and burgesses were summoned to every Parliament but two, and after 1325 no Parliament met without them. The reign of Edward II was the period in which popular representation became an indisputable part of the political process. The irresponsibility of the king threatened turmoil and created a vacuum which Lords and Commons together had to fill.

Edward I's evasive last years created deep mistrust among the parliamentary barons. In 1297 he had even repudiated his confirmation of the basic charters. So low were expectations at the succession of Edward II that a new clause was inserted in the Coronation oath: 'Sire, do you acknowledge that you must hold and keep the laws and rightful customs which the community of your realm shall have chosen?' Their apprehensions were amply justified: Edward's extravagance and his choice of company were both uncontrolled, and in 1310 Parliament had to appoint twenty bishops and nobles as Lords Ordainers to oversee the government of the kingdom. Elected in the Painted Chamber, the first occasion we know it to have been used by Parliament, they declared severe ordinances against the headstrong king, treating him as a dissident child. He was neither to leave the kingdom nor levy war without the consent of the barons in Parliament, which, they declared, must meet at least once a year, and twice if need be. The king was to confer with Parliament about high policy, taxation, and the appointment of ministers. Never had Parliament been more formally defined than in the face of the king's threat to its influence. The Ordainers, doubtless in part as an insurance policy, also affirmed that Parliament was the highest court in the land. The Commons had a voice in the appointment of the Ordainers, for the menace to good order made them an indispensable part of the political community. The *Modus Tenendi Parliamentum*, compiled in Edward's reign, draw a clear distinction between peers, who attend 'for themselves in their own person and for no other', and knights and burgesses who 'represent the whole community of England', so that the two knights who come to Parliament for the shire have a greater voice in the granting and denying (of taxation) than the greatest earl in England.

The roles of Lords and Commons shifted as the crises of Edward's feckless reign deepened. The barons, who had earlier regarded themselves as the voice of the kingdom, now had to sit in judgement on the matters they had been accustomed to raise. They rallied at Westminster fully armed to force the exile of the Despensers in 1321. Now that barons were the judges, the popular representatives became the voice of the kingdom and the natural channel for the raising of petitions. From 1327 petitions in Parliament were presented exclusively by the knights and burgesses. The Commons had acquired an important new role, but the price they had to pay for it was that judicial and legislative authority was vested exclusively in the Lords. The hierarchy was emphatically stated in 1399: 'The judgements of Parliament pertained solely to the king and the Lords and not to the Commons . . . the commons are petitioners and demandants, and the king and lords have for all time had and shall have by right judgements in Parliament.' Apart from their tax-granting powers, the Commons were the king's eyes and ears in the provinces, carrier pigeons reporting grievances and taking political opinions to and fro.

The dominance of the barons was Edward II's doing: he had given them every opportunity to occupy the citadel of power. As his wilful and petulant personal rule spiralled into irreconcilable conflict with the political convictions of his leading subjects, the barons repeatedly seized the initiative: the Ordinances, the removal of Gaveston and the Despensers, and finally, in 1327, Edward himself. Queen Isabella and her lover, Roger Mortimer, invoked the aid of Parliament to legitimise the deposition. The Great Seal was taken from him and used to summon a Parliament. In January 1327 in

Westminister Hall, lords spiritual and temporal assembled, with knights and burgesses, and some of the London mob. 'The community of the realm' had, by a deputation, extracted a deed of abdication from Edward at Kenilworth; now the Archbishop of Canterbury announced his deposition to the gathering, and preached on the text 'Vox populi, vox Dei'.

Parliament in the Ascendant:
the Reign of Edward III

The 50-year reign of Edward III was a golden age for the medieval Parliament. It met regularly throughout his reign, and its proceedings were characterised by a sense of partnership between king, Lords and Commons. Knights and burgesses were summoned to every Parliament after 1325; by 1332 the Commons had established a separate identity and place of meeting; before the end of the reign they would also institute the office of Speaker. Meetings of Parliament settled most frequently at Westminster. Between 1327 and 1338, only thirteen of twenty-nine Parliaments met at Westminster; between 1339 and 1377 all thirty-one did so. The stability of proceedings became banked by habit. Even the raging of plague in 1348–9, when Parliament had to be prorogued several times, failed to disrupt its steadily growing sense of its own importance.

The Parliament of 1330 had cleared the way for the young king by launching proceedings against Mortimer who was drawn and hanged at Tyburn in November. Rogue elephants like Mortimer had no place in the proper conduct of the government of England. Only in Parliament, where monarch and subjects were formally gathered together in partnership, were issues of law and finance to be resolved. The 1327 Parliament ruled that 'a change in the law should not be made except with the assent of the king and of the prelates, earls and barons and other people of the land, and if anything ought to be done, it must be done in Parliament.' In the face of threats from Scotland and Ireland in 1332, the common interest of the king and his people is ingenuously underpinned by the interest of the purse: 'Whereas our Lord the king cannot do these things without the help of his people, the prelates, earls, barons and other magnates, and the knights of the shire, and all the commons, of their free will, to carry out the recommendations and to enable our

Lord the king to live of his own and pay his expenses, and not to burden his people by outrageous prises in any way.'

The mayor and citizens of London had petitioned the new king in 1327 to hold Parliament each year at Westminster, and in the familiarity of a fixed place a sense of orderly procedure soon evolved. Writs of summons always referred to the need to maintain and preserve 'the state of the king and the state of the realm'. Those summoned entered Westminster Hall, showed their writs to the guard, and passed through to the Painted Chamber. Here they would learn the cause of the summons. 'The state of the king' was presented by the Chancellor, the Chief Justice, or the Archbishop of Canterbury, who would assess relations with France, Ireland, Scotland and the Pope, and report on the waging of war and on domestic peace. Parliament's openness to petitions was next declared, and then Lords and Commons divided. 'The magnates and those of the commonalty were commanded to debate and consider among themselves how to meet the king's needs.' The king and Lords moved into the White Chamber; the Commons, until 1352, stayed behind in the Painted Chamber, but from 1352 left the Palace and met first in the Chapter House of the Abbey, later in the Refectory there, and, in the early sixteenth century, in a Parliament chamber at Blackfriars (which was later turned into a theatre for Richard Burbage, the Elizabethan actor-manager). The Painted Chamber was then the place for consultations between the Houses, called 'entre communer', almost certainly by delegations. The physical separation of debating chambers was intended to defend the privacy of discussions, enabling members of the Commons to speak freely without fear. The sense of their proper independence is echoed in the traditional slamming of the door of the Commons in Black Rod's face when he arrives to summon Speaker and Commons to the Lords for either the opening of Parliament or to hear the Royal Assent to bills. The main business of the fourteenth-century Commons was the bringing of public grievances to the seat of justice. It was through petitions being registered as matters of public interest that changes in the law were secured.

Members of the Commons had a fixed rate of pay: 4s. a day for a knight, 2s. a day for a burgess, plus travel expenses. The social distinction implied seems to have pervaded business: knights made formal speeches and acted as hosts at the concluding banquet, and no burgess was ever chosen as Speaker. The Commons became more unified socially in the fifteenth century when successful burgesses turned themselves into gentrified landowners and when the gentry began to seek out borough seats as the status of membership of Parliament increased. In the fourteenth century there was a high degree of unity between the knights in the Commons and the Lords: a flexible class structure guaranteed many common interests. There was a shared conviction that decorum was important. The proclamation opening a Parliament included a 'Cry' against weapons. Archbishop and unruly children alike were subject to rules. In 1341 Archbishop Stratford was denied admission to the Palace by two serjeants-at-arms: 'Father, do not take this ill, but we are forbidden to let you enter the king's Painted Chamber where he is holding his Parliament'; a Royal Proclamation in 1351 declared that, 'on pain of imprisonment, it is forbidden that any child, or other person, shall play in any part of the Palace of Westminster, during the Parliament which is summoned thereto, at bars, or at other games not befitting, and such as taking off the hoods of people, or laying hands upon them, or in other way causing hindrance, whereby each person may not peaceably follow his business.' The Parliament Roll of 1354 records the formal process of assent when the judgement of the meeting is virtually unanimous: 'Donques, vous voillez assentir au Tretie du Pees perpetuele si homme la puisse avoir?' 'Et les dites Communes responderent entierement et uniement, "Oui"'. Such schoolboy French was on its way out, discredited by the triumphant French wars which had fashioned the consciousness of nationhood at home. A statute of 1362 ordered that English was to be the language of the courts, 'the mischiefs of the use of French, too little known in this realm, have been often represented to the king by the prelates, dukes, earls, barons and commons.' In 1363 English became the language of Parliament, and a lasting prejudice against learning foreign languages was institutionalised.

In this period too we first hear the recognisable tones of public men conscious of their status and prickly when they fancy themselves slighted. The Earl of Surrey waxed indignant in the Lords in 1341 at the presence of a group of officials of the royal household: 'How is this Parliament to proceed, sire? Formerly it was not wont to be thus, but now all is topsy-turvy and new-fangled. Those who should be the chief are excluded, while others of the rank and file sit here in Parliament who should not be at such a council but only the peers of the land who can aid and maintain you, O king, in your great need.' His passion won the day: his objection was admitted. The dignity of the Commons was slighted by the Chief Justice in 1352 when he proposed that only a deputation should attend the King in the Painted Chamber to have the purpose of the summons explained, while the rest gathered in the Chapter House. The Commons refused, and had to be mollified by an invitation for the whole Commons to the White Chamber two days later, to meet Prince Lionel, who particularly requested their advice on the French wars. The two houses were united in indignation in 1366 at the proposal to pay an annual tribute of 1000 marks to the Pope in order to secure the restoration of King John of France to his throne: 'Neither King John nor any other sovereign, could reduce the realm to such subjection, without the assent of Parliament, which had not been given.' There was agreement, too, about the problem of lawyers. The importance of the Commons as the channel for petitions attracted ambitious lawyers into Parliament as a platform for advancing their clients' causes. They were quickly under suspicion for 'arranging to present various petitions to Parliament in the name of the commons which do not concern them.' In 1372 an ordinance disqualified lawyers from the king's courts from acting as knights of the shire in Parliament. But then, as now, nothing keeps lawyers out of the Commons. The Parliament of 1404, lacking lawyers, became known as 'the unlearned Parliament', and soon they were back, in full voice.

The 'Good Parliament' and the Speaker

The advancing influence of Parliament in the fourteenth century reached its apogee in the 'Good Parliament' of 1376. The session lasted ten weeks, the longest since Parliaments began. England was in crisis: foreign wars were going badly, and at court Alice Perrers, Edward's mistress in his dotage, and her associates, were living extravagantly. The Lords and Commons acted together to censure court conduct, secure the banishment of Perrers and to affirm that ministers appointed by the king were answerable to Parliament. The Commons withdrew to the Chapter House, 'where they could take their counsel privately without being disturbed or bothered by other folk.' Here they sat in a circle and Sir Peter de la Mare, Steward to the Earl of March and a representative of Herefordshire in five successive Parliaments, summarised the speeches so well and advised them so wisely that they asked him to speak on their behalf in the 'Great Parliament' with the Lords. When the Lords tried to exclude some of the Commons, Sir Peter refused to proceed until all were admitted. Thus the first official Speaker proved his quality of courage, and his passion for Parliament was manifest in his objection to the removal of the wool staple from Calais by the king and his council: 'that it was against the statute made about it in Parliament, and that what was done in Parliament by statute could not be undone without Parliament.' The Commons may have wished to appoint a Speaker because they felt peripheral to 'The Great Parliament' in the Palace, and it was a momentous choice of Sir Peter de la Mare in whom the capacity to defend their interest in negotiations with king and Lords was so highly developed. Though he was an employee in a noble household, and though for over 200 years the choice of Speaker needed royal approval, and was often a member of the royal household, appointed both to spy upon the Commons and to manipulate its will, in practice independence of mind and loyalty to the interests of the lower house was the rule rather than the exception.

At the end of the Parliament which had banished his mistress, the king gave two tuns of red wine and eight deer to a feast laid on by the Commons for the bishops, earls, mayor and worthy citizens of London. As Henry III was the first monarch to discover, to his chagrin, that Parliament could not be ignored, and certainly wasn't going to go away, all his successors were obliged to treat with it. Many, especially those whose claim to the crown was of dubious legitimacy, were eager to have Parliament aboard the carriage of state from the beginning. The story of the interaction of king and Parliament over 200 years is sometimes stormy, sometimes ingratiating, and, during the reign of Richard II, often both at once.

Edward I, who had nurtured a Parliament which became a viper in his bosom, was in desperate need of money for war in Gascony in 1297. He made a passionate speech on a stage outside Westminster Hall to try to secure the popular support that Parliament had not given him by presenting his 13-year-old son as king should he himself not return alive. He was also the first monarch to sense the value of what we now call photo-opportunities. He summoned a Parliament for the knighting of Prince Edward in 1306, and provided a great feast amplified by chivalric ritual. He himself, a sick man, had to be carried in on a litter. From then on, kings expected their Parliaments to endorse the chosen successor, and from Edward's deposition in 1327, the nominal approval of Parliament was sought for every coup which displaced an anointed king, an event which occurred more frequently than elsewhere in Europe. The early precedent for the removal of unsatisfactory kings by means ostensibly constitutional may account for the monarchy's long survival. The 1372 Parliament had approved the succession of Richard II, and, at the death of his father, the Black Prince, in 1376, the Commons requested that the boy he produced in Parliament to be publicly acknowledged 'true heir apparent of the realm'. Henry IV created his son Prince of Wales in full Parliament as soon as he had gained the throne in 1399, and in 1422 the infant Henry VI was brought to Westminster and solemnly addressed by the Speaker. In 1425, aged 4, he was introduced to a full Parliament.

Richard II was broken, partly by his own volatile temperament, and partly by a contradiction that lay at the heart of medieval power. Monarchs were expected both to display strong personal authority and to defer to the views of powerful nobles. This practical impossibility was already, and inevitably, shifting Parliament from a malleable extension of royal will into a body capable of resistance to it. Arrogant and intractable nobles served early notice on the young king of their temper. John of Gaunt undid much of the achievement of the Good Parliament and in November 1381 Lancaster and Northumberland violated precedent by wearing armour in the Parliament House and filling London with bands of armed men in the course of a personal feud. But the notorious extravagance of the court and the tax burdens attributed to it weighing more heavily on the people than on clergy and nobility fuelled deep resentment. In the Peasants' Revolt in 1381 even the Exchequer was broken into. In these tinder-dry political conditions there were plenty of arsonists. Richard outraged Parliament by his absences from it, by his creation of his friend Robert de Vere as the first non-royal duke, of Suffolk, and then appointing him as Chancellor. When Parliament remonstrated, his reply was an intemperate disaster: 'They ought to be silent about such things and should proceed to the business of Parliament and hasten to dispatch it.' The message sent back by Lords and Commons was even more provocative: 'If the King . . .

rashly in his insane counsels exercise his own peculiar desire then it is lawful for [the Lords and magnates] of the realm, with the common consent of the people of the realm, to pluck down the king from his royal throne.'

The Merciless Parliament which met in the White Hall on 2 February 1388, with laymen to the king's left, clergy to his right, and the Chancellor standing behind him, eliminated the court party in a travesty of justice which condemned innocent men to barbaric deaths upon fabricated treason charges. It was a sinister and prophetic consequence of the contest for power between king and barons in Parliament. The subversion both of law and Parliament to remove rivals set a grim precedent which was to haunt English politics for nearly 300 years. The declaration by the Lords that 'it is better that one should die for the people than that all the race should perish' echoes still as a fig leaf for injustice in totalitarian regimes worldwide.

Richard's desperate attempts to reclaim the absolute power of kingship were certain to fail, and equally certain to usher in the dynastic instability and civil violence of much of the next century. At a council in May 1389 he declared that now that he was 21, he was entitled to take the affairs of the kingdom into his own hands. He demanded the keys of the Exchequer, and then the Great Seal from Thomas Arundel, Chancellor and Archbishop of Canterbury, 'placed it in his bosom and quitted his council'. Next day he gave the Seal to William of Wyckham. His final attempt to subject Parliament to his will was a crude show of force in 1398. The gathering was held in a temporary structure in New Palace Yard (the Hall was being rebuilt), with a tile roof and open sides. Richard surrounded it with his bodyguard of king's archers, 4000 men of Cheshire, 'with bowes bent and arrowes nocked in their hands, always readie to shoot'. The Chancellor preached on the text 'One king shall be king overall', and the king pursued his revenge on his enemies by banishment and execution, and by an ordinance charging with high treason anyone who sought to reverse or alter any of the statutes of this Parliament. Two years later, when the statutes were annulled, Richard was no longer king, and Henry Bolingbroke had found Parliament more than ready to work hand in glove with him to legitimise the transfer of power. Richard, a prisoner in the Tower, was visited by Bolingbroke, who disclaimed the initiative: 'My Lord, we cannot do otherwise till the Parliament meets.' It did, on 30 September 1399, in Westminster Hall, summoned by the writ of a king whose abdication had been extracted on the previous day, so technically it was not a Parliament. The Archbishop of York declared the abdication, and put the question whether to accept it or not 'to the estates and people there present'. Only the Bishop of Carlisle demurred: 'You ought to bring King Richard in the presence of the full Parliament to hear what he has to say', but he was led off to prison for his courage. Of the thirty-three charges of misgovernment that were read out, a number concerned violations of the rights of Parliament: interfering with elections and with parliamentary integrity, and using underhand tactics to amend statutes. Then the Recorder of London read out the judgement of the whole Parliament, that 'Richard King of England be sentenced and condemned to be imprisoned in a royal castle . . . If any should raise war for his deliverance he should be the first that should suffer death for that attempt.' Bolingbroke claimed the throne, secured the assent of 'the estates of the realm', and at once issued writs for a Parliament to meet within a week. Prudently throughout his reign he was to show exaggerated respect for the institution, and often fixed the Speaker's seal to documents in order to impress the French with the degree of popular support he enjoyed.

Parliament in Factional Times: the Fifteenth Century

During the confused and often menacing political conditions of the fifteenth century, Parliament struggled to retain its political function. Power was often withdrawn from Parliament and vested in a council of state; when kings felt secure, Parliaments hardly ever met and the Crown had begun to seek out other sources of revenue – customs duties for life, forced loans, benevolences – which made it less dependent on the Commons. It also summoned Parliaments away from Westminster, and infiltrated them with members of the royal household (fifty-three out of 277 in the Parliament of 1447). Besides, Parliament was, of course, still entirely controlled by a royal summons and dismissal, so it followed inexorably that its hold on power was largely conditional on its readiness to cooperate. It was also a period when the Commons had little incentive to take a line independent of the Lords: there was too much to lose by attempting it. In addition, of course, the front line of politics for much of the century often shifted from debating chamber to battlefield.

There is a timeless satirical glimpse of the Commons at work in the alliterative poem 'Mum and the Soothsegger', written around 1400, which serves as a welcome corrective background to the grim headlines of much of the century that followed: 'Some members sat there like a nought in arithmetic, that marks a place but has no value in itself. Some had supped with simony the previous evening so that the shire they represented lost all value from their presence. Some were tattlers who went to the king and denounced as his foes men who were really good friends of his . . . some members slumbered and slept and said very little. Some mumbled and stammered and did not know what they meant to say. Some were hired men and would not take any step for fear of their masters. Some were so pompous and dull-witted that they got hopelessly muddled before they reached the close of the speeches.' Should this anatomisation bring a blush to the cheek of any present members of the Commons, let them recall that less than adequate parts can make a more than adequate whole. These were men who insisted that the king should pay no heed to tattlers seeking to advance themselves, petitioned about corrupt elections and biased sheriffs and secured an indenture between sheriff and electors, bearing the seals of both, to validate the election return. In 1414 they petitioned Henry V in protest at his habit of modifying petitions they had authorised and tried to persuade him to accept their parity with the Lords in law-making: 'It has ever been their liberty that no statute or law be made unless they have given their assent thereto.' And in 1430, as a result of a Commons petition, a right was instituted to the franchise in the shires which was to last 400 years, until the Reform Act of 1832. This fixed entitlement was based on property: 'a freeholding to the value of forty shillings by the year at least above all charges'. In 1430 this criterion included about 5 per cent of the adult male population, and though inflation steadily extended the franchise, the property qualification ensured that members of the Commons from the shires were bound in with the interests of the landed gentry long after the Industrial Revolution had begun to turn society upside down.

Henry V's French wars were the breeding ground for a tranche of aggressive and self-important nobles whose ambitions fuelled the dynastic wars of the mid-century. As early as 1422, Gloucester's claim to the regency, citing Henry V's own will, was denied by the Lords on the grounds that after his death, a king had no power over the three estates of the realm. But at times of great civil disorder, it was hard to bring the Lords together. In 1454 only 45 out of 105 attended, so a system of fines for absence was instituted, graduated according to rank: £100 for a duke or archbishop, 100 marks (a mark was 13s. 4d., or two-thirds of a pound) for an earl or bishop, £40 for an abbot or baron. Those in prison were generously exempted. In 1449 Parliament met in the Painted Chamber, but had to adjourn next day to Blackfriars 'on account of the infection of air in the town of Westminster and in the places adjacent to the Palace'. The conduct of men was infected too. The Commons pursued the Duke of Suffolk on suspicion of treason, and impeachment was in the air. Henry VI summoned his lords to come 'in to his Innest Chambre, with a Gavill window, over a Cloyster', to hear the royal will overrule the Lords in Parliament and substitute banishment. But Suffolk was murdered at sea on his way to the Low Countries; Jack Cade's rebellion broke out; the king's reason was unhinged for a time by the loss of Gascony; the Lords had to appoint the Duke of York Protector and Defender: it is astonishing that any vestiges of constitutional process survived.

It seems appropriate that from these troubled times the mace, a weapon of war, should emerge as the symbol of the Serjeants-at-Arms and, through their use of it to exercise their powers of arrest in legal disputes involving members of the House, it became a symbol of the authority of the Commons as a body. By the early seventeenth century it had become traditional that the Commons could not function in the absence of the mace. Though challenged by the disputacious and radical-minded Pym in 1640 ('it is a new doctrine, that we can do nothing without a Speaker or the Mace'), the tradition has endured, providing at least an occasional theatrical prop for excitable members. Pym would not be pleased to know that the present mace is a Royal Mace made for Charles II.

The authority affirmed by the mace was subverted in the 'Parliament of Devils' after the victory of Lancastrians over Yorkists at Ludlow in 1459. The convenient and swift destruction of enemies was secured by attainder: a Bill of condemnation read in the Parliament Chamber, met with silence from the Commons, could receive royal assent without any further judicial procedure, evidence or arguments. Such a tyrant's dream was not to be lightly set aside by a political and legal system in which aristocratic factions were ruthless and precedent was king.

Three changes of dynasty in 25 years all sought the backing of Parliament: the Duke of York in 1460 and his son Edward IV in 1461 assiduously wooed it; Richard of Gloucester in 1483 seated himself on the throne only after he had publicly assented to a document supposedly from the Lords and Commons asserting the bastardy of Edward IV's sons; the first purpose of Henry VII's first Parliament in November 1485 was to declare his right to the throne, the second to request his marriage to Elizabeth of York, daughter of Edward IV, in an attempt to heal the nation's wounds.

Edward IV was the first king to try to live off his own resources without repeated demands for taxation. So comparatively few Parliaments were summoned in his reign, and in those the influence of the Commons was of less consequence. But we have a glimpse of him as an emollient manager of Parliament in his address of 1467: 'John Say [Speaker] and ye Sirs, comyn to this my Court of Parlement for the Comon of this my Lond. The cause why y have called and summoned this my present Parlement is, that y purpose to lyve up on my nowne, and not to charge my subgettes but in grete and urgent causes, concernyng more the wele of theym self, and also the defence of theym and of this my Reame, rather than my nown pleasir.' A sense of royal support underpinned the stability and confidence of the Commons. Freedom of members from arrest in, and to and from Parliament was a privilege confirmed when Edward consented to a Commons petition after William Hyde was arrested on his way to Westminster for a supposed debt of £69 due to a London mercer. Procedure is ordered and dignified. After a Mass of the Holy Ghost, knights and burgesses answer to their names and progress to the Lords to hear the Chancellor's opening speech. After electing their Speaker, they begin hearing petitions and attending to the reading of Bills. In the Parliament of 1478, these included laws to monitor the quality of cloth and roof tiles, to ban the playing of frivolous games – quoits, dice, football – in favour of archery practice, and to send Irishmen back to Ireland (with just a few exceptions). One member of the Commons at least had an advanced ideal of integrity, that it was sometimes necessary to act independently of king and Lords in order to keep faith with constituents. Nicholas Stathum's will of 1472 restored a bribe of 10 shillings, 'for somoche as I was one of the parleament and should be indifferent in euery mater in the parleament.'

There was no chance to be indifferent in the dynastic upheavals of 1483–5, for Parliament had no part in them. Some lords and gentry who had set out to attend the summons to Edward V's first Parliament arrived in London only to learn that it had been cancelled. They offered the throne to Richard of Gloucester, who could usefully maintain that he was not a usurper, but had been invited by the estates of the realm, even if not constituting a formal Parliament. The only Parliament he summoned himself in 1484 meekly gave the nod to de facto power. Its chief responsibility was 'to quiet men's minds, to remove the occasion of all doubts and seditious language.'

In the turmoil of the fifteenth century, Parliament had been powerless to take any political initiatives. The Commons had a large minority of royal placemen to nudge the house into conformity on major issues, such as Richard's seizure of the throne. Both the conflicts which had split the aristocracy, and the Yorkist building of a strong machinery of central government based on the council rather than on Parliament, laid the foundations of the instinctively autocratic rule of the Tudors. And still in 1485 the Commons found itself, as it had been for 200 years, in the anomalous position of being part of Parliament – necessary to complete the three estates – and yet not part of it, meeting outside the Palace, without a fixed location, not permitted, as remains the case, beyond the bar of the House of Lords, petitioning for legislation, but not assenting to it.

Nonetheless, by 1485 the role of Parliament had become clearly defined. It was no longer primarily a judicial body, but an assembly for law-making, consultation, and for agreeing taxation. The king still had power to dispense with statute, and even Parliament itself, but he was unable to impose taxation on the general population without Parliament's consent. And however deferential the Commons were to king and lords, they were necessary. Their rights to determine taxation and to hear petitions and propose remedies for grievances were not in question. The growth of the authority of their Speaker and their concern for proper electoral practice had increased the status of the lower house, and in 1489 the judgement that valid law needed the assent of both Houses went some way to redressing the political imbalance between Lords and Commons. And somehow, perhaps because of the political and social disorders rather than despite them, an underlying ideal of legality had endured, an assumption intermittently articulated that society could ultimately be governed only with its own consent.

Sir John Fortescue, Chief Justice under Edward IV, had perceived and argued this point in the distinction he drew between absolute and constitutional monarchies, France and England. 'The first king may rule his people by such laws as he maketh himself. And therefore he may set upon them taxes and other impositions, such as he will himself without their assent. The second king may not rule his people by other laws than such as they assent to . . . Blessed be God, this land is ruled under a better law; and therefore the people thereof be not in such penury, nor thereby hurt in their persons . . . Lo this is the fruit of jus politicum et regale, under which we live.' His complacency was premature; Tudor and Stuart kings were reluctant sharers of power, and 200 years more of protracted and bitter struggles lay ahead to bring about a mutually accepted balance of king and Parliament.

The Early Tudors

In the Tudor period, the word 'state', with its overtones of authoritarian government, was first used for the political identity of the land. This was no accident. The painstaking consolidation of the role of the medieval Parliament still culminated in a period of autocratic or near-autocratic rule. The dynastic fracture of 1485 was spanned by the strong preference of the Yorkist and early Tudor kings for summoning a council, consisting of lords only, rather than Parliaments, to advise on policy, adjudicate legal disputes and administer the nation.

Certainly the instabilities of the Tudor period required a strong hand. Religious upheavals had social and economic consequences: the redistribution of wealth and land that followed the dissolution of the monasteries caused acute social instability. Prices quadrupled; the population doubled. The vestiges of the feudal relation between king and nobles were dissolving too. Henry VIII's preference for government through a small Privy Council excluded many nobles from a political role. His French wars were the last occasions on which the nobility with its private armies rallied in support; by the end of the century, county militias had supplanted them. Though the aristocratic order appears stable – 57 peers in 1485, and

55 in 1603 – a quarter of noble families died out every generation, either through natural causes or as the penalty for ill-judged political or religious affiliations. Henry VIII and Elizabeth I were both eager to promote capable lawyers and administrators to manage the growing machinery of government, sometimes, like Wolsey and Thomas Cromwell, from humble backgrounds.

But the need for more professional government, which at first encouraged the rise of autocratic monarchy, led in turn to the growth of Parliament as a useful and appropriate handmaid of royal will. There may have been little real choice, but nonetheless parliamentary endorsement was sought and gained for all the major issues of Tudor rule: the break with Rome, Henry VIII's Acts of Succession, the Acts of Uniformity, Mary Tudor's alliance with Philip of Spain, the Elizabethan religious settlement, and the fate of Mary Queen of Scots. There is one measure of the centrality of Tudor Parliaments: that Robert Cecil in the 1590s called them 'the plagues of Job' is a further index of their capacity to press thorns into the flesh of instinctive autocrats.

Crown, Lords and Commons generally expected to work in partnership for the unity of England against foreign threats, and for the honour of the monarch. There was little conflict of interests. Throughout the Tudor period and beyond, the status of the Commons was far below that of the Lords. Though the judges in 1489 rejected an act of attainder because 'nothing was said of the Commons', we should not be deceived, nor were they, into believing that they were on the instant elevated to the triumvirate. The Commons was viewed as the proper forum for airing grievances, and as a place where the economic temper of the country could most clearly be assessed in its response to demands for taxation. Though knights and burgesses would raise matters of local concern there, the interests at stake were often those of noble families.

Between 1461 and 1529, only the royal need for money kept the political function of the Commons alive. The king was expected, as he always had been, to finance his own government in times of peace, and usually sought parliamentary grants for conducting war. Henry VIII and Wolsey pursued costly military and diplomatic adventures, but did not find the Commons compliant in funding them. Disputes over money were guaranteed by the rising costs of war, Henry's personal extravagance, and the rapid alienation of Crown land in the power-brokering of the fifteenth-century civil

Henry VIII in Parliament
(the House of Lords).

wars, which reduced royal income. The opportunity to restore it with Church land was squandered: by 1558 three-quarters of former monastic land had passed from royal possession. The king's growing inability to finance his own government was to sour relations with Parliament until 1689, and to stoke the fires of revolution between 1603 and 1649.

Meeting Places

The united interests of the Lords and Commons were advanced in the first half of the sixteenth century by their acquiring fixed and adjacent chambers for their meetings. Neither House had ever known a space dedicated to its exclusive use, but had borrowed rooms from king or abbot, or had met out of London altogether, wherever the court happened to be. The lack of a settled meeting place reflected both the king's power to summon Parliaments wherever he chose, and the presumption that meetings would be brief. But Henry VIII's abandoning of the Palace of Westminster after the fire of 1512 left the Lords fully in possession of the White Hall, which soon came to be known as 'the Parliament Chamber', and which they continued to occupy until 1801. In addition, Henry's rejection of the hundred-strong Great Council favoured by his father hastened the crystallisation of 'the House of Lords', a title first used in 1544. The Commons moved into their designated permanent chamber, St Stephen's Chapel, in about 1549. Now Lords and Commons were manifestly two branches of a composite institution, and the Palace of Westminster the exclusive location of parliamentary activity. Both Houses began to keep journals of proceedings, the Lords in 1510, and the Commons in 1542.

Once they were secure, kings were not disposed to summon Parliaments. The new king needed Parliament at the start of the reign, to pass laws, especially acts of attainder to eliminate his enemies, and to grant essential tax revenue. It had no role in policy-making, and after 1497 Henry VII only summoned a single Parliament, in 1504. We know something of its proceeding. It began with a sermon by the Archbishop of Canterbury, as Chancellor, on the text 'Choose justice, ye who judge the world'. He then nominated committees to hear petitions, and dismissed the Commons to choose a Speaker. Not until the fifth day was Edmund Dudley presented as Speaker, and, after formal excuses and protestations of inadequacy, he was entered in the roll. Once Bills had been read and understood, and the advice and assent of Lords and Commons given, the king's answer was, as now, 'Le Roy le veult'. Henry was not persuaded of its necessity: 'After the present Parliament, his highness is not minded, for the ease of his subjects,'(he was thinking of taxation) 'without great, necessary and urgent causes, of long time to call and summon a new Parliament.' Parliament sat for only 25 weeks in his 24-year reign.

Every new king was required to summon a Parliament, and in his early years Henry VIII encouraged it, since his plans for military exploits in Europe needed financing. But during the years of Wolsey's dominance of government (1515–29), only one Parliament met, in 1523, again because there was a financial crisis. Despite summoning only nine Parliaments in his 37-year reign, which sat for just over three years in total, Henry nonetheless altered its sense of its own importance. His nurturing of the anti-clerical bond between himself and the Reformation Parliament from 1529 in what was clearly a marriage of convenience ensured that Parliament became an indispensable legislative assembly, though expected to comply with the royal will as a matter of course, as it did during the protracted divorce from Rome. Its willingness to cooperate may be partly explained by the events connected with the passing of the Bill for suppression of the lesser monasteries in 1536. The Commons delayed, so Henry sent for them and told them that delay would cost some of them their heads. When the matter still dragged, he sent for the influential Edward Montague, who knelt before him. 'Ho man! Will they not suffer my Bill to pass?' He took Montague by the ear. 'Get my Bill passed by tomorrow, or else tomorrow this head of yours will be off!' The Bill was duly passed.

Such a style of management was not in evidence at the first Parliament of the reign, in January 1510, though it was the pretext for a display of royal magnificence, including a High Mass in Westminster Abbey. The crowd outside was so dense that the King had to fight his way across to the Palace. Among the Bills considered by the Lords was one concerning the reform of apparel (third reading), for sending better wools to the staple of Calais, for punishing perjury, and for unloading ships not only in ports but also in other places called creeks (all first reading). After three readings the Clerk of the Parliament sent them on to the Lower House. At the concluding session, after formal praise of the king, the Chancellor commanded all the Acts made and done for the public good to be recited by the Clerk of the Crown. The royal will was noted on the back of each. The Bill for a subsidy was endorsed: 'The King thanks his Commons for their good will in making their grants.' The Chancellor thanked all, and declared Parliament dissolved, with a free privilege to all for their return home.

Wolsey's high-handed ambition alienated the Parliament men. Judicial reform, particularly his raising of the profile of the Court of Star Chamber both for subjects unable to obtain justice through common law and as a statutory tribunal, completed the stripping away of Parliament's judicial role. Wolsey's hostility to Parliaments was confirmed when he was forced to summon one in 1523 to obtain funds for the conduct of war abroad. One member complained that the high cost, in blood and cash, of the acquisition of Therouanne, was 'more than twenty such ungracious dog holes could be worth'. Thomas More, the Crown's nominee, was selected as Speaker when the Commons met, and boldly adapted the usual formal request for the privileges of Parliament to be granted into a persuasive appeal for the right of members to speak freely on any subject before them without threat of reprisal. The anti-clerical mood of the assembly was resistant to Wolsey's control. He sought a subsidy four times higher than any previous one, and when the Commons flatly refused, he came in person with a posse of associates to intimidate them, in full scarlet, scorning them as ungrateful dogs and ordering them to agree the subsidy. There was 'a marvellous obstinate silence'. More, kneeling, explained that there could be no debate in the presence of strangers, and Wolsey had no choice but to depart. His next strategy, to raise money by the extra-parliamentary device of benevolences, also led to conflict with Parliament: benevolences had been outlawed by an Act of 1484. 'A usurper's law,' retorted Wolsey. Parliament's response was assured: 'the act had been passed in Parliament, and its validity was unaffected by the character of the king.' Wolsey did not summon Parliament again. Thomas Cromwell was a member of the Commons for the first time in 1523, but was disillusioned by the discrepancy between words and deeds: 'I amongst others have endured a Parliament . . . where we communed of war, peace, strife, contention, debate, murmur, grudge, riches, poverty, perjury, truth, falsehood, justice, equity, deceit, oppression, magnanimity, activity, force, attemprance, treason, murder, felony, conciliation, and also how a commonwealth might be edified. However, in conclusion we have done as our predecessors have been wont to do, that is to say, as well as we might and left where we began.' But he learned quickly, and in the Reformation Parliament was to become one of the consummate parliamentary managers in history.

In 1529 Henry VIII dropped Wolsey and turned to Parliament to redress both the humiliations of his foreign policy and his marital discontent. The consequence, which he could not have foreseen, was a political and religious upheaval which made England a nation. It was also a turning point in the history of Parliament.

CHAPTER THREE

From Partnership to Division:
Monarch and Parliament
1529–1629

T HE PARLIAMENT summoned in 1529, which became known
as the Reformation Parliament, was to continue meeting
intermittently for seven years. Its early years were dominated
by Thomas More, now Chancellor, and after his fall, by Thomas
Cromwell. More opened proceedings by praising the king as a
good shepherd, and attacking Wolsey as 'the great bell-wether
which had led the flock astray'. A committee of both Houses
presided over by More signed a list of forty-five grievances against
Wolsey, and formal proceedings against him were only deflected
by Cromwell's eloquent opposition, perhaps speaking as the voice
of the king. 'The nether house' was in an anti-clerical mood, and
ready to sing the king's music. It aired six great griefs about
oppression by the spirituality: excess fines for probate of testaments, exaction of corpse presents, monopoly of agriculture,
participation in the leather, wool and cloth trades, neglect of the
poor in favour of 'lying in the court in Lords' houses', and 'ignorant priests with 10 or 12 benefices and resident in none'. These
could not be talked of before, for 'fear of being made a heretic.'
But now God has illuminated the eyes of the king, and men begin
'charitably to desire' a reformation. The spiritual peers 'frowned
and grunted' when they heard of the requests from the lower
house for clerical reform, and More too misjudged the Commons
when he set out to tackle heresy and schism, 'divers new enor-

The Commons in St Stephen's.

mities' which he accused Wolsey of neglecting. But this was not what the Commons wanted to hear. They were ready to echo the king's conviction that the authority Rome wielded in England through Convocation was a threat to royal supremacy, the loyalty of his subjects and perhaps also to Parliament.

The point of no return was reached in 1532. The Act in Conditional Restraint of Annates, ending the payment of fees to Rome by clergy on their appointment to benefices, was passed in the Lords by a majority vote, the first recorded instance of such a procedure. Cromwell pounced, fanned the flames of anti-clericalism in the Commons, and secured the Act for the Submission of Clergy in May 1532. Thomas More resigned the Great Seal in protest that the Act of Parliament was 'directly repugnant to the laws of God and his Holy Church'. More's vain protest was at an alliance between king and Commons which had removed all limitations on the scope of parliamentary statute. Now the dominoes fell: April 1533: the Act in Restraint of Appeals (appeals to be directed not to Rome, but to English Church Courts); 1534: the Act of Supremacy: 'Be it enacted by authority of this present Parliament that the King our sovereign Lord . . . shall be reputed the only supreme head in earth of the Church of England called Anglicana Ecclesia'; 1536: the Bill for Dissolution of the Lesser Houses, which did not affect any of the Lords Spiritual. It was passed 'by the consent of the great and fat abbots in the hope that their monasteries should have continued still, but even at that time one said in the Parliament house that these were as thorns but the great abbots were putrefied old oaks and they must needs follow or many years be passed.'

The session of 1536 was the first to be formally opened in the Lords Chamber, a practice that still continues after nearly 500 years. In his opening address Lord Chancellor Audley praised the king, as he must. Catherine of Aragon was dead, and Anne Boleyn executed. 'Who else would after two such marriages venture upon yet a third, except this great sovereign, who yielded reluctantly and from no carnal desire to the urgings of his nobility, much troubled by the uncertainty of the throne?' Who, indeed?

The elections for the new Parliament of 1539 were systematically influenced by Cromwell, through pressure on shire and borough councillors, in order to secure a 'more tractable' Commons. And in a reformed Lords, with 'the great and fat abbots' removed, the remaining Lords Spiritual were a broken-spirited minority. So Cromwell must have been surprised to be arrested at the Council table in June 1540, and condemned to death by Act of Attainder in the very Parliament he had so dominated for eight years. Hollow accusations against him were the revenge of the great – among them Norfolk, and Gardiner, Bishop of Winchester – against the upstart son of a sheep shearer, 'a person of as poor and low degree as few be within this your realm'. There was deep resentment of the power the 'foul churl' had acquired, and fear of his relentless pursuit of chosen victims through the treason laws. If the Parliament of Henry's last years faltered, the sacrifice of Cromwell's skills was to blame. Yet the development of Parliament in the 1530s had been decisive. With the king's encouragement, it had elevated statute law above all other authority. It had become a unified legislative assembly with a wide remit and a recognised political function. It had new prestige among powerful subjects, though it had no interest in challenging royal power or even in claiming a monopoly of legislation. It delegated to the king power over the Succession Act, the Act of Union with Wales, and control of imported French wines. But the Commons in particular now enjoyed status, and a place in it began to be seen as desirable. Country gentry even infiltrated borough seats, evading the rule that borough representatives had to be residents. The landed interest, the dominant section of society, was to monopolise the Commons until the end of the nineteenth century.

Parliamentary Privilege

An important benchmark of the status of the Commons was its assertion of its privileges. In the Middle Ages, its members enjoyed a modicum of privileges: they were free from arrest at a private suit while on parliamentary business, and the Speaker claimed free access to the king to express Commons' views, free speech in communicating them, and pardon if he misrepresented them. Requests for confirmation of such privileges were a formal element of the opening of a parliamentary session and were, as a matter of course, formally granted. But free speech within Parliament was not a recognised privilege. Thomas Yonge, imprisoned in 1451 for proposing in Parliament that York be named as heir presumptive, petitioned that members of the Commons 'ought to have their freedom to speak and say in the house of their assembly what they think convenient or reasonable, without any kind of challenge, charge or punishment therefore to be laid to them in any wise.' But there was no progress for this desired privilege until Henry VIII's time. Henry was confident enough to allow Parliament surprising liberties, including criticism of his policy and his private affairs. More's eloquent appeal for free speech in the 1523 Parliament had found favour with the king. The Commons should be 'utterly discharged of all doubt and fear . . . every man to discharge his conscience and boldly in every thing incident among us to declare his advice; and whatsoever happen any man to say, that it may like your noble Majesty, of Your inestimable goodness, to take all in good part.' It was a small price to pay for an effective ally of royal policy. By the end of the reign, the Bishop of Winchester could use the liberty of the House proverbially: 'I am like one of the commons House, that, when I am in my tale, think I should have liberty to make an end.'

The Ferrers case of 1543 placed the authority for immunity from arrest in the hands of the Commons itself. Previously an arrested member could be freed only by a request for a writ from the Speaker to the Court of Chancery. But when George Ferrers, a burgess for Plymouth, was arrested in a suit for debt while on his way to Parliament, the Commons sent their Serjeant-at-Arms with a mace, as symbol of the authority of the House, to secure his freedom. When the sheriffs of the City of London defied him, they were themselves imprisoned and forced to apologise. 'By warrant of the mace' the House had exerted its authority. At a meeting of both Houses together, the king supported the action: 'We be informed by our judges that we at no time stand so highly in our estate royal as in the time of Parliament, wherein we as head and you as members are conjoined and knit together as one body politic.'

A parallel freedom was claimed by the Commons for running its own affairs: keeping a full record to furnish legal evidence, the power to resolve disputed elections, the power to judge whether a member was qualified, and the disciplining of its own members. Peter Wentworth, for example, in 1576, was imprisoned and examined 'by order of the House', and was allowed to return only after making 'humble submission' before them.

Thomas Smith, writing in 1565, was able to celebrate Parliament as an expression both of the royal will and of the community of the land: it is 'the most high and absolute power in the realm . . . It bindeth all manner of persons', because 'every Englishman is intended to be there present, privy and parties to all its actions . . . and the consent of the Parliament is taken to be every man's consent.' Members were added in the mid-century from Wales, the Palatinate of Chester and Calais; English boroughs were enfranchised, and the Crown's desire to broaden representation increased the membership from 300 to 462 between 1504 and 1603.

The Commons in St Stephen's

The status of the House of Commons was raised by its occupation of the deconsecrated St Stephen's Chapel as its debating chamber at some point between 1547 and 1550. No one knows exactly when the move occurred, but accounts show the sum of £344 16s. 10d. to cover 'sundry charges made and done in and upon the Parlyament house at Westminster some tyme Saynt Stephen's Chappell' for the year 1549–50, so unless Parliament cohabited with workmen, 1550 seems the earliest practicable date. The Commons found a long narrow building set out collegiate fashion, with rows of stalls facing one another across the width of the chapel, which was five bays long. An existing wooden screen made an ante-chapel of the two western bays, and supported a loft or 'pulpitum', from which services from the Sarum Primer had been sung. In such an inconvenient space the Commons had to improvise procedure: the Speaker's chair was raised up on the altar steps, and the lectern was replaced by a table for clerks and the mace. The ante-chapel became the Commons lobby, and when there was a vote, the Ayes passed through a set of doors in the screen, while the Noes remained in their places. The stalls were the benches for members; their facing one another disposing them to behave in an adversarial manner, an arrangement which fostered the later development of a two-party system. Though the short return stalls inside the screen provided some cross-bench seating, the bar of the house was set in front of these. The disposition of Charles Barry's Commons Chamber of 1852, and of its replacement by Giles Gilbert Scott (1945–50), pays homage to the original St Stephen's both in layout and intimacy of scale. So too, it is said, does the continuing practice of bowing the head to the Speaker when members enter the Chamber, rooted either in reverence to the former altar of St Stephen's, or in the necessity of ducking the head when passing through the screen to avoid losing lofty headgear.

John Vowell, member for Exeter, described the Chamber as he knew it in 1571: 'This House is framed and made like unto a theatre, being four rows of seats one above another . . . upon the lower row, next to the Speaker, sit all such of the Queen's Privy Council and head officers as be knights or burgesses of that House' (the origins of the government front bench), 'but after, everyone sitteth as he cometh . . . because each man in that place is of like calling.' The small gallery was accessible only by a ladder; in 1641 when a member sat perched on it, Speaker Lenthall 'called out to him and desired him to take his place, and not sit upon the said ladder as if he were going to be hanged. At which many of the House laughed.' Over the years the magnificent interior vanished: the wall paintings behind panelling, whitewash or tapestries, the soaring painted vault behind a false ceiling. A door for fresh air remained to one side of the east wall, giving access to Solomon's Porch. Here the younger Pitt sped to vomit after an excess of port, though still listening to a speech by Fox. Having 'yielded to his malady', he returned to reply with 'little less than his usual brilliance', as Wilberforce narrated.

The Commons was now established in the most sumptuous chamber in the former royal residence. Though Lords and Commons were closely linked by family ties, and by social and economic interests, a jocular resentment about the promotion of the Commons to the heart of the Palace persisted in royal circles. When twelve members visited James I at Newmarket in 1620, at their approach he called out, 'Chairs! Chairs! Here be twel' kynges coming.' Pepys in 1668, very grand in the Admiralty, sought to amuse Charles II with a similar allusion: 'April 2. From the Privy Stairs to Westminster Hall, and taking water. The King and the Duke of York were in the new buildings, and the Duke of York called to me whither I was going. And I answered aloud, "To wait on our masters at Westminster", at which he and all the company laughed; but I was sorry and troubled for it afterwards for fear any Parliament-man should have been there; and it will be a caution to me for the time to come.' From the mid-seventeenth century onwards, St Stephen's rather than the White Hall, home of the Lords, was commonly known as 'The Parliament House', a measure of the primacy achieved by the Commons during the political upheavals of the mid-century.

Henry VIII's death in 1547 was concealed for three days, and Parliament kept in session, contrary to all precedent, to ensure Somerset's emergence as Protector during the minority of Edward VI. This fudge was the prelude to 11 years of political and religious instability, intensified when Mary Tudor succeeded her half-brother in 1553. The national Catholic Church was converted into a Protestant one by the Protectors Somerset and Northumberland, but restored again to Rome by the Catholic Mary.

Five Parliaments were summoned in less than seven years in Edward's reign. The Protectors needed money for the Scottish war, to pay off Henry VIII's war debts, and because of inflation and the profligate distribution of Crown land to greedy nobles. They also needed Parliament's authority for a continuing religious reformation because of the precedent set by Henry VIII and the

Reformation Parliament. The 1548 Parliament passed the First Act of Uniformity, which introduced an English prayer book, imposed penalties for non-observance, and ordered the suppression of both images and Latin primers. It was the first occasion when religious practice had been prescribed by a secular authority. The Second Act of Uniformity followed in the 1552 Parliament which required every subject to attend church on Sunday, at one of the rechristened services of morning prayer, evening prayer, or the Lord's Supper. This Act was the beginning of 'keeping Sunday special'. It was accompanied, appropriately, by an Act for the control of alehouses by Justices of the Peace, when liquor began for the first time to be licensed.

Mary's first Parliament in 1553 begged her not to marry abroad, a plea she fiercely rejected. Having legitimised Mary to smooth the succession, it could only lose itself in ferocity, attainting the Dudley family, which had tried to place Lady Jane Grey on the throne, and Thomas Cranmer, and disposing of them. Mary had no choice but to work with Parliament in her attempt to restore Catholicism. A few monasteries were re-founded, some clerical taxes returned to Rome, and tough heresy laws were introduced, but former Church lands had passed beyond her reach. The political nation was divided; there was widespread suspicion of her personal and political alliance with Spain. When the Regency Bill, which sought to exclude Elizabeth from the succession in favour of Philip of Spain, was introduced in Parliament, there were many absences in both Houses. A roll-call was taken; some members were indicted in the Court of King's Bench, and those who failed to appear to answer the charges had their possessions seized. Stephen Gardiner was Lord Chancellor, and drove the legislative programme, but he was not a skilled manager and met strong resistance in the Lords. His death in 1555 left a vacuum, and the parliamentary history of the reign dissolved in brief sessions, absenteeism, slipshod recording of proceedings and the lack of serious domestic issues.

Parliament under Elizabeth I

At the accession of Elizabeth I in 1558, the position of Parliament seemed secure, provided that it did not offend the royal will. Henry VIII had made it an instrument of his religious policy, and it was inevitable that Elizabeth would also have to achieve her religious settlement through Parliament. But it was also inevitable that Parliament would subsequently seek to examine the royal prerogative. The Crown's financial difficulties were increasing, and the granting of taxation was, more than ever, the Commons' lever on policy. Lords and Commons had had their first taste of opposition to Mary Tudor's foreign and religious policy. So it is not at all surprising that the relation between the new queen and Parliament during her 45-year reign was a volatile one. Her attitude to it ranged from the storminess of a severe governess towards errant children, to the romantic allure with which she strove to invest herself, and the shameless flattery and flirtatiousness with which she wooed it. There were continual conflicts, over marriage and the succession, over religious questions, over the fate of Mary Queen of Scots, over monopolies controlled by the Crown, and, above all, over Parliament's freedom to set its own agenda. There were ten Parliaments in the reign, but the queen preferred to restrict the length of sessions in order to minimise provocation. Apart from the religious settlement and the provision of money, Parliament was not wanted. There was little need for new legislation, so Parliament sat, in all, for an average of only three weeks a year, and, when they occurred, sessions averaged about ten weeks. The last Parliament of the reign, in 1601, was the unhappiest.

Thomas Smith, writing in 1565, took a large view of the functions of the monarch in Parliament: 'The Parliament abrogateth old laws, maketh new, giveth orders for things past, and for things hereafter to be followed, changeth rights, and possession of private men, legitimateth bastards, establisheth forms of religion, altereth weights and measures, giveth forms of succession to the Crown, defineth of doubtful rights, whereof is no new law already made, appointeth subsidies, tailles, taxes and Impositions, giveth most free pardons and absolutions, restoreth in blood and name as the highest court, condemneth or absolveth them whom the Prince will put to that trial.' An assembly with so wide a notional mandate proved a magnet for the leading spirits of the time: Grenville, Hawkins, Gilbert, Sidney, Bacon, Drake, Raleigh, Bodley, Cotton, Fulke Greville and Donne all sat in Parliament at some point in the reign. There are attractive glimpses of the sensible and pragmatic Raleigh, first opposing the persecution of sectarians: 'A law against a fact is just, but the law is very hard that taketh life or sendeth into banishment, where men's intentions shall be judged by a jury and they shall be judges what another meant'; later resisting unnecessary state regulation over the sowing of hemp: 'For my part, I do not like this constraining of men to manure or use their grounds at our wills; but rather, let every man use his ground to that which it is most fit for, and therein use his own discretion.'

The membership of the Commons was homogeneous. Over half were landowning country gentlemen, and many of them had received a legal education or been to university. In 1601, 253 out of 460 members had been educated at the Inns of Court. A large minority were members of the royal household, about three-quarters of which served as MPs or JPs. Court and country were, in effect, the same section of the dominant class at different times of year. The growth of London had already bestowed a fashionable season upon it, and fathers thought it fit to send their sons to the Commons as a finishing school, to educate them in statecraft.

The queen opened Parliaments herself, in considerable splendour, riding to the door of the Lords on her own horse in her early years, later in an open chariot or a horse litter. The formal proceedings would sometimes include a royal imperative; in 1571 she wished 'they would be more quiet than they were at the last time.' There is a description by Fleetwood of the assembling of the 1584 Parliament which shall stand for all. The Commons first met in their own Chamber, 'out of all order, in troops standing upon the floor, making strange noises. After this we were all called into the White Hall, and there called by name before my Lord Steward and the rest of the Council; and after that we were sworn.' Then, as now, there were many people in a small space, 'with great thrusting'. The queen commanded the Lord Keeper of the Great Seal to 'show the causes of the Parliament' (a forerunner of the Queen's Speech). 'And after that Mr Treasurer moved the House to make an election of a Speaker, whereupon he himself named my brother Puckering who sat next me; and there was not one word spoken. And then I said to my companions about me, "Cry Puckering", and then, they and I beginning, the rest did the same.'

The Commons usually sat six days a week, from 8 to 11 in the morning, the same hours as the law courts. Afternoons were reserved for committee meetings in smaller rooms in the Palace. Voting was at first by acclamation, but it was soon acknowledged that this method gave undue advantage to the loud-voiced. Shortage of seats caused constant grousing, and the method of division adopted, in which the 'Ayes' left the Chamber and the 'Noes' kept their places tended towards an outcome in which the 'Noes' carried it, 'because divers are loth to go forth for losing of their places. And many that cry "aye, aye, aye" will sit still with the noes.' In the 1601 Parliament, a Bill for the Stricter Observance of the Sabbath received 105 'Ayes' and 106 'Noes'. It was revealed that one 'Aye' member had been pulled back and held in his seat by a 'No' member. Raleigh's comment – 'Why, if it please you, it is a small matter to pull one by the sleeve, for so have I done myself often times' – caused a stir. William Knollys, Senior Councillor, condemned the episode. 'And as for that other gentlemen that said he had often done the like, I think he may be ashamed of it.'

After a Bill had received a second reading, it had to be either 'engrossed' (transferred to parchment), committed (referred to a committee), or rejected. Rules of conduct were agreed: language had to be civil, members must give way to others, no member may speak twice in a day on the same subject, and all remarks must be addressed to the Speaker. The Speaker had authority to license absentees: lawyers were inclined to slip out of the Chamber into the courts to follow their profession. Members wore their hats in the House, and if they wished to speak, stood up bare-headed. But conduct, despite the rules, was habitually rowdy. They sabotaged speeches they disliked with coughing, whistling, spitting or even squaring up to one another. In 1572, Arthur Hall's speech expressed sympathy for Mary Queen of Scots and the Duke of Norfolk over the Ridolfi Plot. 'The House misliked so much of his talk that with shuffling of feet and hawking, they had well nigh barred him to be heard.' When speeches were drowned in the same way in 1601, Robert Cecil rebuked the behaviour as being 'more fit for a grammar school than a Court of Parliament'. The stairs down from the lobby to Westminster Hall were always congested with servants, and the Warden of the Fleet Prison was commanded by the House in 1581 to lay hands on some of the miscreant serving men, to make an example of them for their 'lewd disorder and outrage'.

Direction of this potentially turbulent body of men was attempted in four ways: by the queen personally, by the Privy Council, by electoral manipulation, and by the selection of the Speaker.

Elizabeth watched the progress of a session closely, and used her authority to summon the Speaker or groups of members to White-

Elizabeth I in Parliament.

hall Palace to seek to influence the course of legislation. Her right of veto, and of proroguing or dissolving Parliament, were her weapons of last resort, but she preferred to try more distinctively feminine tactics first. In 1563, under pressure from Parliament about the succession, she won precious concessions with unashamed emotion: 'And so I assure you all that, though after my death you may have many step-dames, yet shall you never have a more natural mother than I mean to be unto you all.' Mother, but also bold father and protector. Steeling hearts against a probable invasion by Spain she declared: 'I protest, I never feared, and what fear was, my heart never knew . . . If I have used my forces to keep the enemy far from you, I have thereby thought your safety the greater, and your danger the less. Now must I give you all as great thanks as ever prince gave to loving subjects.' Such rhetoric, such flattery carried her through many crises, and was hard to resist.

The chief instrument of Tudor government was the Privy Council, between 12 and 20 strong under Elizabeth. Some councillors were peers, others were members of the Commons. Councillors, sitting together as ministers do today on the Treasury bench, were accustomed to manage debate and act as channels of communication between queen and Commons. Privy Councillors also exploited the Commons' occasional preference for confrontation to put pressure on a vacillating Elizabeth to take vital decisions, on the succession, on religious policy, on Mary Queen of Scots.

Through Crown or family patronage, particularly in borough elections where small-time officials were easily influenced, a significant number of royal servants or members of the household secured parliamentary seats. Though never enough to control the Commons, they formed a sizeable minority (50–70) whose loyalties were guaranteed.

The Speaker was generally a royal nominee, hand-picked by Queen and Privy Council, though not necessarily subservient to them, who decided in advance of a Parliament who the Speaker should be. The subsequent 'election' by the Commons was a mere formality. In 1597 Sir William Knollys, Controller of the Household, after the House had sat 'some space of time very silent', delivered his opinion about who was most fit to be Speaker – the House hawked and spat, and after silence he proceeded to name Mr Serjeant Yelverton, who blushed and put off his hat. Knollys invited anyone 'to supply another name as freely as I have done' but the whole House cried, 'Aye, aye, aye, let him be'.

Equally formal were the nominee's 'disabling words' in which he protested his unfitness for the task (transmuted in modern times into the 'show of reluctance' that accompanies a new Speaker's placing in the chair). John Croke, elected Speaker in 1601, protested: 'Who am I that should go on such a service? I am plain bred, of a weak understanding and judgement for so great a work, of frail memory . . . I am of a slow and unready speech.' But he was elected unanimously. The Speaker was an important ally of the Privy Council in the handling of legislation, and the queen, even at the end of her reign, spared no theatrical gesture in wooing him. Yelverton in 1597 reported that 'she pulled off her glove and gave me her hand to kiss, and said "You, sir, you are welcome to the butts, sir", and laid both her hands about my neck and stayed a good space.'

Throughout her reign, conflicts between herself and Parliament were endemic, and intensified as it neared its end. Mary Tudor had faced opposition to her marriage to Philip of Spain and to her religious policy; Elizabeth met a wider recalcitrance from members who felt entitled to raise matters of national importance which the queen regarded as 'matters of state' which Parliament was not entitled to discuss. 'Matters of state' included the royal prerogative, marriage and the succession, the religious settlement, the conduct of foreign policy, the regulation of trade and granting of monopolies. Parliament was as obstinate in pushing against so wide a proscription of subjects as Elizabeth was in asserting her rights, and unremitting attrition was joined. There were occasions, as over the succession question in 1566, and the fate of Mary Queen of Scots in 1572 after the Ridolfi Plot, when the queen stood alone against the Privy Council and both Houses of Parliament. She seems often to have relished the battle, and devised a whole armoury of tactics, not least magnificent rhetoric, with which to conduct it.

For four decades the succession question nagged. Elizabeth had smallpox in 1562, and the Commons petitioned her about the succession. She made no response. The 1566 Parliament fussed about it, and tried to trade a grant of taxation for discussion of the queen's marriage. She was enraged at this impertinence, and told the Spanish ambassador that the Commons was offering her £250,000 to do their will. She opposed the deal with fierce pride: 'I will never be by violence constrained to do anything. I thank God I am endued with such qualities that if I were turned out of the realm in my petticoat, I were able to live in any place in Christendom.' In her dissolution speech she added intimidation: 'Beware how ever you move your prince's patience as you have now done mine.' But Parliament was not persuaded of her immortality: she had a severe fever in 1572, and the assassination of William of Orange in 1584 displayed the flimsiness of the life of a Protestant monarch in an unstable Catholic-dominated Europe. In the 1570s Elizabeth continued to temporise: 'I know I am but mortal . . . but let good heed be taken that, in reaching too far after future good, you peril not the present and begin to quarrel, and fall by dispute together by the ears, before it be decided who shall wear my crown.' But the years, and the anxiety attendant on them, could not be stayed. In 1593 a Succession Bill was drawn up by Peter Wentworth and Henry

Bromley. Royal outrage instructed the Council to see to them, and two councillors tried to dissuade them from proceeding. Unyielding, they were committed to the Tower and the Fleet Prison, and three days later the Speaker delivered to the Commons a peremptory message from the queen: 'It is in me and my power to call Parliaments; it is in my power to end and determine the same; it is in my power to assent or dissent to anything done in Parliaments.' And that was that.

The Commons was just as insistent on discussing issues of religion, which tangled at many points with the succession question and which Elizabeth again regarded as her exclusive province. It was difficult enough for her to maintain the middle ground of her religious settlement under pressure from both Puritans and Catholics, but a Commons that had tasted power over religion in the 1530s was unlikely to abdicate its interest now. Puritan elements in Parliament desired a preacher to read a 45-minute discourse to members at 7 o'clock each morning; they attacked the authority of bishops despite a royal injunction not to do so; they requested public fasting by members to begin each day. Elizabeth was provoked: 'no public fast could be appointed but by her, and therefore their action impeached her jurisdiction.' At the discovery of the Duke of Norfolk's Ridolfi Plot in 1572, in which Mary Queen of Scots was implicated, the Privy Council demanded an emergency session of Parliament to seek immediate execution for both. Norfolk went to the block; Elizabeth spared her cousin. In the same session she vetoed a Bill concerning rites and ceremonies because it had not been first considered by the bishops. A diarist commented: 'The message that forbade the bringing of bills of religion into the House seemed much to impugn the liberty of the House, but nothing was said unto it.' She again forbade debates on religion in the 1584 Parliament, which this time voiced its discontent and invoked the Reformation Parliament: 'when the Pope first began to stagger in England, very many of the church matters took their beginning from the Nether House.' At the end of the session, the queen was censorious: 'I see many overbold with God Almighty, making too many subtle scannings of His blessed will, as lawyers do with human testaments.'

Catholic fanaticism intensified in the 1580s: Elizabeth was branded 'the impious Jezebel' and 'the monster of the world'. Mary Queen of Scots' implication in the Babington Plot in 1586 confirmed that Elizabeth's life was in jeopardy while Mary was alive. The Privy Council and Parliament joined forces to extract a death sentence from Elizabeth; the national interest could be fobbed off no longer. Parliament met in November. Job Throckmorton denounced the Scots' queen: 'The daughter of sedition, the mother of rebellion, the sister of unshame fastness . . . a Scottish of nation, a French of education, Papist of profession, a Guisan of blood, a Spaniard in practice, a libertine in life . . .' To destroy her would be 'one of the fairest riddances that ever the church of God had'. But is it Parliament's business? 'Under the warrant of God's law what may not this House do? I mean the three estates of the land. To deny the power of this House, ye know, is treason . . .' The Speaker sought an audience with Elizabeth. She would be pleased to forbear the taking of her blood if by any other means the safety of her majesty's own person and of the state might be preserved. The Privy Council and Parliament were adamant: There is 'none other way of safety'. Elizabeth was irresolute for some weeks, and only when panic and rumour swept the land early in 1587 did she consent to Mary's execution, on 8 February. Her moral agonising over the choice may be set against the response of Mary's son, James VI of Scotland, later James I of England: 'How fond and inconstant I were if I should prefer my mother to the title!'

Elizabeth was much less relaxed than her father had been about the subject matter and tone of Commons debates, and the quest of a handful of members for freedom to discuss what they thought touched the national interest was a continual provocation to her. In particular the brothers Paul and Peter Wentworth were in turn provoked to seize every opportunity to argue for freedom of discussion uninhibited by the rumours and messages sent indirectly to the Commons by the queen to influence proceedings, and the Privy Councillors acting as royal spies who took information in the other direction. But at every opening of a parliamentary session the Queen, through a member of the Privy Council, unvaryingly granted the Commons the freedom of speech they formally begged, but always reminded them of its limits, 'not to deal with her estate'. They were not 'to frame a form of religion or a state of government as to their idle brains shall seem meetest. She saith no king fit for his state will suffer such absurdities.' This warning was given to the 1593 Parliament, in the course of which seven members were imprisoned or suspended by the queen. The Commons passed a motion to have them set at liberty, but the official reply was brusque: 'The House must not call the Queen to account for what she doth of her royal authority. She liketh no such questions.' In such a political climate, the Wentworths of the Commons needed rare courage to advance, ahead of their time, the case for an uninhibited Parliament, and the price they paid was continual harassment and royal displeasure. In 1576 Peter Wentworth pleaded: 'In this House, which is termed a place of free speech, there is nothing so necessary for the preservation of the prince and state as free speech, and without, it is a scorn and mockery to call it a Parliament House, for in truth it is none, but a very school of flattery and dissimulation.' But for such a Parliament as this the nation was not yet ready.

Money, the most prized prerogative of the Commons, was always a quicksand for relations between monarch and Parliament. Elizabeth was scrupulously careful about her requests, but both her pride and the increasing gap between income and expenditure, especially in time of war, which necessitated further sale of Crown land, were obstacles in the path of easy agreement.

Two economic aspects of the Crown's prerogative, purveyance and monopolies, aroused widespread outrage, and fomented the most serious of all the conflicts between Elizabeth and Parliament in the last two assemblies of the reign, in 1597–8 and 1601. Purveyance was the Crown's right to purchase provisions for the household at below half the market price; the granting of patents for monopoly of trade in specific commodities, also a function of the prerogative, was widely abused by courtiers and government officials as lucrative sources of income, and was partially responsible for the serious inflation that afflicted Elizabethan England. Raleigh, for example, held monopolies for tin, playing cards, and the licensing of taverns. The 1597–8 Parliament was indignant about the effect of monopolies, and unmoved by Elizabeth's emollient rhetoric: 'Her Majesty hoped that her dutiful and loving subjects would not take away her prerogative – which is the chiefest flower in her garland and the principal and head pearl in her crown and diadem.' Elizabeth, a mistress of elegant vacillation, did nothing, and the 1601 Parliament was fractious. Robert Cecil, opening proceedings, hoped there would be no new laws made, and counselled against 'fantastic speeches and idle bills'. He had been outraged at the sight of a popular demonstration crowding the stairs and lobby of Parliament, the first on record, beseeching the Commons to take compassion of their griefs, for they were being spoiled, imprisoned and robbed by monopolists. Cecil's ill-judged anger against them welled up from his conviction that the business of Parliament was no concern of the populace: 'Whatsoever is subject to a public exposition cannot be good. Why, Parliament matters are ordinarily talked of in the streets!' And, of members who aired issues outside the House, 'I think those persons would be glad that all sovereignty were converted into popularity.'

But in debate members excoriated the abuse, and the prerogative which upheld it. Mr Martin listed the commodities that are ingrossed into the hand of those 'blood-suckers of the commonwealth': currants, iron, powder, cards, ox shin bones, train oil, transportation of leather, lists of cloth, ashes, aniseeds, vinegar, seal-coals, steel, aqua vitae, brushes, pots, saltpetre, lead, oil of blubber, dried pilchards in the smoke. 'Is not bread there?' 'Bread,' quoth one. 'Bread,' quoth another. 'No,' quoth Mr Hakewill, 'if order be not taken for these, bread will be there before the next Parliament. But what purpose is it to do anything by Act of Parliament when the Queen will undo the same by her prerogative.' The granting of monopolies is derogatory to her own majesty, odious to the subject, dangerous to the Commonwealth. In vain did Mr Secretary Cecil chide them for behaving like schoolboys.

But when the storm was at its fiercest, Elizabeth sent a message of gracious capitulation. She promised to reform anything that produced evil consequences: some should be repealed, some suspended, and none put in execution but such as should first have a trial according to the law for the good of the people. The conflict dissolved in good humour. Cecil was joyously utopian: 'Every man shall have salt as cheap as he can buy it or make it. And aqua vitae, and vinegar. Train oil shall go the same way; oil of blubber shall march in equal rank. The sowing of woad shall be free – though the Queen prays that when she cometh on progress to see you in your counties, she be not driven out of your towns by the stench.' Elizabeth's judicious concession succeeded in deferring the first statutory inroads on the royal prerogative until the next reign, provoked, again, by the issue of monopolies.

The queen was faced with opposition in all her Parliaments, and feelings on both sides often ran high. Yet the relationship held, because Elizabeth's manipulative skills shamelessly fostered a mystique of romance with her subjects capable of transcending radical differences of opinion, notably on the role of Parliament itself. By the end of her reign, some of the Commons had come to associate with the qualified privilege of free speech the right of unrestricted agenda and debate. They were confused rather than angry at the collision that ensued: 'either they must offend this gracious Sovereign, towards whom they dared not so much as to lift up one evil thought or imagination; or else suffer the liberties of their House to be infringed.' Even at times of friction members were ready to air the most extravagant panegyrics upon the queen's majesty. Job Throckmorton, he whose rhetoric had savaged Mary Queen of Scots, opened a different set of floodgates for his own sovereign: 'if it so pleased God, the last day of Queen Elizabeth's life might be the last day of this earth, that when she fleeteth hence we may then behold Jesus sitting in His throne of Judgement, to our endless and everlasting comfort.' A more earthbound prognosticator might have speculated about the political destiny of England under a monarch less capable of both managing and charming his Parliament, and also more likely than the parsimonious queen to be seen as extravagant with money and favours. At the end of the 1601 Parliament Elizabeth made her last public speech, able still to assert the bond that had united her with her people, especially in time of peril: 'This testimony I would have you carry hence for the world to know: that your Sovereign is more careful of your conservation than of herself, and will daily crave of God that they that wish you best may never wish in vain.' She took a final audience of her entire Parliament in Whitehall Palace, and in what became known as her 'Golden Speech', showed that even as a decayed old woman near death, she knew exactly how to play upon the heartstrings: 'Though God hath raised me high, yet this I count the glory of my crown, that I have reigned with your loves . . . There will never Queen sit in my seat with more zeal to my country, care for my subjects, and that will sooner with willingness venture her life for your good and safety, than myself. For it is my desire to live nor reign no longer than my life and reign shall be for your good. And though you have had and may have many princes more weighty and wise sitting in this seat, yet you never had nor shall have any that will be more careful and loving.'

The Early Stuarts

Thomas Smith's recipe for a good kingdom was 'peace, liberty, quietness, little taking of money, few Parliaments'. He was writing in 1565, and could he have looked back, 60 years later, on the reigns of Elizabeth and James I, he would have been well satisfied. For both monarchs, Parliament was a necessary nuisance, to be humoured by minor concessions into granting acutely needed subsidies. It was a period in which Parliaments met in short and infrequent sessions and conducted minimal legislative business. Most practical government at the time was local government, and, since national policy was initiated by the Privy Council or royal favourites such as Buckingham, there was little for Parliaments to do beyond responding to the royal need for money. They were not essential to the machinery of government. Foreign ambassadors reported home that the king possessed practical supremacy in all matters. The Venetian ambassador described the Commons as 'semi-rustics, noisy in their claims to order everything, but mostly unaccustomed to any authority.' Until 1689 there was not even a constitutional guarantee that Parliament would sit; each was conjured by the king, when he wanted one, with 40 days' notice given in his writ of summons, and each was dismissed, at the king's pleasure, with 'the king's majesty doth dissolve this Parliament.' A Parliament in session was automatically dissolved on the sovereign's death as late as 1830.

Why did a king summon a Parliament at all? Apart from the practical need for cash, there were two political advantages. The first was advisory. From Saxon times there was a precedent, even an obligation for a ruler to take wise counsel in order to bolster the practice of personal rule. The giving of counsel was the foundation of the privilege of free speech, yet Tudor and Stuart kings regarded counsel not as a right, but as a duty, to be given only when sought by the monarch, and only upon matters of his choice. Secondly, Parliament was a convenient way of ensuring that laws were binding, beyond dispute, on the whole of the kingdom, and was useful evidence that the ruler was not a tyrant. It was not only a point of contact between the king and his subjects in the provinces, but also a symbol of national unity, and celebrated as such by Henry VIII and James I. The nation was united in its Parliament, unlike its Continental rivals. 'The nation is not a nation until it is unus grex making law,' declared Sir Edwin Sandys in 1607. The established predisposition in favour of harmony between king and Parliament persisted in the early seventeenth century; a 'father–son' relationship was seen as the norm. As James himself defined it at the 1621 Parliament: 'A Parliament is composed of a head and a body. The head is the monarch and the body the three estates.' Power could only be exercised through the monarch, and it was still a contradiction in terms to exercise it against him. The king was himself a member of Parliament, exercised his right to sit in the Lords, and even claimed parliamentary privilege for his servants. Nor was Parliament power-seeking. It was not a settled body of men with a political agenda. Wide absenteeism had been a problem in Elizabeth's Parliaments, and continued in the next century. Most members were country gentry, for whom parliamentary service would be a distraction from routine activities. The disruption of travel and lodging in the city was seldom welcome, and the end of a session and permission to go home again was a relief. In the great crisis of 1641 the Commons failed to muster a quorum. They were reluctant to assume power in the 1640s, and only too ready to hand back to the Protector, to his son, and to the restored monarchy the additional burdens they had had to shoulder in troubled times. They expected stable government by the king in Parliament, exercising power in the interests of the dominant class. Until the Civil War, there was less call for regular Parliaments than there had been in the Middle Ages. There was nothing remotely threatening about Parliament's attitude to the monarch. Yet by 1629 relations between king and Parliament had broken down so completely that Charles I resolved to rule without a Parliament at all and might, but for serious misjudgement, have continued to do so indefinitely. A representative assembly could easily have died out at this point in history, as the States-General had in France in 1614. The mishandling of Parliament by the first two Stuart kings brought to an end a limited but mutually accepted partnership between monarch, Lords and Commons.

James had good intentions. Though an absolutist by inclination, he was ready to uphold his Coronation oath to respect the laws and customs of England, and to defer both to the structure of common law and the existence of a Parliament that saw itself as an integral part of government. He acknowledged Parliament's right to make

James I in Parliament.

law and to grant taxation. Yet he and his Commons were regularly at one another's throats. The period from 1600 to 1630 was a time of great economic hardship, and money was one source of mutual irritation. For 300 years the Crown's income had been insufficient to sustain the cost of government, even in peacetime, and the gap was ever widening. James lamented 'the eating canker of want'. From the 1590s Parliaments would not grant their rulers enough to live on, and also insisted that they should not raise revenue from other sources. The Jacobean Commons wanted to abolish the feudal rights which gave the Crown a measure of financial independence, not least because members needed Parliament for the advancing of local interests. A decline in the importance of subsidies threatened Parliament's very survival. But James was not only extravagant, but also took criticism as a personal insult and was contemptuous of almost all opinions the Commons offered, which he ascribed to 'idle heads and trouble makers'. His attitude needled members into airing grievances. Neither he nor Charles I had any capacity for managing their Parliaments as Elizabeth had done, lacked understanding and sympathy for them, and a successful partnership never blossomed. Instead, faction, conflict and premature dissolutions by James bred a minority of 'fiery spirits' who relished opportunities for dissent. The Commons was dominated by landowners, and completed by lawyers and merchants. They regarded themselves with some pride as the representative element in government, and James, at his first Parliament in 1604, confirmed their opinion: 'You who are here presently assembled to represent the body of this whole kingdom and all sorts of people within the same.' But his interest in demonology seemed unluckily to rub off on to parliamentary business: the Commons had failed to be summoned to the Lords to hear this speech, and members who sought access were roughly repelled by one Brian Tash, a yeoman of the guard, who thrust them out crying, 'Nay, goodman burgess, you must stay a while.' When the Commons began to discuss religion, he gracelessly prorogued it: 'I can not enough wonder that in three days after the beginning of the Parliament, men should go contrary to their oaths of Supremacy . . . There was nothing but curiosity, from morning to evening, to find fault with my propositions. I wish you would use your liberty with more modesty in time to come.'

This unhappy start set a tone that would not be dispelled. In 1610 James whinged to the Privy Council: 'The lower house have imperilled our health, wounded our reputation, emboldened all ill-natured people, encroached upon many of our privileges, and plagued our purse with their delays' – this last despite the Commons having been more open-handed with subsidies than they had ever been to Elizabeth. Bargaining came close to delivering a 'Great Contract' to resolve financial disagreements, but broke down over the king's refusal to concede his supremacy over religious policy and new demands from him for additional revenue. His intransigence provoked attacks on Scottish favourites and court extravagance, and in a temper he dissolved Parliament.

The 'Addled Parliament' of 1614 was ill-tempered and mistrustful. James dissolved it as a cross he resented having to bear: 'The Commons is a body without a head. The members give their opinion in a disorderly manner. At their meetings nothing is heard but cries, shouts and confusion. I am surprised that my ancestors should ever have allowed such an institution to come into existence.' In 1621, though his foreign policy needed financing, he was determined to exclude Parliament from any influence upon it. So they aired their grievances about monopolies, which had multiplied since 1603, and made a formal 'Protestation' disputing the king's right to imprison members at his will and asserting the propriety of debating foreign policy in the Commons. He summoned them to a council meeting, tore their protestation from the Commons' *Journal* on the grounds that it had been passed with less than one-third of the House present, and petulantly dissolved Parliament, accusing it of meddling. His view, that it was a merely consultative gathering on matters of policy, was increasingly at loggerheads with theirs, which his tactless conduct had done much to provoke. His last Parliament, in 1624, was comparatively tranquil. He conceded on foreign policy, declaring that 'no man dying of thirst longed for water more ardently than he desired a happy conclusion to his Parliament.' But no public Bills at all were sent from the Lords to the Commons. 'See what care they have for the Commonwealth, who were wont to be the chief statesmen and should be pillars of the commonwealth,' groused one disaffected member.

James's handling of Parliament was, without a doubt, clumsy, but a man as superstitious as he was would not quickly have recovered from the attempt to blow him up on 5 November 1605. The previous March Catholic plotters, desperate at the inconsistent persecution of Catholics that James had adopted, had secured a lease on a 'cellar' linked to the house of John Whynniard, Keeper of the King's Wardrobe, a ground-level room once part of the medieval kitchens and directly below the Parliament Chamber. The Palace was at this time a labyrinth of ramshackle buildings, some used by tradespeople, some by parliamentary administration, some as residences for officials of the Royal Household. All such residences needed cellarage for coal and wood. The leased cellar had easy access from the river, and hence from the Lambeth lodging of Robert Catesby, who was at the centre of the conspiracy. Between March and July, gunpowder was ferried across the river and stored in the cellar, using small barrels (firkins) for transport and large ones (hogsheads) for storage. By the end of July 36 hogsheads were in place. By late August, however, the powder was discovered to be 'decayed' – its components separated out harmlessly. More gunpowder was brought in, and more firewood to conceal it.

But the extensive spying network of the state had picked up the scent of conspiracy from an agent in Flanders. Confirmation came in a mysterious letter delivered on 26 October to Lord Monteagle at his house in Hoxton, warning him to stay away from Westminster: 'I say they shall receive a terrible blow this Parliament, and yet they shall not see who hurts them.' Monteagle passed the letter to Robert Cecil in Whitehall, who showed it to the king on 1 November. On behalf of the plotters, Guido Fawkes had checked the cellar on 30 October to confirm that all was ready. On 4 November Lord Suffolk and members of the Privy Council searched the Parliament buildings 'both above and below'. Suffolk noted in one cellar a greater volume of wood than the house it served needed. The tenant, Thomas Percy, kinsman of the Earl of Northumberland, was also known to have his main residence elsewhere.

A second search party, initiated by the king, and led by Sir Thomas Knevett, a Justice of the Peace for Westminster, visited the cellars on the night of 4–5 November. Around midnight 'a very tall and desperate fellow', giving his name as John Johnson, booted and spurred, and wearing a cloak and dark hat, was seized near the suspect cellar. The Commons' *Journal* for 5 November records: 'This last night the Upper House of Parliament was searched by Sir Thomas Knevett; and one Johnson, servant to Mr Thomas Percy was there apprehended; who had placed 36 Barrels of Gunpowder in the Vault under the House with a Purpose to blow the King, and the whole company, when they should there assemble.'

The apparatus of the state was swift and efficient in investigation and pursuit of the conspirators. Though Fawkes was defiant and assured at a first questioning, which included the king himself, fascinated and horrified by that terrorist dimension to the scheme which contemplated the death of innocent people, he was broken by the usual methods. James wrote on 6 November to the Lord Chief Justice, Sir John Popham: 'The gentler tortures are to be first used unto him . . . and so God speed your good work.' Manacles and the rack in the Tower worked their magic, and Fawkes talked. Most of the plotters had fled to Holbeach House, in Staffordshire, where on 8 November there was a shoot-out worthy of a classic Western. Catesby, Thomas Percy, and two brothers named Wright

The Gunpowder Plot.

were shot and mortally wounded, stripped and mutilated while in their death throes. The gunpowder had been taken from Westminster to the Tower, where it was classified as 'decayed'; had the fuse ever been lit, there would have been no explosion.

On 9 November James addressed Parliament, claiming that he himself had discovered the plot, dwelling on its cruelty, but maintaining a spirit of mercy towards innocent Catholics (which did not last long). Had it succeeded, his one consolation would have been his death 'in the most honourable and best company rather than in an ale-house or a stew'. The trial of the surviving conspirators for high treason was staged in Westminster Hall on 27 January 1606. They were exhibited on a specially built scaffold to a great crowd of spectators, including the king and queen and Prince Henry, who had a secret vantage point. It was more of a state ceremony than a trial; their guilt having been determined by Privy

Council interrogations, and all that remained was for the establishment to milk the opportunity for political ends by high melodrama. The accused fingered rosaries and took tobacco throughout, 'as if hanging were no trouble to them'. The King, whose 'Counterblaste to Tobacco' had appeared in 1604, would doubtless have found this practice a confirmation of their desperate condition.

Seven of the eight pleaded 'Not Guilty': Edward Phillips, serjeant-at-law, delivered the declaration: 'The tongue of man never delivered, the ear of man never heard, the heart of man never conceived, or the malice of hellish or earthly devil ever practised such a treason, to murder such a king, such a queen, such a prince, such a progeny, such a state, such a government.' Sir Edward Coke, Attorney General, spoke at length, blaming the Jesuits, evoking the horrors had the plot succeeded, and relishing the penalties in prospect. Each man was to be drawn backwards to his death, at a horse's tail, because he hath been retrograde to nature; his head at ground level, not entitled to the common air. To be hanged halfway between heaven and earth – unworthy of both. His privy parts cut off and burnt before his face since he had been unworthily begotten, and so unfit to leave a generation after him. The bowels and heart which had devised the plot were to be hacked out, and the head which had imagined the mischief was to be cut off. The dismembered bodies would be exposed as prey for the fowls of the air.

The king's verdict was not in doubt. Four were put to death on 30 January, at the west end of St Paul's Churchyard. On 31 January, Wintour, Rookwood, Keyes and Fawkes went to the scaffold in Old Palace Yard. Of Tom Wintour the spectators demanded a speech. He declared: 'This is no time to discourse: he was come to die.' He crossed himself and cried out that he died a true Catholic. He was cut down and mutilated after only 'a swing or two with the halter'. Rookwood confessed his sin and asked for God's blessing on the king and his family – but he besought God to make James a Catholic. He was granted a long hanging. Keyes ascended the platform with a brisk defiance. With his neck placed in the halter, he jumped off into space, hoping to die quickly. But the halter broke, and he was taken fully conscious to the quartering block. Last Fawkes, weak with torture and sickness. He made a short speech asking forgiveness, but kept up his 'crosses and idle ceremonies'. Scarcely able to climb the ladder, he had to be helped by the hangman. His neck was broken by his fall. An Act of Parliament decreed public rejoicing every 5 November. Bonfires, a traditional form of celebration, were permitted, provided they were 'without any danger or disorder'.

1625–9: Strife

Charles I was immediately at odds with his Parliament over money, his religious policy, the war with Spain, and the Duke of Buckingham. Buckingham was a serious threat to good government. Earl, Marquis and Duke in quick succession under James I, he was Lord High Admiral, a manipulator of influence at court, profligate both in distribution of peerages and in his abuse of monopolies. Though ignorant of foreign affairs, he was convinced of his destiny to rule England de facto. The hostility to him of men such as John Eliot and Dudley Digges in the Commons was heroic and rash: both were committed to the Tower in mid-session in 1626 for supposed seditious language. Buckingham tried to pack the Lords with the sale of peerages – its numbers rose from fifty-five in 1603 to 126 in 1628 – but his tactics failed: established peers were displeased at the upstarts, who were themselves fickle, and for a time the Lords joined forces with the Commons in resisting the royal will. When Buckingham was impeached, Charles summoned both Houses to Whitehall Palace. 'Remember Parliaments are altogether in my power for the calling, sitting and continuance of them, therefore as I find the fruits of them good or evil, they are to continue or not to be.' The prophetic Dudley Carleton was prompted to warn the Commons that the king might abolish representative assemblies, as other European monarchs had done: 'Move not his Majesty with treading upon his prerogatives, lest you bring him out of love with Parliaments.' Buckingham was saved from impeachment only by Charles's dissolution of Parliament, but after his military disaster at La Rochelle, nothing could save him from assassination at Portsmouth as he was preparing another naval venture.

The Parliaments of 1628 and 1629 provoked Charles into displaying the qualities that would destroy him: arrogant defiance followed by capitulation. The issue was money, as it had been since the reign began. His first Parliament in 1625 had voted him only one-seventh of what he asked for, and aired grievances until the king's impatience dissolved it. But the threat of war with France caused him to summon another in 1626. Laud preached at the opening. 'A royal command is God's glory, and obedience to it the subject's honour.' This was not what the Commons wanted to hear. Charles was wounded by the Commons' refusal of subsidy, and sought other sources of funding, including forced loans, and appeals from the nation's pulpits, which yielded insufficient. His third Parliament in 1628 brought to a head the conflict between the king's prerogative and the subject's liberties. The Commons was incensed both by forced loans and the arbitrary punishment of those who refused to pay them, and passed resolutions to prevent extra-parliamentary taxation and imprisonment without cause shown. The king made a provocative demand for money, veiled as a threat. The Commons granted him five subsidies, totalling £275,000, which they saw as generous. But the king needed four times that sum. The Crown's needs were rising, because of the increasing cost of warfare and defending the kingdom, while the value of money and yield of the taxes voted by Parliament were both falling. But, rubbing salt into the wound, the Commons voted their subsidies only in exchange for royal confirmation of their liberties. The Petition of Right for the redress of grievances, supported by the Lords, and invoking the precedent of Magna Carta, was accepted by Charles. He undertook not to levy taxes without consent, not to imprison subjects without cause shown, not to billet soldiers with civilians without consent, and not to impose martial law on civilians. The Petition was followed by remonstrances protesting at abuses in Church and State, naming Laud and Buckingham, and resisting Charles's claim to tunnage and poundage (customs' dues) which Parliament had not granted. The king prorogued Parliament. Before it next met Buckingham had been assassinated.

When it reassembled in 1629 it was spoiling for confrontation, not because of any revolutionary temper, but because of its essential conservatism. The king was perceived to be breaking the settled political and economic moulds. There were dramatic scenes in the Commons in March 1629. The goods of John Rolle, MP had been seized and he had been committed to Star Chamber because of his refusal to pay tunnage and poundage. The nub of the outrage of the Commons was parliamentary privilege, fuelled further by the king's desperate sanctioning of unjust and illegal conduct by customs officers. The Commons boiled over, and a series of adjournments failed to reduce the temperature. Members attacked the king's religious policy, particularly 'the disease of Arminianism' rooted in the court. The Commons seemed to be claiming sole right to define the national religion. Charles rose to the defence of his Church and ordered the Speaker to adjourn the House for eight days. War had been declared. John Eliot stood up, but the Speaker repeated that the king had forbidden all business. When he tried to leave the House, Holles and Valentine forced him to back into the chair and held him there. 'By God's wounds, you shall sit till we please to rise!' Eliot asserted that it was a fundamental liberty of the House to adjourn itself. Three resolutions were passed: any person supporting Arminianism was a capital enemy of king and kingdom; no tunnage and poundage without Parliament's approval; anyone paying tunnage and poundage voluntarily was a betrayer of the liberties of England. John Eliot offered a statement of the House's intentions, and threw the paper on which they were written to the floor. It was picked up and given to the Clerk, but the Speaker repeated the command to adjourn, and refused to allow the paper to be read, despite shouts of support for Eliot from the benches. He was condemned for his failure to obey the House, but he refused to yield. Eliot declared his loyalty to king and country, and attacked the insidious advance of popery. Two days later, Eliot and eight fellow members were arrested by order of the Privy Council. The treatment of Eliot, who was kept in prison until his death in the Tower in 1632, provoked bitter feelings amongst members. On 10 March Parliament was dissolved. The king declared that it had exceeded its functions, blaming 'the undutiful and seditious carriage of the lower house, provoked by "some few vipers"'. The king had entirely failed to understand the widespread appeal of Puritanism and the threat posed by his embracing of high Anglicanism. There was no pressure for new laws, and Charles had concluded that he could raise more money without Parliament than with it. He was to rule without it for the next 11 years. There was no compelling reason why it should ever be summoned again. The Puritan Symons D'Ewes declared of the dissolution of the 1629 Parliament that it was 'the most gloomy, sad and dismal day for England that happened in five hundred years last past'.

CHAPTER FOUR

Two Revolutions: 1629–1689

The Short and Long Parliaments

YET THE MOST extraordinary two years in parliamentary history lay ahead. Between November 1640 and June 1642, Parliament extended its powers by a systematic attack on the royal prerogative which culminated in Charles's descent on the Commons in January 1642 in an attempt to arrest five of its members. The king fled the city, and Parliament declared its own sovereignty. Not only did Charles lose his prerogatives to the Parliament he had wooed so roughly; by 1646 he had also lost the war between them, and in 1649 he lost his life.

It was the Scots who brought the English Parliament back to life. They resisted the king's attempt to impose the English Prayer Book on the Scottish Kirk in 1638; he stumbled into war with them without securing parliamentary support, and lost. For the first time since 1629 Parliament was summoned in April 1640 to provide money for that war. Instead it delivered a deluge of grievances and discovered, in John Pym, a radical voice. He at once seized the initiative, and directed the course of events until his death in December 1643. 'A Parliament is that to the Commonwealth which the soul is to the body, which is only able to apprehend and understand the symptoms of all such diseases which threaten the body politic'. The old imagery of the king as the head has been discarded. Ship money, a levy on subjects supposedly for the better defence of the kingdom, was abolished. This tax had been one of the ways in which Charles raised income independently of Parliament, at least until 1638 when Hampden's ship-money case was decided so narrowly in the king's favour that it then became virtually impossible to collect. Benjamin

Rudyerd's declaration that 'His subjects' hearts are the king's treasure' was not a practical financial substitute. Faced with protests about forcible charges on the shires to maintain the army, and with a petition in favour of peace gaining momentum, Charles, on Strafford's advice, dissolved Parliament again in early May. It was indeed the 'Short Parliament'.

But the triumphant Scots still had to be pacified. Money talks, so Parliament was summoned again in November. Charles was now trapped in the payment of Danegeld. The Scots refused to accept peace terms unless they were ratified by Parliament. So the king had to cede to the Lords the negotiation of a treaty, and to the Commons the payment of the armies. But security for the treaty, and for the loans secured to pay off the armies on both sides, depended upon the existence of Parliament. So Charles now had to accept the Triennial Act and the Act against Dissolution to guarantee the peace. Pragmatism dictated these developments, which turned Parliament in a trice into a necessary institution with security of tenure. The Long Parliament was launched, on a wave of rapidly increasing authority. The Earl of Leicester understood what was happening: 'The parliaments of England heretofore were like tenants at will, but now it is as tenants for years or for life, not determinable at the will of the king . . . it is not likely that they will be weary of their immortality.'

Elected member for Cambridge in both the Short and Long Parliaments was a country squire who made an extremely unfavourable impression. Sir Philip Warwick saw 'a gentleman speaking, very ordinarily apparelled, for it was a plain cloth suit which seemed to have been made by an ill country tailor. His linen was plain, and not very clean, and I remember a speck or two of blood upon his little band which was not much longer than his collar. His hat was without a hat band, his stature was of a good size, his sword stuck close to his side, his countenance swollen and reddish, his voice sharp and untunable, and his eloquence full of fervour.' Sir Philip was disconcerted to find that 'he was very much hearkened unto'. Lord Digby asked Hampden about the new man. 'That slovenly fellow which you see before us, who hath no ornament in his speech: I say that sloven, if we should come to a breach with the King (which God forbid!) in such case will be one of the greatest men of England.' The slovenly fellow was Cromwell.

As the struggle between King and Parliament began to polarise, how did sympathies in the Lords and Commons stand? In 1640 Charles had called a Great Council and appealed to the Lords for support. But their response displeased him. There was no automatic support for the King there – indeed many of the commanders in the parliamentary army later on were peers – and the Lords sought to be brokers between king and people. Though they opposed Strafford's attainder and the Militia Bill, and, with bishops and Catholic peers among its members, became a target for popular anger, in 1642 they sided with the Commons in voting to limit the king's power to control appointments, reflecting their deep suspicion of his judgement. In the Commons, Charles had no supporting faction who were placemen, members of the household. Nonetheless, among the active members were a substantial number of moderates who found themselves under pressure from the volatile conduct of the king on one side and the policies of Pym on the other. Many of the crucial votes in the early stages of the struggle were a close call. Charles acquired support only gradually as the excesses of the parliamentary leadership began to drive some of these moderates into his fold. When war broke out, two hundred of the five hundred members joined the king's party and were expelled from Parliament. These were the men who would have responded in good part rather than sceptically when Charles assured Parliament in January 1641: 'I ingenuously confess that frequent parliaments is the best means to preserve that right understanding betwixt me and my subjects which I so heartily desire.'

But the Long Parliament was on the march, and rapidly consolidated its strength. The prerogative courts and conciliar government were abolished: the crown had now no independent means of effecting policy. The Tunnage and Poundage Act gave the king the customs revenue, but only for two months at a time. The Triennial Bill passed both houses, and Charles was forced to accept it even though he had announced he would never consent, because of popular demonstrations in the city. His irritated response – 'you have taken the government all in pieces, and, I may say, off its hinges' – was a mirror image of how the Commons had judged his conduct in the early years of his reign. Pym's strategy of making Parliament indispensable led him to attack the king's ministers. He initiated the impeachment of Strafford as soon as the Long Parliament assembled: 'A king and his people make one body: the inferior parts confer nourishment and strength, the superior sense and motion. If there be an interruption of this necessary intercourse of blood and spirits, the whole body must needs be subject to decay and distemper'. The ferocity of Strafford's conduct in Ireland was suspected as a rehearsal for the disciplining of England, and mercy was not his for the asking. Though impeachment failed, a Bill of Attainder was brought in to settle his fate. He was a sacrificial victim, trapped between greater forces, and his final attempt to defend himself to the House of Lords before going to the block, though just, was unavailing: 'My Lords, do we not live by laws, and must we be punishable by them ere they be made? These gentlemen tell me they speak in defence of the commonweal against my arbitrary laws; give me leave to say that I speak in defence of the commonweal against their arbitrary treason.'

The successful intimidation of the Lords and the King, partly with the lever of armed mobs, over Strafford's attainder, encouraged further challenges, and can be seen as a rehearsal for what was to follow a few months later. After Strafford's execution, the Commons sent to the Lords the Ten Propositions. The third sought to vest effective power over the king and his ministers in 'the High Court of Parliament', 'to commit the affairs of the kingdom to such councillors and officers as the parliament may have cause to confide in'. Charles's tactics, to buy time by making concessions, merely fuelled the next parliamentary demand. So at no point was equilibrium attained as the see-saw of power tilted. A second wave of expanding parliamentary authority followed in the autumn of 1641. Rebellion broke out in Ireland in October, and was blamed by Pym and Parliament on the king's councillors. Troops had to be raised to suppress the Irish, but the leaders of the Commons were not prepared to concede royal control over this force. Cromwell moved in the House that the Earl of Essex, by an ordinance of Parliament, be empowered to command the forces of suppression. By a vote of 151–110, Parliament thus sought to gain control of the defence of the kingdom; Charles also issued ordinances to raise troops. Pym responded to the crisis by summoning the London trained bands to guard Parliament. The King was in Scotland, but set out for his capital in November, expecting to rout the 'juggling junto' of his opponents. But three days before he arrived, the Commons passed the Grand Remonstrance, by a majority of eleven votes, on 22 November. The

Remonstrance was a wide-ranging attack on royal policy and royal authority, and was the cause of violent scenes in the Chamber. The large minority opposed to it was howled down when they tried to record their protest, and members were close to a riot. It was a pivotal moment. Cromwell told Lord Falkland that if it had been rejected, 'he would have sold all he had the next morning, and never seen England more'. It was also the event which polarised Parliament between the self-righteous 'saviours of the nation', and the moderates, accused by the former of engaging in 'conspiracies of self-interest'. It was a turning point, too, for the new rapport between the Chamber and the streets. The abolition of the Court of Star Chamber had freed opponents of the government from the fear of prosecution for treasonable matter. There was suddenly a deluge of pamphlets printing versions of parliamentary events, and a weekly broadsheet summarising debates. Officially such publications infringed privilege, but leading politicians turned a blind eye to them because they sensed that a public platform was in their interest. Throughout November and December the streets were turbulent, especially in the City. There were rumours of a military coup against Parliament. Gangs of apprentice boys picketed the Palace, shouting 'No Bishops', in support of Pym's proposal to remove the voting rights of bishops in the House of Lords. But there were respectable citizens there too, fearful of popery, stopping the coaches to prevent bishops and 'popish lords' from entering. John Williams, Archbishop of York, had to be rescued from a fracas. On 7 December the Militia Bill was debated, vesting in Parliament appointments in the armed forces, and thus absolute control over the military. Colonel Lunsford, Lieutenant of the Tower, was jostled by apprentices in Westminster Hall and drew his sword on them. Later in December the same combatants had a proper fight there, with several wounded or taken prisoners. 'Roundhead' (the skinheads of Stuart London) and 'Cavalier' first began to be exchanged as terms of abuse.

Charles Invades the Commons 1642

In such volatile days, some kind of disaster was inevitable. On 30 December 1641 the bishops protested at their exclusion from the Lords by mob violence. The Commons voted to impeach them.

Charles I attempts to arrest the five Members. Lenthall, kneeling, courageously asserts the privileges of the House of Commons.

The Lords supported the Commons, and twelve bishops were led off to prison 'in all the extremity of frost'. Charles, having in effect rejected the Grand Remonstrance, then launched in the Lords accusations of treason against leading members of the Commons. On 3 January 1642 the Commons sat, and claimed a breach of privilege which, deliberately or not, incited the king to attempt force. On 4 January the Commons sat in St Stephen's with the five named members present. News was brought of Charles's approach, and they skipped out to the river and took a boat to the city. The king crossed Westminster Hall and entered the Chamber, leaving the door open so that members could see the troops 'making much of their pistols'. Charles removed his hat, and walked towards the Speaker's chair. The members stood in silence, also bare-headed. 'Mr Speaker, I must for a time make bold with your chair'. Speaker Lenthall vacated it. 'Is Mr Pym here?' Silence. He asked the Speaker if the five were present. Lenthall, on his knees, spoke. 'May it please Your Majesty, I have neither eyes to see, nor tongue to speak in this place, but as the House is pleased to direct me, whose servant I am here; and I humbly beg Your Majesty's pardon that I cannot give any other answer than this to what Your Majesty is pleased to demand of me.' It was the first time a Speaker had declared his allegiance to the liberty of Parliament rather than the

Flight of the five named Members (a painting in the Palace of Westminster).

will of the monarch. Lenthall's courage at this moment of confrontation was extraordinary. The king paused. 'Tis no matter; I think my eyes are as good as another's.' He studied the benches 'a pretty while'. Then 'all my birds have flown'. He left the chair and walked out 'in a more discontented and angry passion than he came in'. His crass effort to arrest the five for endeavouring 'to subvert the fundamental laws and government of the kingdom' rebounded catastrophically upon him. Within a week he had fled the city for Hampton Court, not to set foot in his capital again for seven years, and then only for his trial and execution. On 11 January the five members returned in triumph by barge to Westminster. 'Every countryman's mouth almost is full of breach of privilege of Parliament'. He had forfeited the sympathy of the moderates. The Militia Bill was now issued as an Ordinance, affirming the authority of Parliament above that of a wayward king. The Commons was heady with the first taste of sovereign power, and issued a bold declaration justifying itself. The first signs of serious intolerance followed: Ralph Hopton accused them of condemning their sovereign 'upon less evidence than would serve to hang a fellow for stealing a horse'. He was committed to the Tower. The 'company of giddy heads' hunted down dissent, and multiplied committees from which royalist sympathisers were excluded. It was too late for reconciliation; 'King Pym' now ruled in London.

The Breach between King and Parliament
and Civil War 1642–6

The breach became geographical as well as ideological in May 1642 when the king ordered the law courts to accompany him to York. Parliament declared this to be illegal, and the order was disobeyed. The Great Seal was taken to York, but Parliament subsequently commissioned its own Great Seal. The king was declared to be making war on his Parliament, and lawful authority was claimed by the Lords and Commons. This move required a doctrine which distinguished between the king's person and his office. His office was now declared to be exercised by Parliament 'after a more eminent and obligatory manner than it can by personal act or resolution of his own'. In the same month Charles's wife, Henrietta Maria, was negotiating with France for support.

On 1 June, Parliament issued the Nineteen Propositions, effectively a declaration of war, demanding parliamentary control of all offices in the land, laws against Catholics, and reform of the Church. Charles's reply measured the great gulf that had opened between them: 'The House of Commons is an excellent convenor of liberty, but was never intended for any share in government, or the choosing of them that govern'. A royal proclamation in May had forbidden his subjects to accept the ordinances of Parliament, 'raisers of sedition and enemies to my sovereign powers'. The Lords and Commons declared in answer: 'The King by his proclamation cannot declare the law contrary to the judgement and resolution of any of the inferior courts of justice, much less against the High Court of Parliament'. Impasse. In July members of both Houses were appointed to a Committee of Safety wielding full executive power, which Parliament continued to exercise, for the only time in its history, until 1653. At once it seized for its own safety and use warships, dockyards, ports and magazines of ammunition. In August the Royal Standard was raised in Nottingham and the Civil War began. The inconclusive Battle of Edgehill in October, and the king's failure to take advantage of the chance it offered to return to London, committed the land to a long and bitter attrition.

Yet at the very moment when Parliament took control of the helm, it revealed that it had no idea where the ship was heading. It was as if the loss of so many familiar political landmarks had consigned it to wholly uncharted waters. In the short term the battlefield had primacy over the debating chamber, but the Chamber was deeply divided, first between radicals and a peace party, and later between independents and Presbyterians. The death of Pym in 1643 deprived the Commons of its experienced helmsman; Cromwell's absence on army service deprived it of its next natural leader. Between 1640 and 1642, the volume of work and press of events had turned part-timers into professional politicians, but now, like professional politicians, they found many of their tasks thankless.

Financing the war cost them dear in public sympathy. In November 1643 an ordinance compelled a contribution to war expenses by all property holders. The land tax outraged the gentry, and a variety of 'imposts', first on tobacco, wine, cider and beer (first aid post for many subsequent Chancellors of the Exchequer), then, as war spread, to imported textiles and foods, then to soap, paper, domestic cloth, leather, meat and salt. Riots forced the withdrawal of the taxes on meat and salt, and the promise to repeal the rest when the war was over. But in 1654 Cromwell extended such tax to almost everything sold. So taxation by Parliament without royal consent replaced taxation by the Crown without parliamentary consent. Though the Commons continued to house a fairly wide spectrum of opinion until Pride's Purge in 1648, the puritanical cast of some of its legislation could only further sap the spirits of the populace. Theatres were closed in 1642; regular public fasts and condemnations were ordered, and in December 1644 even Christmas was abolished: 'the sins of our forefathers have turned this feast, pretending the memory of Christ, into an extreme forgetfulness of him, by giving liberty to carnal and sensual delights, being contrary to life which Christ himself led here upon earth'.

The current of events was sweeping the Long Parliament along with it. The Commons had shrunk to only 200 of an original 600; the Lords barely mustered a dozen members. Charles set up a rival Parliament – 'my mongrel Parliament' – in Oxford in 1644, and in the same year, after the Solemn League and Covenant with the Scots, the Committee of Both Kingdoms, a prototype of executive government, wielded most of the political influence. There was a triumph when victory at Marston Moor led to the capture of York in July 1644, and conquered standards, with strips torn off by soldiers for mementoes, were laid at the bar of the

House. But there was no settlement, because although Parliament pursued a treaty, the king was not prepared for serious negotiation at this point. Moreover, mob rule threatened all ordered government. Archbishop Laud was the next sacrificial victim of ignorant fervour. He was charged with treason, which was not provable by legal process, so like Strafford in 1641, he was condemned by an Ordinance of Attainder. The rabble ruled the streets, demanding his execution and agitating against the lords who, they believed, wished to spare him. The Bill of Attainder against him passed the Lords on 4 January 1645, the same day that the Commons abolished the Prayer Book, and he went to the block on 10 January, an ecclesiastical sacrifice to match Strafford's secular one. Charles sent a general pardon on Laud's behalf, but Parliament disregarded it because 'the authority of Parliament must prevail'.

The ebbing of members from the Upper House had, by 1645, handed parliamentary dominance to the lower: 'The House of Commons is called the lower House in 20 Acts of Parliament, but what are 20 Acts of Parliament amongst friends?' was John Selden's rhetorical question. But parliamentary authority in both Houses was threatened from without by the kind of mob rule that had claimed the head of Laud. 'Is this the liberty which we claim to vindicate by shedding our blood? Our posterity will say that to deliver them from the yoke of the King we have subjected them to that of the common people,' deplored the Earl of Essex. In December 1644 Cromwell had briefly appeared, to implore the Commons to 'save a Nation out of bleeding, nay almost dying condition'. Within the Commons there was a division between the peace party and the war party; the latter group secured the passing of the Self-Denying Ordinance, which disqualified military commanders from membership of the House and led to the foundation of the New Model Army.

There were other omens of an intemperate future. Parliament's Ordinance for the New Model Army of February 1644 appointed Fairfax as Commander, but his commission contained no clause for the preservation of the king's person. Moderates in the Lords objected, but were defeated by one vote. Parliament offered the king peace terms in May, but since they included the establishment of Presbyterianism as the national religion, and permanent control by Parliament of the army and navy, Charles's rejection of them can have been no surprise. Then, in June 1645, after the Battle of Naseby gave the military victory to Parliament, Cromwell's dispatch to the Commons had its final sentence censured before printing. It had read: 'He that ventures his life for the liberty of his country, I wish he trust God for the liberty of his conscience, and you for the liberty he fights for.' But both political liberty and liberty of conscience seemed to recede with military victory: from the pulpits radical fervour stirred unrest and threatened anarchy, as if the collapse of royal authority had equally undermined the authority of the state embodied in Parliament. And all across the country fervent Presbyterians were advocating the promotion of spiritual authority and threatening to unsettle the English precedent twice battled for, between Henry II and Becket and between Henry VIII and Rome.

In 1646 there was talk of peace, but the king's strategy had again been disastrous. The draft of a secret treaty between Charles and Irish Catholic supporters reached Westminster, where no one was any longer able to trust his word or his motives. In June 1646 the royalists had to accept capitulation. Parliament's peace terms were stringent: accept the Covenant agreed between the English and the Scots, abolish the Episcopal Church, impose penalties on Catholics, surrender control of the armed forces; agree to the exemption from pardon of a long list of royalists. Charles refused, continuing to delude himself that some accommodation of views was possible, or that his enemies would fall out, as they so nearly did. But he was now a prisoner, first of the Scots in Newcastle, then of the English Commissioners at Holmby House in Northamptonshire. In September 1646 the Commons declared that the king should be disposed of as both Houses thought fit. In December he appealed for a free journey to London in order to negotiate: 'A King who would not hear a subject would be thought a tyrant, how could they his subjects refuse to hear their King?' They could and did. In June 1647 he was seized by Cornet Joyce on behalf of the army and incarcerated at Hampton Court. When rumours of a plot to kill him surfaced, he fled to the south coast, and took refuge in Carisbrooke Castle in the Isle of Wight. Various schemes of escape were thwarted by bad weather and his irresolution, and Carisbrooke remained his place of detention until he was brought back to London.

The Trial and Execution of the King

An uneasy stalemate followed. Parliament was under suspicion in the streets, by the leaders of the New Model Army, and from the Levellers. The Putney Debates of 1647 revealed a swelling tide of radicalism tinged with republicanism. John Lilburne's pamphlets demanded that the Long Parliament declare a term to its existence, and advanced proposals for democratic government which included triennial elections and universal suffrage (but for men only). Cromwell was alarmed: what will be the outcome if 'men that have no interest but the interest of breathing' were to vote? He foresaw the overthrow of property and collapse of civil society; his reaction is already an argument for the Restoration. But the existing Long Parliament was increasingly unpopular. It had imposed punitive taxation, violated laws and the constitution and chosen a course which had led to slaughter, all without identifiable achievement except keeping hold on power. It had become a cosy oligarchy: 'it were endless to name the father and son, brother and brother that fills the House; they come in couples more than unclean beasts to the Ark.' But they were under threat. The dominant Presbyterians in the House tried to impose a Presbyterian settlement and disband the army without satisfying its grievances: arrears of pay and immunity from prosecution. The army resisted, first among the ranks, and then with the support of the officers, to preserve unity. The invasion of the Commons by mobs further intimidated the Presbyterians, and their supremacy was broken in 1647. Parliament had assumed powers more despotic than Charles had ever claimed, and considered itself invulnerable, but in the course of 1648 it became seriously divided between doves and hawks: those who wished to negotiate with Charles with the aim of restoring him, and those who wished to put him on trial. Army officers had also been negotiating with the king, but increasingly came to doubt his good faith. The flaring of the Second Civil War in 1648 convinced them that he was inexorably a man of blood who had to be brought to justice. But among members of the Commons the peacemakers had the initiative, and sent commissioners to treat with the king in the Isle of Wight. They returned in early December, but the army marched on London and occupied Whitehall. On 5 December the Commons defied the threat by voting 129–83 to continue discussions with Charles. That evening, a secret meeting of three members and three army officers 'went over the names of the members one by one, giving the truest character we could of their inclinations'. Next morning, at Ireton's instigation, Colonel Pride and a troop of soldiers blocked access to Parliament, arrested about forty members, and subsequently forbade about seventy more to enter the Palace. The purpose of Pride's Purge was to free the Commons to proceed with the trial of the king, and, despite the crude method used, showed that the army still needed parliamentary sanction for its policy. Cromwell hailed the purge as a process that 'sifted, winnowed and brought to a handful'; Clement Walker, one of the excluded members, gave it its historical identity: 'this fag end, this veritable Rump of a parliament with corrupt maggots in it'. Now the way was clear to break the political stalemate. The purged Parliament voted that to continue negotiations with the king was 'highly dishonourable, and destructive of the peace of the kingdom.' It determined 'to proceed by way of justice against him.'

On New Year's Day 1649 the Commons declared it to be High Treason for the King of England to levy war against the Parliament and kingdom of England. An Ordinance for the trial followed at once, which the Lords refused to pass, so on 4 January the Commons passed three resolutions claiming exclusive power: 'That the Commons of England, in Parliament assembled, do declare, That the people are, under God, the original of all just power: And do also declare, That the Commons of England, in Parliament assembled, being chosen by, and representing the people, have the Supreme power in this nation: and do also declare, That whatever is enacted by the Commons . . . hath the force of law . . . although the consent and concurrence of King, or House of Peers, be not had there unto.' On 6 January followed the act setting a High Court of Justice to try the king. That the authority to proceed had been secured from a hand-picked oligarchy which was unrepresentative of the people was not acknowledged. On 19 January Charles was brought from the Isle of Wight to St James's. Cromwell ran to the window, looking on the king as he came up the garden; he turned 'white as the wall': 'My masters, he is come, he is come, and now we are doing that great work that the whole nation will be full of.' He asked for advice on how to answer the king's inevitable first question, 'By what authority do you proceed?' There was a pause. Henry Martin then said, 'In the name of the Commons and Parliament assembled, and all the good people of England.' Algernon

Sydney was nominated as one of the judges. He arrived in the Painted Chamber for discussions before the trial opened, and opposed proceedings. 'The King could be tried by no court; no man could be tried by that court.' Cromwell was adamant: 'I tell you we will cut off his head, with the crown upon it'. At 2 p.m. on Saturday 20 January Charles was brought to Westminster Hall to hear the charge. 'He had traitorously and maliciously levied war against the present Parliament and the people therein represented.' John Cook, prosecuting, moved the impeachment of 'the said Charles Stuart as a Tyrant and Murderer, and a public and implacable enemy to the Commonwealth of England.' At this Charles laughed in the face of the court, and challenged its authority. Throughout the proceedings, he refused to remove his hat, as a gesture of defiance of the court. Since he was seated with his back to the body of the Hall, his tall black hat was all of him most spectators ever saw. Bradshaw, the President of the court, adjourned it upon the king's protest. Hugh Peter, one of the commissioners, was seen holding up his hands to the dispersing crowds: 'This is a most glorious beginning of the work.' But there had been loud protests from women in the galleries, on whom the troops were ordered to train their muskets and fire if the interruptions continued. Next day, Sunday, the commissioners fasted upon a diet of three sermons, whose texts were: 'He that sheds blood, by man shall his blood be shed'; 'Judge not, that ye be not judged'; and 'I will bind their kings in chains'. In further short sessions on the following Monday and Tuesday afternoons, 22 and 23 January, the impasse continued. Charles refused to plead. If the prisoner refuses to plead, declared Cook, it will be taken as an admission of guilt. The king, usually a poor public speaker, was roused to eloquence: 'if power without law may make laws, I do not know what subject he is in England, that can be sure of his life, or anything that he calls his own.' The heart of his challenge, which was unanswerable, caused Bradshaw to lose his temper. 'The Commons of England was never a Court of Judicature. I would know how they came to be so.' On the Tuesday, Charles's implacable defiance terminated public proceeding. 'You are to find you are before a court of Justice,' reiterated Bradshaw. 'I see I am before a power,' observed the king, and rose to go. On the next three days the commissioners heard witnesses in the Painted Chamber in private sessions, and on 26 January produced the draft sentence. On the afternoon of the 27th,

The Trial of Charles I in Westminster Hall.

Charles was brought to the Hall to hear the sentence read. Charles had a new proposal for the peace of the land, and asked to be heard by the Lords and Commons in the Painted Chamber, but Bradshaw strongly opposed it, and the request was rejected. Bradshaw, summing up, advanced a theory which, though only tacit in 1649, was to become explicit forty years later in the Bill of Rights: 'There

A redrawing of the death warrant of Charles I.

is a contract and a bargain made between the king and his people, and your oath is taken: and certainly, Sir, the bond is reciprocal – the one tie, the one bond, is the bond of protection that is due from the sovereign . . . Sir, if this bond be once broken, farewell sovereignty.' Farewell indeed. Sentence was read. 'The said Charles Stuart, as a Tyrant, Traitor, Murderer and a public enemy, shall be put to death, by the severing his head from his body.' The king tried to speak both before and after the sentence, and was refused the right. 'I am not suffered for to speak: expect what justice other people will have.' And the guards hustled him away to Whitehall through the crowds and lines of soldiers who puffed tobacco and little explosions of gunpowder in his face, and cried out 'Justice. Justice. Execution. Execution.' His execution in Whitehall followed swiftly, on 30 January. He cut a brave figure, but his words from the scaffold revealed how little he had learned from his ordeal: 'Truly I desire (the people's) liberty and freedom as much as anybody whomsoever, but I must tell you their liberty and freedom consists in having of government those laws by which their life and their goods may be most their own. It is not for having a share in government.'

K.Charles I.murthered. *Pf. 31.*

Into thine hands I comit my Spirit: thou haſt re-deemed me O Lord God of truth v.5. For I have heard the ſlander of many while they took coun-ſel together againſt me, to take away my life. v. 13

Execution of Charles I.

Parliament During the Commonwealth 1649–60

It was a brave new world. The Rump Parliament was able to savour its creation. It resolved in February that 'the House of Peers in parliament is useless and dangerous, and ought to be abolished'. On 7 February the monarchy was voted out of existence – 'the office of a king being unnecessary, burdensome and dangerous to the liberty, safety and public interest of the people.' The mood of the Rump was not dogmatically republican, but the experiences of the 1640s had so confronted Parliament with double-dealing by the king and obstructiveness by the Lords that there seemed no practical alternative to the political supremacy of the Commons. After all, it had demonstrated that it was capable of governing no less satisfactorily than a Stuart king, and had risen so high in its own esteem that many of its members were more affronted by Pride's Purge than by the execution of Charles. But ideology was curiously selective: titles were still recognised, and three members of the abolished Lords sought election to the Commons, as they were entitled to; though 'king' was removed from all legal documents (replaced by 'Keepers of the Liberties of England'), and the King's Highway renamed, in an early outbreak of political correctness, 'the Common Highway', many parliamentarians still believed that parliamentary supremacy was perfectly reconcilable with a monarchy.

On 13 February the functions of the monarchy were transferred to a Council of State, forty strong, thirty-one of whom were MPs and five were peers. The Commons delegated to it responsibilities for defence and the army, foreign policy and trade. So executive authority largely passed into its hands, while the Rump began to lose its way in a tangle of procedural and constitutional nit-picking. It undertook to dissolve itself 'as soon as may possibly stand with the safety of the people'. But that moment, in its own view, never seemed quite to arrive; it lingered on in a kind of half-life until Cromwell wearied of it in 1653. He was himself distanced from it in August 1649 when he was sent to Ireland, leaving behind an unloved Parliament which neither seized the political initiative nor made any effort to win hearts. Yet the spring had heralded the new order: 'The people of England shall from henceforth be governed as a Commonwealth and free state by the supreme authority of this realm, the representatives of the people in Parliament.'

The parliamentary history of the Commonwealth years of 1649 to 1660 makes sorry reading. Cromwell had no clear idea of how he was going to create a godly settlement, and ruefully summarised the struggles: 'our passions were more than our judgements.' The period was beset by constitutional problems (who or what is the ultimate authority?), by rivalry between radicals and moderates in the army and Parliament, by fiscal problems (how to raise taxation to pay the army and to fight wars against royalists in Scotland and Ireland, and against the Dutch), and by the distractions of ideological debates, some of them fanatical, about the nature of government. There was a huge burden of business in the absence of the king, Lords, Privy Council and Star Chamber, and the machinery of government was unable to respond to the pressures. 'The petitions of poor sufferers are used only to light tobacco', grumbled one disillusioned citizen. And absenteeism from Parliaments compounded the difficulties.

The Rump essayed the wrong kind of control. In October 1649 an Oath of Engagement to the Commonwealth was required of MPs, officers, judges, barristers, clergy, schoolmasters and university fellows. The next year the death penalty for incest and adultery, three months imprisonment for fornication, 'wherewith this land is much defiled', graduated fines for 'profane swearing and cursing'. In 1652 the celebration of Christmas was again attacked by radicals, and the Rump forced London shops to close and observance of the festival was repressed. The national mood was poisonous. The army was impatient with the Rump's slowness to embrace reform, and feared that Parliament intended to disband a threateningly politicised army. Cromwell's efforts to make peace between them failed. Possessed preachers attacked the Rump from wild pulpits: 'Sunday last a glazier preached in Somerset House, and told his auditors they should see ere long a greater destruction fall on the Parliament than ever befell the Cavaliers.'

It did on 20 April 1653. Cromwell took his seat, and listened to the debate. As the House prepared to put the motion, he stood up and, walking up and down the House like a madman, and kicking the ground with his feet, he harangued them. 'You have sat too long here for any good you have been doing. Depart, I say, and let us have done with you. In the name of God, go!' A member rose to protest. 'Come, come, I will put an end to your prating. You are no Parliament. I say you are no Parliament. It is not fit you should sit here any longer.' He called in Thomas Harrison with five or six files of musketeers. Cromwell pointed to Speaker Lenthall in his chair. 'Fetch him down.' Lenthall, facing the second great challenge in his career to the authority of Parliament, sat on, in silence, because the House had not been constitutionally adjourned. 'Take him down.' Harrison, condemned to death as a regicide after 1660, later gave this account. 'I went to the Speaker and told him, Sir, seeing things are brought to this pass, it is not requisite for you to stay there; he answered he would not come unless he was pulled out; Sir, said I, I will lend you my hand, and he putting his hand into mine came down without any pulling, so that I did not pull him.' Cromwell went to the table where the mace lay, and said, 'What shall we do

Cromwell dissolving the Long Parliament.

with this bauble? Here, take it away.' So the soldiers took away the mace, and the House was cleared. Cromwell took the act for the perpetual sitting of Parliament from the table and put it under his cloak. 'All being gone, the door of the House was locked, and the key with the mace was carried away.'

The Rump began and ended violently. Cromwell had succeeded where the king eleven years before had failed, in bringing the splinter of the Long Parliament elected in 1640, the sole repository of constitutional and legal authority, to an undignified close. It was 'a glorious parliament for pulling down,' said Arthur Haslerig, and now it had met an appropriate end. 'I have sought the Lord night and day,' said Cromwell, 'that he would rather slay me than put upon me the doing of this work,' but the Lord's ears were deaf. There was now a horrible vacuum. Bradshaw, at a Council of State meeting the same afternoon, confronted Cromwell with it: 'Sir, you are mistaken to think that the Parliament is dissolved; for no power under heaven can dissolve them but themselves; therefore take you notice of that.'

Cromwell, now in sole charge, took stock for two months and then, in conjunction with army officers, initiated a series of unhappy constitutional experiments. For the Barebones (or Nominated) Parliament which met in July 1653, the system of representation was reconstructed: the distribution of members was proportionate to the tax burden, and Scotland and Ireland were included. One hundred and forty men were chosen, 'fearing God and of approved fidelity and honesty' by church congregations. Cromwell naïvely thought that godly men would guarantee godly rule, but their morality exceeded their political sagacity. The great number were 'inferior persons, of no quality or name, artificers of the meanest trades, known only for their gifts in praying and preaching.' It passed some worthy legislation, introducing civil marriages, the registration of births and deaths, and probate for wills, and also improved the care of lunatics, prisoners and debtors, but was hijacked by around sixty fanatics who abolished the Court of Chancery, proposed the abolition of universities and the public ministry. One Vavasour Powel even clamoured for the replacement of Common Law by the Laws of Moses, perhaps encouraged by Cromwell's likening Parliament to the Sanhedrin. Faced with a legislative momentum out of step with public opinion and driven by doctrine, Cromwell's moderate supporters arrived early for work on 12 December, and proposed and carried the dissolution. At this point Cromwell took the oath as Lord Protector.

The next experiment, the first Protectorate Parliament, was elected, with a new system of four hundred constituencies, and was dominated by independent gentry. They were ordered to assemble on the Lord's Day 3 September 1654, the anniversary of Cromwell's victories at both Worcester and Dunbar, but the righteous were displeased by such irreverence. It was greeted and briefed in the Painted Chamber by Cromwell, who had taken the precaution of locking them out of the Parliament House. Sitting in a chair of state, and surrounded by lifeguards and halberdiers, he gave them an ultimatum: 'I must profess this to you, that if this day prove not healing, what shall we do?' But at once republicans challenged the authority of the Protector. Cromwell had them back in the Painted Chamber: They were 'a free Parliament only so long as they accepted the authority that summoned them there.' But they continued to attack the basis of Cromwell's power, questioning his authority, his finances and his right to raise and employ a militia. They wanted absolute sovereignty for Parliament. So, dispiritedly, Cromwell dissolved it in January 1655, with words of reproach and frustration: 'Is there not yet upon the spirits of men a strange itch? Nothing will satisfy them, unless they can put their finger upon their brethren's consciences, to pinch them there . . . What greater hypocrisy than for those who were oppressed by the bishops, to become the greatest oppressors themselves, so soon as their yoke was removed? You have wholly elapsed your time, and done just nothing.'

A Council of Officers now divided England into ten districts ruled by Major Generals, who set about executing the laws of the Commonwealth and arousing fierce unpopularity by their repressive methods. They forbade race meetings, and even closed brothels, believing them to be patronised by royalists. Cromwell had issued a series of extra-parliamentary ordinances, redefining treason, for example, and appointing Commissioners to eject 'scandalous, ignorant and insufficient ministers and school masters' (an embryonic OFSTED). But the validity of such ordinances was widely questioned, and a disillusioned Cromwell had to summon yet another Parliament in order to ratify his own authority. The major generals tried to select a Parliament of their own persuasion, and the army council issued tickets to admit members to the House. About one hundred and twenty members were rejected at the door, thereby violating all preceding assumptions about representation. Another crude tactic backfired, for the exclusions undermined all confidence in this 'rag of a Parliament', as one of its own members described the Second Protectorate Parliament. This assembly first offered Cromwell the crown, which he refused, and then, in the Humble Petition and Advice in May 1657 offered him the Protectorship for life, the nomination of his own successor, and the re-establishment of the 'other house', a second parliamentary chamber again nominated by him.

On 26 June 1657 Cromwell was installed as Lord Protector in Westminster Hall. The Coronation chair was brought across from the Abbey, and a stage draped with cloth of state and pink velvet. On a table were placed a Bible, a sword of state, and a sceptre of 'massy gold'. At 2 o'clock Cromwell arrived by river. In the Painted Chamber he assented to the Humble Petition and Advice, and joined a procession to the Hall, preceded by heralds and the Lord Mayor of London. The Speaker invested him with a robe of purple velvet lined with ermine, and he swore a solemn oath, as 'Chief Magistrate of these three nations', to uphold the reformed Protestant religion and the peace and safety, just rights and privileges of

the people. There was, of course, a sermon, and an acclamation by trumpeters. 'God Save the Lord Protector,' cried the heralds, echoed by some of the spectators.

But God would save neither his peace of mind nor his person. Because he had nominated many of his own supporters to the 'other house' and refrained from vetting membership of the Commons, he had left fanatical republicans, fierce in opposition to the settlement proposed by the Humble Petition and Advice, to dominate it. They fiercely attacked the existence of the 'other house', and refused to recognise its authority. Like many Parliaments before them, they tried to bargain by demanding the redress of grievances before they would provide a subsidy. By January 1658 all tempers were at breaking point. 'We must live long on a little time', advised the shrewd Haslerig, 'for it may be questioned whether we shall sit in a fortnight.' Within a week, Cromwell dissolved them in despair. All his hopes and experiments had failed. 'You not only have disquieted yourselves, but the whole nation is disquieted. Let God judge between you and me.' 'Amen,' cried the defiant republicans. The whole tragicomic sequence is a salutary lesson for proponents of constitutional change who slide around on the surface rather than think through the consequences. The machinery of government presupposed the seamless authority of hereditary monarchy as the lynchpin; once that was taken away, the entire system dissolved.

The Death of Cromwell and the Restoration 1658–60

Cromwell died on his 'lucky' date – 3 September – in 1658, and the land was possessed by political inertia. Richard Cromwell, Oliver's son and heir, summoned a Parliament in January 1659 in another effort to release the costive machinery of state, but the Council of Officers persuaded him to dissolve it again in April. The young Cromwell resigned. Junior officers and men of the ranks demanded the return of the Rump, which was greeted with public derision, and when the army disbanded it in October, rumps were roasted in the London streets in rejoicing. Authority had melted away, and there was relief when General Monk occupied London in February 1660, readmitted to Parliament the members excluded by Colonel Pride twelve years earlier, and, after twenty years of interruptions, the Long Parliament of 1640 was at last able to dissolve itself and

Statue of Oliver Cromwell, outside Westminster Hall.

authorise a new election. The Convention Parliament met on 25 April, opened negotiations with Charles II and voted for the restoration of the monarchy. There was enough political goodwill to secure a reasonable settlement. The legislation of the Long Parliament up to 1642 was largely preserved. The Triennial Act was replaced by an act requiring the king to meet Parliament every three years. High levels of taxation for two years enabled Parliament to pay off the army, and an Act of Indemnity and Oblivion extinguished the resentments of the Civil War, with the exception of the regicides. Parliament was authorised to determine Church discipline and approve forms of public worship and the suitability of clergy. The 1642 statute excluding bishops from the House of Lords was repealed by the Cavalier Parliament in 1662.

It was all very civilised, except for the dishonouring of the bodies of Cromwell and some of his partners. A stage was created on which the political fortunes of the first two Stuart kings were to be played once again, with variations: another Long Parliament, the Cavalier Parliament which sat from 1662 to 1677, stridently anti-Catholic, colliding with its monarch over the Exclusion crisis, finding itself suspended, and finally another king losing his throne. Yet in the decisive year of 1688, no Parliament sat. It was the last constitutional crisis from which Parliament was excluded.

Parliament under Charles II

After so much apparent upheaval, it was remarkable that political and social life should re-establish themselves so swiftly. The Civil War had not elevated Parliament at the expense of the Crown: both appeared to emerge the stronger for the ordeal. The 1661 Parliament voted Charles customs revenues for life, which freed him to rule without summoning Parliament at all if he wished, and as indeed he chose to from 1681 to 1685. He often visited the Lords, which he thought 'as good as a play'. He sat 'not decently on the throne', but warmed himself at the fire. But when members began to gather round him, and he took the opportunity to ask for favours, he had to be urged to appear less often. Conduct in both chambers returned to normal.

In 1666 Pepys observed an altercation in the Lords between the Duke of Buckingham and the Marquess of Dorchester about Buckingham's intrusive elbow. Buckingham knocked off Dorchester's hat and pulled him by the periwig. The Lord Chamberlain committed both to the Tower for contempt of court. The Commons was no better. Sir Allen Brodericke and Sir Allen Apsley were both drunk in the Chamber one evening, and caroused together for half an hour. They 'could not be laughed or pulled, or bid to sit down and hold their peace.' Pepys was doubtful about the Commons. It is 'a beast not to be understood, it being impossible to know beforehand the success of almost any small plain thing, there being so many to think and speak to any business, and they of so uncertain minds and interests and passions.' But it was united in two crusades which soon began to dissipate the amity of the Restoration, against Catholics and against the Lords. In 1673 in reaction to Charles's Declaration of Indulgence promoting religious tolerance, Parliament passed the Test Act, which excluded both Catholics and dissenters from public office. The Exclusion crisis of 1679–81, when the Commons sought to exclude the Catholic James Duke of York, younger brother to the king, from the succession, and the erosion of the relationship between Charles and the Commons which accompanied that crisis, was already predictable. In 1678 hysteria about an alleged Popish plot swept the country and engulfed Parliament. There was more anxiety about the cellars, where noises had been heard. Christopher Wren inspected them and advised that for safety's sake they should be cleared 'so that soldiers and sentinels may walk day and night there'. The real Popish plot was the secret Treaty of Dover between Charles and Louis XIV, in which Charles had undertaken, in return for a French subsidy, the elimination of Parliament and the handing of the English throne to Louis upon Charles's death. The Commons was also at war with the Lords, especially over their fiercely guarded right to initiate money bills, and over the Lords' claim to act as a court of law. Buckingham, declaring the dissolution of the Cavalier Parliament, Charles II's 'long parliament', in 1677 rebuked the Commons for being 'less respectful to your lordships . . . than any House of Commons that were ever chosen in England . . . they look upon themselves as a standing senate, and as a number of men picked out to be legislators for the rest of their lives . . . my Lords, it is a dangerous thing to try new experiments in a government.'

Commons' pressure on Charles II steadily grew, over the Exclusion Crisis, over his prerogative to make peace and war, over his choice of ministers. The king refused an address in 1680 begging him to remove the Earl of Halifax as the source of distrust and jealousy between the king and the loyal Commons. The royal response to this pressure was corruption: the packing of Parliament with placemen, and by bribing MPs in order to create a tractable 'court party'. Both Charles and James rigged elections by issuing new charters to boroughs which removed the franchise from the inhabitants and vested it in corruptible petty officials, and, by royal command, making it a criterion of suitability for election to favour the repeal of the Test Act and penal laws against Catholics. JPs were ordered to establish 'what persons of such as are willing to comply with these measures have credit enough of their own to be chosen Parliament men, or may be chosen if assisted by their friends.' The result was a parliament in 1685 containing barely forty opposition members but 'a furious and violent majority who wanted to put everything in the king's power, and ruin all those who had been for the exclusion.' Like the Cavalier Parliament before it, it granted James II customs revenues for life, and made itself dispensable: James did not summon another. The Stuart campaign to corrupt Parliament was a major cause of the revolution of 1688–9, and the political settlement that followed it.

The English were quite experienced at changing kings, but had never been able to avoid violence in the process. The protracted dispute between Parliament and Stuart kings that simmered between 1679 and 1688 not only achieved a bloodless replacement of the monarchy, but also anticipated the emergence of the party system in national politics.

Charles's attempt to promote religious toleration aroused deep suspicions about his motives. Parliament, with good reason, feared a hidden Catholic agenda, and three times, in 1679, 1680 and 1681, brought in an Exclusion Bill to prevent James's succession. Each time Charles dissolved Parliament. The Earl of Shaftesbury, who had promoted the Exclusion Bill, organised petitions in defence of Parliament. Some saw his tactic as an attack on the royal prerogative: they were the 'abhorrers' opposed to the 'petitioners'; neither epithet was very catchy, and both factions quickly attracted new titles, both derogatory: 'Tories' and 'Whigs', slang terms for Irish vagabonds and Scots Covenanters respectively. The Celtic fringe again shaped political consciousness at the centre. Charles backed the Tories, dissolved Parliament and purged the Whigs through treason charges and dismissal from office. Shaftesbury fled to Holland and died there.

William and Mary presented with the Bill of Rights.

The exposure of the Rye House plot of 1683, to assassinate both Stuarts, completed the rout of the Whigs. James succeeded to the throne in 1685, and defeated risings against him. But he at once aroused the hostility of both Houses of Parliament by proposing to repeal the Test Act, excusing army officers from its provision, and assembling a large standing army in which Catholic officers were prominent. So he dissolved Parliament and set about promoting his supporters to control local government. In 1687 and 1688 he issued Declarations of Indulgence towards Catholics and dissenters, intimating that he was prepared to suspend laws that Parliament refused to repeal. The second of these was ordered to be read in every church in the kingdom, but seven bishops petitioned him in protest. They were charged with seditious libel, and put on trial in Westminster Hall. The acclamations of the mob at their acquittal in June emboldened seven public men, Whigs and Tories, to invite William of Orange to cross the North Sea to defend English liberty.

The Glorious Revolution 1688–9

William arrived in London on 18 December 1688. The House of Lords assembled on Christmas Day and formally invited him to assume responsibility for public affairs. Another Convention Parliament met in January 1689 to discuss how the country should be governed. On 27 January the Commons resolved that 'King James the Second having endeavoured to subvert the Constitution of the Kingdom by breaking the original contract between King and People . . . and having withdrawn himself out of this Kingdom has abdicated the Government and that the Throne is thereby vacant.' The Lords struck out 'abdicated' and substituted 'deserted', and voted against a proposal to declare William and Mary joint king and queen. The impasse was only resolved by William's threat to go home again, and the Lords accepted the Commons resolution as it stood. 'We must not leave ourselves to the rabble' was the inglorious reason for the capitulation.

In February 1689 the Lords and Commons agreed the basis of the Bill of Rights which established the settled relation between king and Parliament. The terms were not so much a revolution, as an insurance against the abuses of recent memory. Parliament asserted its rights in articles eight and nine: 'That elections of members of Parliament ought to be free. That the freedom of speech and debates or proceedings in Parliament ought not to be impeached or questioned in any court or place out of Parliament.' There would be no standing army in peacetime, and no royal levying of revenue without Parliament's consent. It had learned the hard lesson of its generosity to Charles and James. The new monarchs were awarded the revenues for four years only: 'by keeping the king poor, his poverty may necessitate him to call frequent parliaments.' The expenses of the royal household were to be determined by Parliament so that the ruler became, in effect, a paid servant of the state; the army and navy also ceased to be his private forces, and were answerable instead to the national will embodied in Parliament. Parliamentary government arrived at a time when it had little or no place in mainland Europe, and the constitutional partnership of monarch and Parliament established in 1688–9 has survived all subsequent challenges and crises. The political order we still recognise was born in these decisive years.

CHAPTER FIVE

From the Glorious Revolution
to the Great Reform Bill
1689–1832

OR THE HUNDRED years after the Restoration, English political life was deeply conservative. The 'revolution' of 1688 was
intended to alter the established order as little as possible.
Whigs hailed it as 'a preserving revolution', which rescued the
country from the twin perils of popery and absolutism. Memories
of civil and constitutional disorder rendered all notions of political
reform abhorrent, and retarded significant reform of Parliament
until 1832.

In the 1680s, England might easily have lapsed into the political
absolutism common on the European mainland. After 1688, described by Bertrand Russell as the occasion when 'my family and a
few others, gave one king notice, and hired another,' it would have
been extremely perilous for an English monarch to challenge the
nation represented in Parliament, and none did. Parliament has sat
in every year since 1689. Satisfaction at the Settlement, and the
desire to preserve it, dominated the political scene for much of the
eighteenth century. It was the foundation of a long aristocratic
supremacy, and 50 years of Whig ascendancy after 1714, during
which the 'Revolution Settlement' was a shibboleth for moderate
politicians across the spectrum. The new constitution was for so
long regarded as a pattern of perfection that any criticism of it was
deflected by the kind of complacency satirised by Swift in *Gulliver's
Travels*: 'We are lucky to be English, and not living under despotism.'

The commercial, colonial and military successes that befell the country in subsequent decades confirmed the perfection of the constitution and blocked all reappraisal of a representative system which equated power with the aristocratic and landed interests.

The supposed excellence of this constitution lay in the notion of a balance of interests: the benefits of Crown, Lords and Commons without the troubles that would arise if any one of the three was dominant. The Commons had notional power over the king, the king had power over the Lords, and the Lords wielded the power in practice. This questionable theory was supported by some more solid advantages, however. One was economic. At a time of wars and great expansion of trade, Parliament had the function of managing national resources to meet demand. Annual sessions became the norm because of the need to vote taxation for the French and subsequent European wars. Responsibility for the armed forces, increased taxation and a low-interest national debt required an increasing role for state government and administration. The Bank of England, founded in 1694, provided security for finance by funding the national debt. Such security, and the involvement of commercial interests in the heart of government, was the source of a remarkable eighteenth-century expansion which made Britain a greater power than her wealthier and more populous neighbour. Parliament was integral to this process. The second advantage was constitutional. Through the years of settlement after 1688–9, Parliament grew as the recognised forum for the resolution of constitutional conflicts or dynastic disputes. Even the Jacobites, who continued to oppose the settlement for 50 years, were committed to the working of Parliament.

So devoted was the Act of Settlement to achieving a balance of power that one clause in it which was to become binding on the death of Anne specified: 'No person who has an office or place of profit under the king, or receives a pension from the Crown, shall be capable of serving as a member of the House of Commons.' Had the clause taken effect, the executive and legislative branches of government would have separated, as they have in the United States, and neither the cabinet system of government nor the political supremacy of the Commons would have developed. But the clause was repealed by the Regency Act of 1706, which stipulated that anyone appointed to office had to leave the Commons, but could offer himself for re-election. So the decision about a minis-

Queen Anne signing the Articles of Union, 1707.

ter's integrity was thrown back to his constituents. This practice continued until 1918; Winston Churchill lost the by-election that followed his appointment to the Board of Trade in 1908.

Yet there could be no balance of religious interests. The Revolution Settlement was virulently anti-Catholic. The Bill of Rights asserted that the English monarch could not be a Catholic; the Catholic Insurrection in Ireland was brutally suppressed between 1689 and 1691, and the Anglo-Irish Protestants given the supremacy which has poisoned the life of that troubled island for 300 years and is still defiantly celebrated by Orangemen at Drumcree and elsewhere. The religious bigotry of the Revolution Settlement excluded Catholics from civil and political rights until the nineteenth century and ensured the disruption of national politics, including the fall of many prime ministers, by 'the Irish question' apparently until the end of the world. The Act of Settlement of 1701 vested the succession in the Electress Sophia of Hanover and 'the heirs of her body, being Protestants'; Parliament was in no doubt that it was the proper authority to determine the succession after the death of Anne in order to safeguard the revolution settlement. The same consideration prompted both the Regency Act of 1706, which decreed that Parliament would automatically be summoned to bridge the potentially perilous gap between Anne's death and the arrival of her Hanoverian successor, and the Act of Union with Scotland in 1707.

From his deathbed William of Orange had sent a message to the Lords, telling them of his 'earnest desire that they would consider of a Union between England and Scotland'. The 'blessed union' was inspired and largely negotiated by the Whigs, who desired to see the same succession binding on Scotland as on England, but it was also supported by the Tory leaders Godolphin and Marlborough. Bribery and bully-boy tactics forced the Scottish Parliament to allow Godolphin's ministry to nominate the negotiating commissioners for Scotland, in order to minimise Scottish influence and produce terms acceptable at Westminster, where high Tories resisted Union, fearing that the taint of Presbyterianism would infect the Church of England. Their opposition was discredited by the suspicion that they were closet Jacobites; Scots Presbyterians broadly favoured Union as a shield against Jacobitism. In practice there was no real option for Scotland but the threats of internal division, commercial blockade and dynastic war. The Union, popular with the queen who called it the happiness of her reign, was approved by the Scottish Parliament in January 1707, and at Westminster in March. Sixteen Scottish peers and forty-five more members of the Commons joined the first united Parliament. On 1 May 1707 'Great Britain' came into statutory existence, and there was a thanksgiving service in St Paul's. Godolphin was less thankful, and wrote to Harley in April: 'All the Scots will pour in upon us next week. I wish before they come we could pour out the English and that I might go Monday to Newmarket.' In Scotland a third of the shires and a quarter of the royal burghs petitioned against the Union, and elections to the new unified Parliament at Westminster were suppressed by the fear of a massive anti-Union vote, and thirty-one dead whales washed up on the sands at Kirkcaldy were viewed as a particularly sinister omen for the future of Scotland.

Crown, Lords and Commons

How had the political functions of Crown, Lords and Commons changed as a result of the Glorious Revolution? The Bill of Rights removed the suspending and dispensing power of the king, and the Triennial Act of 1694, which William vetoed several times, reduced his prerogative of summoning and dissolving Parliament. The Crown had become largely dependent on cash supplied by Parliament, and from 1702 a civil list was voted for the expenses of the

Royal Household. William was so displeased by limitations on his power that he seriously considered returning to Holland, especially in 1699 when the Commons compelled him to disband his Dutch guards, who constituted a standing army under royal control. George II was to complain that he had more power in Hanover than in England where, he believed, ministers were truly the kings. The royal prerogatives of making war and peace, and conjuring Parliaments into existence, had been brought under a measure of political control, and though the monarch still exercised his prerogative of choosing his ministers, his choice was limited to the politicians who could muster enough support in both Houses of Parliament to get business done. Anne, in 1708, was the last monarch to veto a Bill; after the Hanoverian Succession in 1714, 'the king in Parliament' had effectively replaced royal prerogative, as George II was to discover when he had to ask William Pitt to head a government in 1757, despite intense personal hostility to him.

The landed aristocracy in the Lords gained most from the Glorious Revolution, and established a political ascendancy that was to endure for about 200 years. The Lords emerged as mediator between Crown and Commons, and was described by Fox as 'the proper poise of the constitution'. Until the Reform Act of 1832, the Lords had more prestige than the Commons, and wielded more power, though it never commanded the same degree of excitement that the Commons was able to generate. Peers dominated the ministries for 150 years, because the only practicable system of government was founded upon the landed interest. Throughout this period the peerage flourished: twenty-three dukedoms were created between 1688 and 1720; Anne raised twelve to the peerage in one swoop in 1711 to save Harley's ministry from defeat. In all cases the necessary condition for elevation was the possession of land. The landed aristocracy was an open elite always capable of renewing itself; through an oligarchic alliance with the monarchy it developed extraordinary staying power in English politics and society which extended, through family connection and patronage, into the Commons as well. Disraeli termed it a 'Venetian oligarchy'. As late as 1818 Lord Liverpool, then Prime Minister, commented that 'the House of Commons is in sentiment much more a body of aristocrats than is commonly supposed.' As a younger man, debating reform in 1793, he had had no doubt that the landed interest, 'the stamina of the country', should have preponderant weight

View of the House of Commons, 1742.

in Parliament, next the manufacturing and commercial interest, and lastly the professional classes. Thomas Paine, sniping at titles as 'mere foppery', at the same moment found his darts to bounce harmlessly off a well-armoured system: peers had the monopoly of power in national and local government, in the armed forces and through their economic dominance. Yet there were elections, and public opinion could not be entirely ignored. Though politics was in no sense either democratic or uncorrupt, it was still more developed than in any other European nation. It was, as the Whig politician and historian Macaulay described it when urging the passage of the Reform Bill in 1831, 'government by certain detached portions and fragments of property, preferred to the rest on no rational principle whatever'.

The House of Lords, with about 220 regular members in the eighteenth century, usually supported the king uncritically. A government could always expect a comfortable Lords majority as long as it was known to enjoy royal favour. Ministers in the Lords could use the prospect of opposition from the Commons to force the king's hand on policy. So by 1714 and the Hanoverian succession, the Lords were in a strong position to control the machinery of government. Their sycophancy and acquiescent instincts did not endear them either to wits or independents: 'A tame, subservient, incapable set of men, governed entirely by the Duke of Newcastle,' judged Horace Walpole. Henry Fox claimed that only the Commons blocked the Crown's subversion of the function and privileges of Parliament. Yet strong ministers such as Robert Walpole, Pelham, Lord North and the younger Pitt commanded wide support in both houses.

The Lords' monopoly of power and influence extended to the Commons too. Throughout the eighteenth century, over half the 558 seats in the Commons were controlled by the Lords, and occupied either by peers' sons, peers' nominees, or Irish peers. Political society was inbred in both Houses: Joseph Aske in 1710 had fifty relatives who were also MPs; family allegiances as much as political ones fashioned pressure groups; all political groups were headed by landowners in the Lords. The Lords and Commons were socially homogeneous (Chatham described the Commons as 'a parcel of younger brothers'), and therefore had no essential divergences of interest.

Parliament in Action

Parliament met each year, but usually sat for not more than five months of it, and generally not beyond 4 o'clock in the afternoon. Up to 1740 most sessions began after Christmas, and ended in June. After 1740, under pressure of business, it began to be summoned in November. Walpole established a five-day week 'for the sake of his hunting, and was then much complained of, but now every body is for it,' said Speaker Onslow. Throughout the eighteenth century, the bulk of legislation was local and personal, 'a mere quarter sessions, where nothing is transacted but turnpikes and poor rates,' rather than a programme introduced by government. The Commons was more important for its traditional function as controller of finance, and for a new function as 'the grand inquest of the nation'. Parliamentary questions evolved in both the Lords and Commons in the eighteenth century, and ministers were made answerable to interrogation and comment. 'The certainty of discussion keeps administration in awe,' commented Horace Walpole, 'and preserves awake the attention of the representatives of the people.' All finance measures began in the Commons, jealous in preserving its authority from interference by Crown or Lords. The right to grant money, declared Speaker Onslow, cannot be given up 'without betraying the liberties of our constituents'. When the Lords dared to send across a Bill that involved levying taxation, the Speaker would throw it on the table, or to the floor, where it was sometimes kicked by members to the door, and the whole Bill was rejected. One familiar expression of the financial authority of the Commons began in 1753, when Prime Minister Pelham 'opened the budget'.

St Stephen's Chapel was falling down, reported Christopher Wren in 1691. Members were understandably alarmed, and sent a humble address to William III asking him for a new home. He, not an instinctive estate agent, replied 'it would be difficult to find a convenient place on a suddaine.' Wren, working with a Commons committee, decided on repair, and with a degree of vandalism reserved for celebrated architects, demolished the heavenly vault, inserted a false ceiling, blocked in the soaring windows and lined the room with wooden galleries and panelling. The supreme work of medieval Gothic had become a Methodist chapel. The lower ceiling caused members who had formerly complained of cold to complain of heat. A ventilation committee sat for many years. Forty-five more members arrived from Scotland after the Act of Union in 1707; Wren had to extend his new galleries to provide more seats; the air was still more foetid. In 1715 the Speaker invited Dr Desagulier, FRS, to 'propose a method to evaporate the unhealthful breathing in the House of Commons.' He was the first of many oddballs appointed to solve the problem; his system involved the generation of still more hot air with huge fires. It failed because Mrs Smith, the Housekeeper, refused to light the fires, which made her private rooms too hot. Defeated, the Commons passed the first recorded ban on smoking in public places, and in 1732 petitioned George II for another new Parliament House. By the time William Kent produced designs in 1739, they seemed to have become reconciled to their ramshackle old home.

Seating in St Stephen's was very restricted, with room for about 300 in the body of the Chamber. Seats could be booked only by those present at Prayers, and shortage of space often persuaded members to stay put and vote against their inclinations rather than risk losing their places for later business. From the seventeenth century it had become customary for opposition to sit on the Speaker's left, and the phrase 'Opposition Bench' was in use from 1770. Rounding up members to fill the Commons was a continual challenge. When turnout was poor, a 'call of the House' was held, a roll-call after which those absent without excuses were taken into custody by the Serjeant-at-Arms. But since every trifling excuse was allowed at that stage, the threat was not very serious. 'Fox-hunting, gardening, planting or indifference' all dissuaded country members from travelling up to town. The need to bring in country members led, appropriately, to the use of the term 'whip'. In 1742 'the Whigs for once in their lives have whipped in better than the Tories', and Burke reported in 1769 that the ministry had sent for their friends, 'whipping them in'. The habit of 'pairing' absent members began occasionally from around 1730, and was in regular use by 1770. Many members were practising lawyers, and sometimes the Serjeant-at-Arms was sent with the mace into Westminster Hall to collect them up. When a debate had a doubtful outcome, word would be passed round in the locality (what is now the division bell area), so that the minister could 'collect his hands from the coffee houses, to make them leave their dinner and their bottle, and come staggering into the House to decide on the fate of their country.'

Pastor Moritz, visiting the House in 1782, recorded its casual, almost undignified atmosphere. Members brought their sons, while quite little boys, and carried them to their seats along with them. They entered the House in their great coats, and with boots and spurs. Wigs were worn, with or without hats; office holders wore full court dress with swords. Behaviour was extremely informal: they stretched out on the benches, cracked nuts and ate oranges. James Boswell's respect for it, like that of some modern spectators, was 'greatly abated by seeing that it was such a tumultuous scene'. However, courteous conventions largely controlled debate: members were not referred to by name, and attacks on the king were strongly disapproved of. The Jacobite Shippen in 1717 criticised George I: 'the only infelicity of his Majesty's reign is that he is unacquainted with our language and constitution.' He refused to withdraw the words, and was committed to the Tower. In the small but intimidating St Stephen's, speaking was a challenge and a threat. It was a rite of passage. 'You must first make a figure there if you would make a figure in your country,' wrote Lord Chesterfield to his son. But there were some notable failures. Addison, elected member for Lostwithiel in 1708, rose to speak for the first time but was so intimidated by the loud cries of 'Hear him! Hear him!' that he collapsed back on the bench and never spoke again (though he still rose to high office); Edward Gibbon, elected for Liskeard in 1774, sat silent for eight sessions: 'I am still a mute, it is more tremendous than I imagined, the great speakers fill me with despair, the bad ones with terror.' He remained 'chained down to my place by some invisible unknown power, a dumb dog.' There was no such problem for pachydermatous dullards such as David Hartley, who rose to speak about 5 o'clock one day in 1779. Mr Jenkinson, later Lord Liverpool, took the opportunity for some country air, and rode out on horseback to his retreat some miles out of town, dined, took a walk and rode back to Westminster to find Mr Hartley still speaking. His rising 'always operated like a Dinner Bell'. In 1783, in somnolent flow he moved that the Riot Act be read to elucidate a point. Burke laid hold of him by the coat – 'The Riot Act! My dear friend, the Riot Act! To what purpose? Don't you see that the mob is already completely dispersed?' Yet when there was excitement, it was in the Commons, and the Lords could never match its magnetism. Lord Hervey moved to the Lords in 1734, and there was commiseration on his going to 'so insignificant a place'. Walpole and Pulteney, elevated into Oxford and Bath, met in the Lords, and Walpole observed that they were now two of the least significant men in the kingdom.

The Commons was not divided into parties in the eighteenth century, but interest groups. Party affiliation was deeply suspect at the end of the seventeenth century, when a political party was described as 'only a kind of conspiracy against the rest of the nation'. The majority of the eighteenth-century members were independents, who deplored 'party', which compromised the integrity of individuals. No government could be, exclusively, a 'party' government; the majority of members were uncommitted to party or ministry, and so their support had to be wooed to ensure a ministry's success. The great part of independents had no political ambitions of their own, and so were well suited to serve as watchdogs over abuses and corruptions without the risk of being summoned to assume power themselves. So the majority of members were sedate, and only stirred at times of crisis or when their pockets were threatened. Not until the time of Disraeli and Gladstone did ministers expect a committed parliamentary majority; Lord Liverpool in his long ministry could only rely on about 150 'solids'. He would 'never attempt to interfere with the individual member's right to vote as he may think consistent with his duty upon any particular question.'

No sooner had the new political order of 1689 been born than questions were raised about its integrity. A tract called *The Danger of Mercenary Parliaments* in 1690 compared Parliament to 'an organ where the great humming basses as well as the little squeaking trebles are filled but with one blast of wind from the same sound board.' The seventeenth-century Stuarts had tried to pack Parliament; their eighteenth-century successors made a better job of it. The use of royal patronage to reward biddable members installed over a hundred 'placemen' in Anne's reign, and Walpole extended the practice of ensuring a solid basis of parliamentary support by handing out pensions and offices: 'This chief minister plumes himself in defiances, because he finds he has got a Parliament like a packed jury, ready to acquit him of all adventures.'

The Franchise and Elections

There are few, if any, features of eighteenth-century representative government that would now be regarded as democratic. It was a commonplace of politics unchallenged by any except a lunatic fringe that suffrage was rightly confined to those with interests, chiefly money and property, at stake. Cromwell had shared that view; so too did Macaulay, a champion of the 1832 Reform Act, who saw no contradiction in declaring, in the 1840s, 'I believe that universal suffrage would be fatal to all purposes for which government exists, and that it is utterly incompatible with the very existence of civilisation.'

There was no electoral revolution in 1688, nor again when opportunity offered in 1707. After the towns of Durham and Newark were enfranchised in the 1670s, there were no more significant changes until 1832. In the early eighteenth century the electorate numbered about 250,000, or roughly 5 per cent of the population. In the shires the criterion was still that of the forty-

'Chairing the Member' after the election – one of William Hogarth's celebrated 'Election' series, 1758.

shilling freeholder set in 1430; the boroughs employed a bewildering variety of criteria, ranging from self-sufficiency (those not in receipt of charity) through scot and lot payers (those who paid church and poor rates) to potwallopers (men able to boil their own pot). Some boroughs were corporation boroughs, where the right to vote was restricted to a small number of local officials, who were easy to influence by bribery. Buckingham was such a borough, in which the member was chosen by only thirteen burgesses. Constituencies were unevenly matched, ranging from Westminster and Bristol, each with several thousand voters, to Gatton, which had two, and Old Sarum, which was just a vacant tract of land, where a solicitor handed the seven electors title deeds to property which were taken back as soon as they had voted. There were forty-nine two-member constituencies each with fewer than fifty voters. Sixteen boroughs in Cornwall each had fewer than one hundred electors, and so to 'cornwallise' came to mean using gold to win an election. Many ministers sat for pocket boroughs such as these, and in 1830 even the upright Peel had to be returned for the pocket borough of Westbury when he was rejected by his constituency, Oxford University, because of his reluctant support for Catholic Emancipation. In 1793, nearly half the members of the Commons were returned by only 11,000 voters in total. The complications of electoral law enriched lawyers and occupied much parliamentary time: after every election committees had to sit to adjudicate disputed results, claims from fifty or sixty constituencies at a time being not unknown.

Patronage dominated electoral choice. About four-fifths of MPs were returned by influence, chiefly that of the local landowners, most of them aristocratic. The Duke of Newcastle offered the Boroughbridge seat to Cecil Bisshop: 'It is a seat in Parliament entirely my own but I am very cautious not to choose anyone but such as I can entirely depend on in everything.' In Malmesbury the electors said it was no odds to them who they voted for, 'it was as master pleased.' Leominster was likened to a farm, 'where the good wife beating the bottom of the pail, all the hogs run to the wash.' Because of the power of patronage, elections were rare. In the 1761 election, only four counties voted out of forty, and only forty-two boroughs out of 203. Two-thirds of the boroughs were controlled by patrons. Shropshire saw no election between 1722 and 1831; the borough of St Germans had no election between the Restoration and the Reform Act. The non-contesting of seats was a convenient way of evading the requirement that members appointed to office should seek re-election. The elder Pitt only once had to fight an election campaign. When elections did take place, they were a rich man's playground. In 1711 a property qualification was set for membership of the Commons: an income of £600 a year for knights, £300 for burgesses. The purchase of votes through bribery and treating was a common practice: 32s. 6d. was the going rate for a vote in Wotton Bassett in 1690, but by 1754, 30 guineas was being demanded. Borough seats were also purchasable until an Act of 1809 prohibited the sale of seats in the Commons, though even after that date the purchase of property which pre-empted electoral selection continued. In 1807 Samuel Romilly looked for a seat to buy, but found the prices inflated: 'the new Ministers have bought up all the seats that were to be disposed of, and at any price' – partly with the help of the King's Privy Purse, wielded by the

THE DEVONSHIRE, or Most Approved Method of Securing Votes

The Duchess of Devonshire, caricatured by Thomas Rowlandson, soliciting votes for Charles James Fox (himself orating in the background) in the 1784 Westminster election.

Prince Regent, who wished to support the new ministry. Eventually Romilly bought Wareham for £3000, and justified his move with the thought that only money could help a man to steer clear of patronage. The upright William Cobbett, in Honiton for an election in 1806, told the inhabitants 'how wicked and detestable it was to take bribes, but most of the corrupt villains laughed in my face; but some of the women actually cried out against me as I went along the streets, as a man that had come to rob them of their blessing.' Even if a member had come through his Eatanswill ordeal as a victor, there still might be a petition against him from a defeated candidate to the Commons Committee of Privileges and Elections, in which an ostensibly impartial appraisal of electoral corruption was shamelessly used by the ministry in power to secure seats for candidates whose votes would be reliable. It is easy to deride such tricks, but at the time it seemed entirely natural that family, land and money should manipulate the political process. Besides, there was an unquestioned consensus that sovereignty lay not with the people, but with the king in Parliament. The conflict of assumptions between then and now is at its clearest in Lord Liverpool's pronouncement: 'We ought not to begin by considering who ought to be the electors, and then who ought to be elected; but we ought to begin by considering who ought to be elected and then constitute such persons electors as would be likely to produce the best elected.' The chief consequence of eighteenth-century electoral practice was that politics became dominated by a broadly aristocratic oligarchy from which the lesser gentry and the professional middle classes were excluded.

Executive Government

Alongside what must seem a highly idiosyncratic parliamentary system, the machinery of executive government evolved in the first part of the eighteenth century. In the Middle Ages, executive responsibility was invariably in the hands of churchmen; after the Reformation it passed to secular figures. Usually the Lord Chancellor was the chief minister of the executive; Clarendon (1660–7) was the last Lord Chancellor to play this role. After him the Chief Minister, Danby for example, presided over the Privy Council, but the Lord Treasurer (or First Lord of the Treasury), who was usually responsible for Parliament, was a rival in status. As the Privy Council grew in number and became an unwieldy instrument (in Anne's reign it numbered eighty), a Cabinet or Cabinet council emerged from it, which contained members of both Houses and was answerable directly to the king. A reduced unofficial Cabinet, the 'Lords of the Committee', consisting of the Lord Treasurer, the two Secretaries of State, the Commander-in-Chief, the Lord Admiral, the Lord Chancellor and the Lord President, met once a week with Anne, and twice a week without her. This select executive group was further reduced by Walpole, and known as the 'lords of confidence'. Most were peers, though Walpole himself remained in the Commons for over 20 years. Within this inner Cabinet there was a crucial role for the member best able to manage the king; for such a man the term 'Prime Minister' emerged as a satirical title used by his enemies. In this exclusive group lay executive control, though it never offered a detailed programme or manifesto, but only general principles (e.g. 'the Revolution Settlement'). For much of the century the machinery of government remained archaic despite its rapidly increasing remit: two Secretaries of State, with a total staff of twenty-four in 1726, were responsible for administering foreign and domestic affairs, Scotland and Ireland, the colonies, the armed forces – everything except finance. Courthand – a script unintelligible to all except initiates – and wooden tally sticks were used in the Exchequer throughout the century. It seems a ramshackle way of conducting the affairs of a great nation.

The Hanoverian Succession in 1714 reversed the fortunes of the party groups in Parliament. The Tories were perceived to be disloyal; even moderates refused to take office under George I. The Whigs came to power in the 1715 election; Bolingbroke, the leader of the Tories, fled to France: 'The grief of my soul is this, I see plainly that the Tory party is gone.' The Jacobite rebellion that followed the election consolidated Whig power for a generation. In 1716 the Triennial Act was replaced by the Septennial Act, as the Whigs strove to make their hold on power everlasting. Frequent elections, the argument ran, made government 'dependent on the caprice of the multitude and very precarious'. Stanhope was chief minister, but in defending the Peerage Bill with fervour in the Lords burst a blood vessel and died, opening a path to power for the first of the century's great Parliamentarians, Sir Robert Walpole.

Walpole was an assured manager both of men and finance. His astute financial control after the fiasco of the South Sea Bubble speculation was the foundation of a programme of peace, prosperity and stability which kept him in power for over 20 years. Throughout this time, the inner Cabinet was almost entirely aristocratic, but Walpole chose to remain in the Commons, which was his power base, until his ministry ended. Through his commanding political position, he was a master of patronage as well as finance, and built up a court party of placemen, numbering around one-third of the House. His majority was never certain, however, and he was adept at winning the support of independents and delivering their votes by the persuasiveness he could exercise at meetings. Part of his strength was his skill in projecting 'character': he carefully preserved the image of a rough-hewn country squire, with his Norfolk accent, his love of fox-hunting, his plain language, rustic metaphors and bawdy stories. His manners were coarse: during Commons debates he made a point of chewing home-grown apples very noisily. He had no ideology beyond a gut commitment to the Revolution Settle-

Sir Robert Walpole with the Speaker, Arthur Onslow.

ment. His position was briefly threatened by the death of George I in 1727 (family relationships were never happy among the Hanoverians). Other politicians cultivated the new king's mistresses, but Walpole shrewdly made friends with Queen Caroline, and regained his position. As he admitted, he had 'seized the right sow by the ear'. His mastery of Parliament was widely suspected as a threat to its independence. *The Craftsman*, an opposition pamphlet, crudely compared the Commons to a monster, 'Polyglott, who had about 500 mouths and as many tongues, and fed on gold and silver'; its master 'could make more than 300 of his tongues at once lick his foot or any other part about him.' The pragmatism of his policy and dexterous management of politics and politicians with which he pursued it could not compete, however, with Jenkins' ear. In 1738 Jenkins appeared before the Commons with his ear, cut off seven years earlier by a Spanish coastguard, pickled in a bottle. The sight of it roused the House to patriotic fervour, and Walpole, who had maintained peace for so long, realised that he had lost control of the Commons, and had to defer to the war party. 'It is your war,' he said to the Duke of Newcastle, 'and I wish you well of it.'

For 20 years Walpole had been the 'minister with the king' in the Commons. His loss of power was the overture to a period of uneasy relations between George II and his ministers: the Duke of New-castle, his brother Henry Pelham, and William Pitt the Elder. Mon-archs had to be humoured; the Hanoverian insistence on choosing or vetoing ministers often flew in the face of political realities. Gov-ernment was no longer fully royal, nor yet fully Parliamentarian. 'That damned House of Commons!' fumed George II as if hoping that an expletive might blow it away.

William Pitt established a popular reputation as a patriot during the 1740s by denouncing a foreign policy that seemed more aligned to Hanover than to Britain. England was reduced to the role of 'a province to a despicable electorate'. Small wonder he was never a favourite with either George II or George III. When the Pelhams wanted Pitt to join the Cabinet as Secretary at War in 1746, George II, offended, asked Granville and Bath to form a new ministry. All the Pelham supporters resigned, and the new ministry lasted barely 48 hours. It won satirical praise: 'the minister never transacted one rash thing and what is more marvellous, left as much money in the Treasury as he found in it.' Pelham resumed office, and for a time there was placidity in politics: 'A bird might build her nest in the Speaker's Chair, or in his peruke. There won't be a debate that can disturb her.' But in 1754 Henry Pelham died, and the king was hor-rified: 'Now I shall have no more peace.'

Pitt came to power in November 1756, when early reverses in the Seven Years' War unnerved Newcastle. Pitt had stirred up popular feeling in the Commons and in the streets, and when the mob cried 'To the block with Newcastle,' the Duke thought it prudent to resign. George II made Pitt Secretary of State and, in effect, chief minister. But the king's loathing for Pitt intensified on closer acquaintance, and he dismissed him in April 1757. At once a new phenomenon burst upon the scene: Pitt became the first political pin-up. There was popular adulation for a true patriot betrayed by lesser men. 'For some months it rained gold boxes upon him,' wrote Horace Walpole; he was given the freedom of more than a dozen cities. Public acclamation on this scale could not be ignored, and it restored Pitt to power: in June he formed a joint ministry with the pusillanimous Newcastle, and proved himself a tri-umphant war minister. He was, wrote Boswell, 'the first minister

A medieval painting depicting scenes from the Bible in St Stephen's Chapel – a 19th-century restoration.

The 14th-century Chapel of St Mary Undercroft.

Boss in St Mary Undercroft, depicting St Lawrence.

Ivory and ebony carving depicting Oliver Cromwell and the execution of Charles I, on display in the Speaker's House.

Detail from Canaletto's view of Westminster from Lambeth, 1746.

Westminster Hall threatened by the fire that destroyed the rest of the Palace in 1834.

Westminster Hall, 2001.

Big Ben, the largest bell in the Clock Tower, has given its name to the tower itself.

Facing page: *The author looking at the inside of one of the tower's four clock faces.*

Part of the clock mechanism.

The Clock Tower.

The Palace of Westminster looking south from Portcullis House.

The Palace of Westminster from the Millennium Wheel. Portcullis House is to the right of the Clock Tower. Parliament Square, St Margaret's and Westminster Abbey can be seen above Portcullis House.

The Speaker's Procession in the Central Lobby.

The Commons Chamber viewed through the Churchill Arch from Members' Lobby.

The House of Commons awaiting Black Rod, State Opening of Parliament, 1999.

Black Rod summoning the newly elected Commons to hear the Queen's Speech, State Opening, 2001.

A Member of the House of Lords (left) with a parliamentary researcher in the Royal Gallery.

Door furniture designed by Augustus Pugin.

The House of Lords in session, 2001.

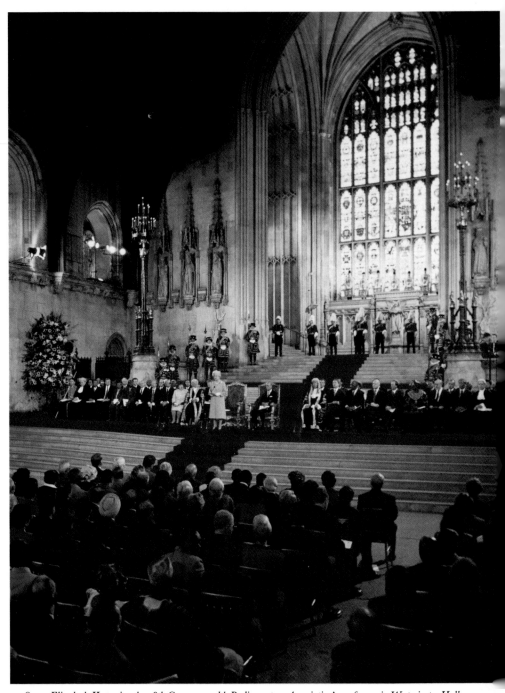

Queen Elizabeth II opening the 48th Commonwealth Parliamentary Association's conference in Westminster Hall, 2000.

Lord Mansfield, Lord Chancellor, 1738.

Lord Irvine of Lairg, Lord Chancellor, 2001.

Speaker Martin, 2001.

Speaker Lenthall, 1635.

Courtyard of Portcullis House, 2001.

given by the people to the king'. Newcastle was less dazzled: 'Mr Pitt is less to be feared inside the ministry than outside it.' Pitt had an extravagant sense of his own destiny, and was a quite insufferable colleague. His manic fervour was more terrifying than sympathetic: 'I am sure I can save this country, and no one else can.' With war across the globe in 1758 and 1759, Pitt was transfigured, and revelled in 'the year of triumphs' when 'our bells are worn threadbare, ringing for victory'. But he resigned in 1761 because of a disagreement about policy towards Spain. Subsequent appearances in Parliament were characteristically melodramatic. His was a driven temperament menaced by ill-health, and in 1762 he was carried to Westminster wrapped in bandages and spoke for three hours denouncing British treachery towards Frederick the Great. He was Prime Minister again, in the Lords, as Earl of Chatham, in 1766, and returned there as an old man from his sickbed in 1778 to denounce the conduct of the American War of Independence. He had to be supported into his place, but the whole House rose in reverence to greet him. Shrunken with illness he rose to speak, propped on his crutches, but freeing one hand to raise towards heaven: 'I am risen from my bed to stand up in the cause of my country – perhaps never again to speak in this House.' He lost his thread for a time, but suddenly found it again: 'Shall a people that 15 years ago was the terror of this world now stoop so low as to tell its ancient inveterate enemy, "Take all we have, only give us peace." My Lord, any state is better than despair; if we must fall, let us fall like men.' He sank back to his seat, tried to rise again, but fell back apparently in the agony of death. He was carried to an adjacent room, and revived sufficiently to be driven home after two days, but he never left it again, and died the next month.

In 1760, when George III succeeded his grandfather, the frame of politics had been fixed for 100 years. But between 1760 and 1830 this stability began to erode. The Whigs lost their hold on power, and a renewed Tory party took office. Though it ruled for half a century, the years were turbulent. Hopes of political reform rose and were dashed again; the American War of Independence, the French Revolution and the Napoleonic Wars unsettled complacent assumptions; Union with Ireland in 1801 dislodged the monolith of the Revolution Settlement; a Prime Minister was murdered in the midst of Parliament; a time of desperate social and economic instability caused by demographic and industrial change put England on the rack between 1815 and 1820. At last, painfully slowly, and confronted by opposition which foresaw in it the end of civilisation, the Reform Act of 1832 brought to birth a modest extension of the franchise, and the beginning of a more professional system of government.

The long political slumber was disturbed. The new king, George III, unwisely appointed his friend the Marquess of Bute to lead a ministry. Opinion was alarmed by royal disregard of the public interest. The instability was compounded by cider. A ministry could not survive in the eighteenth century if independent members, over half the Commons, turned against it, as they did against the cider tax Bute proposed in 1763. Pitt, always dangerous when out of office, spellbound them with his passion, and they developed 'a restless aversion to all government'. The City of London petitioned against the Bill, and the king was appalled: 'What times do we now live in, when a parcell of low shopkeepers pretend to direct the whole legislature?' he complained to Bute. Bute's effigy was burned in the cider counties, and that was the end of him. But the aristocratic monopoly of national and local government was facing challenge, and not only from low shopkeepers. Towns were already increasing their populations, and the concentration in them of literate middle-class people encouraged the proliferation of newspapers and magazines which sharpened political consciousness: the *Gentleman's Magazine* (1731), the *London Magazine* (1732), the *Monthly Review* (1749) and the *Annual Register* (1758). Circulating libraries came into being in the 1740s. The lesser gentry and professional classes who patronised them resented their exclusion from political life by an electoral system controlled by their social superiors. Distress among the urban poor in the 1760s because of bad harvests, high prices and unemployment added to the climate of discontent which the Wilkes affair brought to a head, and challenged the established order.

Ugly as sin, a libertine and member of the notorious Hell Fire Club, John Wilkes had entered Parliament in 1757 with a reputation for brilliance: 'It takes me only half an hour to talk away my face.' He idolised Pitt, loathed Bute, and applied his talents and prejudices to the production of a political scandal sheet called *The North Briton*. Issue number 45 asserted that George III had been persuaded by his ministers to lie. Committed to the Tower on a charge of seditious libel, he pleaded parliamentary privilege, and was released, to general rejoicing. Not content with £4000 in damages, he challenged the 'general warrant' used for his arrest. The Lord Chief Justice ruled that it was indeed illegal, and 'subversive to the liberties of the subject'. But issue number 45 was still burned by the public hangman and Wilkes was expelled from the Commons, denounced by his hero Pitt as 'the blasphemer of his God and the libeller of his king'. Now the ministry tried to overturn the common law and legalise 'general warrants'. It was a tactical blunder: there was not a sufficient majority, the issue was dropped and Wilkes became a cause célèbre, adulated in the press as a saviour of liberty. He was elected for Middlesex in 1768, but arrested as an outlaw. There were riots in London, and a 'massacre' at St George's Fields (seven died; fifteen injured). The ministry foolishly praised the magistrates for their firmness, and passions were rekindled. Again Wilkes was expelled from Parliament, and re-elected without a contest. He was expelled a third time, and one Lutterell was per-suaded to contest the election against him. Lutterell was defeated but the Commons voted to declare him the winner. The high-handed conduct of the government turned Wilkes into the people's champion that he scarcely merited to be. He was at last allowed back into the Commons when he again won Middlesex in 1774. In 1776 the Commons rejected his proposal for universal male suffrage, and the reform movement faltered: there was no body of support for it inside Parliament until the 1820s, and no widespread demand for frequent elections, a wider franchise, or a secret ballot. The very word 'democracy' aroused the kind of horror that 'com-munism' was to in twentieth-century America. But the Wilkes affair had issued a successful challenge to complacent authority, and had established the right of the press to report debates. Parliament could no longer be a private gentlemen's club which excluded reporters and ignored public opinion and political dissent.

Parliament was directly threatened by popular discontent in June 1780. Lord Gordon's petition against Catholics was to be considered by Parliament. The mobs were out in support of Gordon, and the streets around Westminster heaved with an angry crowd which attacked members of the Lords and Commons. The Bishop of Lin-coln was seized by the throat; Lord Mansfield narrowly escaped with his life. To escape injury they had to wear blue cockades and 'join in the cry of "No Popery"'. Soldiers were summoned to prevent the mob from forcing the doors of the Parliament Chambers. The Lords

Chamber 'resembled the pit at a Garrick play'. While the mob thundered outside, most of the participants kept their heads. For an hour the wild Duke of Richmond advocated annual Parliaments and manhood suffrage. The Commons affirmed that 'no act of theirs could be legal whilst the House was under apprehensions from the daring spirit of the people', and that obstruction and insult to members was a gross breach of privilege. The House then adjourned. For some days London was anarchic: Newgate prison was burned down, and the militia had to be ordered by the King in Council to restore order. Between 300 and 400 were killed, and 50 executed for their part in the riots.

The American War of Independence rearranged the political landscape. Both colonists and North's ministry believed they were adhering to the ideals of liberty enshrined in the 1688 Revolution, and there was genuine bewilderment on both sides at the conflicts arising from a common ideology rooted in that 'perfect' settlement. Pitt the Elder collapsed in the Lords while opposing the feebleness of Lord North's Government; his son united critics of the war in the Commons to force North from office: 'The war was conceived in injustice; its footsteps were marked with blood, slaughter, persecution and devastation; in truth everything which went to constitute moral depravity and human turpitude were found in it.' Pitt was 21 when he turned this salvo on the unfortunate North, who had sometimes been so depressed about America that the king had to summon the Cabinet himself. The war inflamed discontent with royal influence upon policy, and in 1780 the Commons in committee passed the motion: 'the power of the crown has increased, is increasing, and ought to be diminished.' George III, in despair, threatened to quit England forever. Rockingham, who followed North, sought to reduce royal patronage and place constitutional restraints on the monarchy, but he died, perhaps of divine displeasure, in July 1782. After an unstable 18 months, when Pitt was briefly Chancellor of the Exchequer, the East India Bill proposed by the 'infamous coalition' of Portland, North, and Fox was rejected by the Lords in November 1783, after a blunt message from George III that 'any peer who voted for the Bill would be considered his enemy.' So in a crisis of his own creation, the king turned to Pitt in December to form an administration. He was 23 years old. Wags called it the 'mince-pie administration', in the conviction that it

'Wrangling Friends, or Opposition in Disorder', Charles James Fox and Edmund Burke, by John Nixon, 1791.

wouldn't survive the Christmas recess. But Pitt was to be in office for 17 years, a period which aroused some of the most celebrated political confrontations in parliamentary history, between Pitt, Burke and Charles James Fox. In the Commons Fox attacked the proceedings which brought Pitt to power ('we shall certainly lose our liberty when the deliberations of Parliament are decided by the illegal and extraordinary exertions of prerogative') and rounded on Pitt as an ambitious turncoat. They remained implacable enemies until 1806, the year of both their deaths.

Pitt's personality was chilling. His manner was formal and unbending. 'Smiles were not natural to him, even when seated on the Treasury bench where, placed at the summit of power, young, surrounded by followers, he maintained a sullen gravity.' Except for an addiction to the bottle (gout carried him off at the age of only 47), his dedication to the national interest was rigorous. He brought a new professionalism to politics: his ministry's trademarks were industry, economy and integrity, and his conduct of his lonely destiny seemed

'The Giant Factotum amuses himself', William
Pitt the Younger, by James Gillray, 1797.

wholly free from self-interest. Edward Gibbon, returning to England in 1786, discovered that 'the country seems to be governed by
a set of most respectable boys.' Pitt's priority was clear: to restore
national self-esteem after the loss of America. He set standards of
administrative and economic competence which would long out-
live him. He was certainly an inventive tax-gatherer: horses,
windows, bricks, hats, ribbons, candles and hackney coaches all
yielded funds to transform government revenue. He was the man
who introduced income tax, in 1799, though it was dropped again
when the Napoleonic Wars ended. He instituted open bidding for
government contracts, and ran an 'efficient cabinet', directed with
personal authority. After him the Prime Minister would have
unchallenged dominance in an administration. George III had
appointed him as defender of what he perceived as a threatened
constitution: 'Where is the independence, nay where is even the
safety of any one prerogative of the Crown if its prerogative of naming ministers is to be usurped by this House?' Though Pitt diluted
the Crown's influence by reducing the number of placemen in Par-

liament, his instinct was to defer to the king, who remained a major political force until his descent into madness in 1810. After the Wilkes affair, many radical societies had been formed to promote Parliamentary reform, and Pitt had early on crossed swords with Burke in expressing support for them, but he backed off when he met royal disapproval.

The French Revolution and the English Reform Movement

Liberty was in the air. Radical reform clubs were flourishing in the cities, in Sheffield and Manchester, and through the widely imitated London Corresponding Society; their aim was to arouse political consciousness among the working classes. Dissenters were restless after their failures in 1787, 1789 and 1790 to secure the repeal of the Test and Corporation Acts which excluded them from polit-ical activity. In May 1789 Pitt introduced a Bill to abolish slavery. It was eloquently supported in the Commons by his friend William Wilberforce: 'Let us put an end at once to this inhuman traffic – let us stop this effusion of human blood. . . . Setting millions of our fellow-creatures a-hunting each other for slaves, creating fairs and markets for human flesh through one whole continent of the world, and, under the name of policy, concealing from ourselves all the baseness and iniquity of such a traffic.' But Pitt's Bill failed, because Parliament was still composed not primarily of parties, but of vested interests, and the slave trade touched so many pockets that enough support could not be gathered. Besides, the quest for liberty nearer home soon fixed all attentions. The French Revolution increased the pressures on all shades of political opinion. It was first a stimulus to the reform movement, but subsequently a stimulus to its repression. The first response to the Fall of the Bastille was one of general approval. Fox was the most extravagant: 'much the greatest event that ever happened in the history of the world'; Pitt more guarded, hoping that France 'will enjoy just that kind of liberty that I venerate.' Burke was one of an apprehensive minority: if they 'establish a mob of democracies they will establish a very bad government – a very bad species of tyranny.' His *Reflections on the French Revolution*, published in November 1790 provoked Thomas Paine's reply, *The Rights of Man*, in April 1791, and the debate became polarised. Paine stirred up criticism of government tyranny and calls for social and political reform. Two hundred thousand copies of *The Rights of Man* were sold in 1793. His popularity among the labouring classes forged a menacing bond in many minds between parliamentary reform and social revolution. Godless republicanism and the dissolution of wealth and property were just around the corner. Propagandist material was disseminated by the Corresponding Society through a network of provincial branches. It is 'The Mother of all Mischief,' declared Burke, coining a metaphor with staying power (and not unknown to Saddam Hussein). The progress of the French Revolution confirmed Burke's fears, and made English politics feverish. Pitt's ordered government was particularly cherished, and wild men such as Fox were swept out of the mainstream. Fox confronted Burke in the Commons at three in the morning on 14 April 1791. Fox had celebrated the Revolution and *The Rights of Man*; Burke, his friend and 20 years his senior, felt compelled, under the pressure of intense emotion, to defend the liberties of England whatever the cost of his friendship: 'It certainly is indiscretion, at any period, but especially at my time of life, to provoke enemies, or to give my friends occasion to desert me; yet if by a firm and steady adherence to the British constitution I am placed in such a dilemma I will risk all; and as public duty and public prudence instruct me, with my last words exclaim – "Fly from the French Revolution".' Fox leant across and whispered to him: 'There is no loss of friends.' 'I am sorry,' Burke replied in a loud voice, 'but there is. I know the price of my conduct. I have done my duty at the price of my friend: our friendship is at an end.' Fox's attempt at peacemaking quickly collapsed into recrimination, and they were irreconcilable for the rest of their lives.

Fears for public order soon swept in repressive measures to which governments instinctively turned in the crises of the next 30 years. In 1792 a royal proclamation against seditious writings was issued, aimed at Paine and his sympathisers. In 1794 the Habeas Corpus Act was suspended after fierce debates in the Commons, and radical leaders arrested. A violent demonstration in 1795 when the king went to open Parliament was the pretext for further repression: the Treasonable Practices Bill extended treason to cover the expression of contempt for king, government or constitution in speech and writing; the Seditious Meetings Bill forbade assemblies of more than fifty people without notice. Stamp duties on newspapers delivered control of the press into the hands of government, and the Combination Act of 1799 even branded working-men's clubs as political conspiracies, and banned such organisations as the Corresponding Society. The government was in panic: political and social unrest, the naval mutiny of 1797 and the Irish rebellion of 1798 forced the suppression of the reform movement. The melodramatic scene in which Burke flung to the floor of the Commons a dagger inscribed 'Rights of Man', one of thousands he claimed to have evidence for, convinced members that there were Jacobins, republicans and revolutionaries among the protesters. Pitt, who had earlier been sympathetic to reform, had turned into its implacable enemy. In 1793 he had declared war on France after the execution of Louis XVI and his queen, 'to oppose those principles of ambition and aggrandisement which have for their object the destruction of England, of Europe, and of the world.' Like his father before him, Pitt ran a good war, and was proud of a peace treaty signed in 1801. But he was dismissed by the king in the same year because of his support for Catholic Emancipation. War was resumed in 1803, and Pitt returned as Prime Minister in April 1804 until his death in January 1806 when he was still only 47.

The nineteenth century had opened with a shotgun wedding. Fearing common cause between Catholic France and Catholic Ireland, the political union of Britain with Ireland took place in 1801. Wolfe Tone and Grattan, who had campaigned hard for an Irish Parliament 20 years earlier, now found it snatched away again. Grattan made a terrible threat: 'You have swept away our constitution, you have destroyed our Parliament, but we shall have our revenge. We will send into the ranks of your Parliament and into the very heart of your constitution, a hundred of the greatest scoundrels in the kingdom.' He was a man of his word, as the story of Parliament later in the century will show. Irish Catholics had had the vote since 1793, and therefore the supposedly indissoluble unity of Church and State embodied in the Revolution Settlement was under threat. Pitt recognised the realities, but his advocacy of Catholic Emancipation was rejected by the king. But a fuse had been lit and smouldered until 1829 when the Duke of Wellington dared to pick it up. By then it had become inseparable from the issue of political reform.

A more immediate problem was how to fit a hundred new

members of the Commons into a chamber only 60 ft. long, and already choc-a-bloc. The solution, as in Wren's time, lay in vandalism. James Wyatt, 'the Great Destroyer', stripped out both Wren's panelling and the magnificent fourteenth-century wall paintings which it had preserved, in order to make the chamber a foot or two wider. The Lords, inflated by Irish peers, simply moved from the White Chamber, their home for many centuries, into the old Court of Requests.

After the death of Pitt in 1806, the war went badly for England. Spencer Perceval, Prime Minister in 1809, reacted to the crisis engulfing Europe by ceasing to call Parliament on a Monday so that members should not have to travel on the Sabbath. He was assassinated on 11 May 1812 (not a Monday) in the Commons lobby by John Bellingham, who had become unhinged by trading losses in Russia, and irrationally held government responsible. The lobby was then open to all: servants, idlers, orange girls dangling their ankles at members, so it was an easy matter for Bellingham to wait there with his pistol. William Gordon, a journalist, was behind Perceval when he entered the lobby. 'There was an instant noise, but as a physical fact it is very remarkable to state that, though I was all but touching him, and if the ball had passed through his body it must have lodged in mine, I did not hear the report of the pistol . . . I saw a small curling wreath of smoke rise above his head, as if the breath of a cigar; I saw him reel back against the ledge on the inside of the door; I heard him exclaim, "Oh God!" or "Oh my God!" and nothing more or longer, and then making an impulsive rush, as it were, to reach the entrance to the house on the opposite side for safety, I saw him totter forward, not halfway, and drop dead between the four pillars which stood there in the centre of the space, with a slight trace of blood issuing from his lips.' A clerk in the Vote Office pointed at Bellingham and called, 'That is the murderer.' Bellingham made no effort to flee, but sank slowly to a bench near the fireplace. His neckcloth was stripped off, his vest unbuttoned, his chest laid bare, and his brace of pistols removed. Within a week, fit to plead or not, he had been tried and hanged.

Perceval's assassination brought Lord Liverpool to office, and his 15-year ministry marked the overlap of the old order of society and the old way of conducting politics, and the new. It was also, in the four years after Waterloo in 1815, a roller-coaster ride through eco-

The assassination of Spencer Perceval.

nomic distress and social disorder which underlined the need for change. In 1812 politics was still dominated by the aristocratic landed interest, and Parliament was still viewed by members as an occasional interruption of their lives elsewhere. It was inconvenient for the Irish members to come till after Christmas, and it was inconvenient for the English members to sit after midsummer. The bulk of legislation was still local and personal rather than initiated by government; indeed, in Liverpool's view the state's role was extremely limited, especially in social matters: 'By far the greater part of the miseries of which human nature complained were in all times and in all countries beyond the control of human legislation.' The government's duty was to act as an umpire and hold a balance between the nation's principal interest groups. Parliament was the meeting place for these interests: India, shipping, railways, the military and, above all, agriculture. Such interest groups were more important than parties in the configuration of the Lords and Commons; parties were still tentative and fluid associations, with their leaders in effect selected by the king when he asked someone to form a government. Ministers had few ways of enforcing party discipline: most members were not in Parliament because of a party label, but because of their status and influence in their locality. The prevailing view of the function of government was fostered by the universal assumption that it had to be cheap. Taxation was an outrage justifiable only in a great crisis; 'retrenchment' was the common theme of electors from Liverpool's ministry at the beginning of the century through to Gladstone's at the end, and it was the most pervasive single pressure imposed on members to act 'in the public interest'. So as the explosion of social problems associated with industrial cities compelled government to abandon Liverpool's laissez-faire assumptions in favour of interventionism, successive nineteenth-century governments had problems raising enough income to fund social policies.

Despite the prevalence of old attitudes to Parliament, after Waterloo it was forced to become more professional. The growing volume of public business, especially associated with Ireland and agricultural enclosures, required two days a week to be reserved for government business. The conduct of debate became less theatrical, from Burke's style to Peel's. In 1818 a working library was created to assist members to be better informed. They needed to be, to understand the causes of the extreme social disorder that swept the country after 1815. The root cause was the widespread misery spread by rapid economic upheaval, but a nervous establishment, fearing widespread attacks on property, was disposed to read political revolution into it and to apply ill-judged repressive measures. The unrest began in March 1815. 'There is a great clamour out of doors,' recorded Peel. 'Some members did not make their escape without the loss of half their coats and a little personal injury.' In January 1817 a hostile crowd gathered outside Parliament for the opening of the session by the Regent. He arrived in silence, and was hissed on his return, and his carriage attacked. Either bullets or pebbles shattered the windows. Parliament, in panic, suspended the Habeas Corpus Act and set up a secret committee to investigate the disturbed state of the country. In panic too, it opted for melodrama, and reported that dark forces were exploiting the distress of the labouring classes to induce them to look for immediate relief not only in a reform of Parliament, with universal suffrage and annual elections, but 'in a total overthrow of all existing establishments'. First France, now England. There was more

The Peterloo massacre, when eleven people were killed and about 400 wounded by local yeomanry at a parliamentary reform meeting, in St Peter's Fields, Manchester.

repressive legislation: the Seditious Meetings Act of 1817 and the Six Acts of 1819, when the threat of revolution triggered the carnage at Peterloo. When Parliament reassembled in November 1819, the Regent's speech pointed a finger at seditious proceedings aimed 'at the subversion of the rights of property and of all order in society'. Government spies abounded: in 1820 the Cato Street Conspiracy, to assassinate ministers at a cabinet dinner, was infiltrated by one of them, and swift revenge was taken. The thoughtful Peel perceived in the disorder pressure for some undefined change in the mode of governing the country, however nurtured, even by 'that great compound of folly, meanness, prejudice, wrong feeling, right feeling, obstinacy and newspaper paragraphs, which is called public opinion.'

Peel was right. There were many indices both of the need for change, and of the will to do so. England's first census, in 1801, revealed that four of the seven largest towns in the country, Manchester, Birmingham, Leeds and Sheffield, had no representation in Parliament. The abolition of slavery in 1808 was a pointer to a shifting political consciousness; journalists, especially Cobbett in the *Political Register* and Leigh Hunt in the *Examiner*, were loudly beating the drum of reform. Yet the movement had gained little ground in 50 years, partly because it was itself divided and poorly organised, partly because of external events which bred reaction, and partly because no party within Parliament was prepared to embrace the cause. The Whigs were at odds with the radicals, and the radicals themselves disunited. The banner of reform was carried by Francis Burdett in the Commons, 'the only spot in the world where the people of England are spoken of with contempt,' though before the disorders he had only fifteen supporters. In 1810 he was sent to the Tower (old practices died hard) for contempt of the House. He had condemned in print a decision of the Commons to imprison a city radical called Gale Jones. The stirring of the mob in Burdett's support secured his release. Bentham's *Parliament Reform Catechism* of 1817 lent authority to the movement for change, arguing that only equal electoral districts and household franchise could rescue England from being governed by a minority in the interests of minorities. In 1817 Parliament was inundated by petitions, most presented by Burdett: 600 in March alone, representing a million people. 468 were rejected by the Speaker because, contrary to the rules of the House, they were printed. But the petition campaign had little effect: Burdett's motion for annual Parliaments, manhood suffrage, secret ballots and equal constituencies was defeated in 1818 by 106 votes to nil.

The faulty analysis and punitive measures adopted by Liverpool's Government had done their utmost to provoke revolution. That the people were not provoked owes something to their decency, something to a gradual easing of distress in the 1820s, and a little to royal soap opera. The hulk that had been George III died in 1820, and at last it was the Regent's turn. But the return of his wife Caroline from Italy, where she had been living adulterously with Signor Bergami, set London in a frenzy. She was put on trial in Westminster Hall, which became the centre of mass hysteria, and had to be turned into a military garrison. The Regent was unpopular, his promiscuity notorious, and the prosecution case feeble. The queen's party was cheered; everyone else, including Wellington, hissed. The case collapsed; Liverpool tried to bring in a Bill of Pains and Penalties to deprive her of her title and dissolve the marriage,

The Prince Regent in the House of Lords.

but that too was abandoned, with the Commons in utter disorder, in November 1820. Parliament was quickly prorogued, to reduce the embarrassment. When Caroline left Westminster, even the soldiers abandoned their weapons to cheer her. Six months later she decently died, and again there were disorderly scenes at her funeral, which gave Peel the idea of a police force for London. George IV was now free to indulge his longing for magnificence and John Soane was commissioned to improve the buildings at Westminster to suit his majesty's taste: a new royal entrance to the Lords, the King's staircase and a Royal Gallery. The White Hall, the former House of Lords, which had stood since the eleventh century, was demolished. The Commons meanwhile suffered as never before in their congested Chamber: how could they give proper attention to reform when they were suffocated daily by bad air and smells, especially since the arrival of a hundred more members from Ireland. The Marquis de Chabannes was asked to install a ventilating machine to improve the atmosphere. It was another failure. But purification by fire, both for the antiquated Commons and Prinnie's candy-floss decorations, would be the best reform of all. Wellington's observation of George IV and his brothers that they were 'the damndest millstone about the neck of any government that can be imagined', was at least as applicable to the ossification of an outmoded political order in decadent premises.

Despite the perception that the foundations of the state were being shaken between 1815 and 1820, politicians turned back into ostriches when the threat faded, and saw little cause to initiate change. Peel's scheme for a London police force was rejected by a parliamentary Committee in 1822 because it was incompatible 'with that perfect freedom of action and exemption from interference which are the great privileges and blessings of society in this country.' The view of the country gentleman did not include the swelling metropolis, its rapid rise of serious crime and concentration of misery where neither privilege nor blessing could be invoked. The *Annual Register* for 1824 pitched into the landed interest as the most querulous and litigious of all classes, the least accustomed to suffer and the most incapable of struggling with difficulties when difficulties presented themselves. The landed interest continued to dominate the House of Lords (because of George IV's profligacy with titles, it increased from 339 to 400 between 1820 and 1830), which therefore was conservative to the very depth of its instincts, and remained so throughout the century. Many members of the Commons were tarred with the same brush; a newly elected member in 1830 complained in the House about 'the hordes of needy adventurers, whom the power and influence of great men has sent into this House to prostitute the little talent which God had given them and to make use of subservience and corruption from their inability otherwise to distinguish themselves.' If the quality of members needed reforming, so too did the burden of government. The strains were dramatically manifested. Castlereagh, Foreign Secretary and Leader of the Commons, committed suicide in 1822, his reason a prey to overwork; Canning, his much distrusted successor, branded by Hobhouse as 'talent without character', a sophist tolerated only by a corruptly elected Parliament, collapsed in a faint having 'called the New World into existence to redress the balance of the Old' in a debate in 1826 on the French threat to Spain, and also died of overwork a few months later. Liverpool, not an old man, was felled by a stroke in 1827 and had to leave office.

Canning's death removed a compelling opponent of reform, but progress was barely perceptible. Boroughs that had been found to be corrupt were punished by the removal and reallocation of their seats. A Bill in 1828 to give Penryn's seats to unrepresented Manchester 'on account of the increased wealth and population' was rejected by the Lords without a division. 'In that single sentence', declared Lord Salisbury, 'were embodied the wildest doctrines of radical reform.' Manchester was roused to fury. The total population of one hundred parliamentary boroughs was less than the unenfranchised parish of the city.

Resolution 1828–32

The indestructible Wellington came to the premiership. He was not a natural politician. De Tocqueville watched him one day from the Gallery and was disappointed: 'It was the strangest sight to see the man who had won so many battles and defeated Bonaparte as embarrassed as a child reciting its lesson before a pitiless pedagogue. The hero of Waterloo did not know where to put his arms or legs, nor how to balance his long body. He picked up and put down his hat, turned to the left and the right, ceaselessly buttoned and unbuttoned the pocket of his breeches as if he wanted to seek his words there, words to be sure that did not flow easily from his mind.' His army experience made him impatient at the time he had to spend humouring 'what gentlemen are pleased to call their feelings'. Though no radical, he was a realist, and secured the repeal of the Test and Corporation Acts which had excluded dissenters from participation in politics, and then he was forced to tackle Catholic Emancipation. It was an unpopular issue. Politicians and the public were strong in opposition, for they had no wish to see agitators elected to Parliament. But Parliament was hoist with its own petard, the Union with Ireland. In July 1828 the Catholic Daniel O'Connell was elected for County Clare in a by-election, and there was a strong possibility of the rest of Ireland's following Clare's lead in a general election by selecting Catholics. Wellington, ever the strategist, accepted that Catholic Emancipation was urgently needed to head off revolution in Ireland, or even civil war at home. The legislation was rushed through, to the great discomfiture of Peel, the 'Protestant champion' whom Wellington depended on to steer the measure through the Commons by 320–142, and a few days later it squeezed through the Lords by 111–109. It received the royal assent within three days. Wellington and Peel had earned themselves the labels of traitors, split the Tory party, and opened the gates to reform. Irish Catholics were now eligible for election to the Commons and some Catholics in Britain had the vote for the first time. O'Connell had learned the value of large-scale political agitation as a lever for reform; radicals in England observed his success, and would try to emulate it in Chartist demonstrations. Once in the Commons, of course, O'Connell devoted himself to repeal of the 1801 Act of Union.

But Catholic Emancipation represented the limits of Wellington's flexibility. The new Parliament which was elected following the death of George IV in 1830 met amidst serious distress, unrest and arson in the rural counties. Grey and Brougham, for the Whigs, at last declared for reform; Wellington announced in the Lords that the legislature and system of representation possessed the full confidence of the country, and that he would always resist measures for change. His blunder split his party and united the opposition. Within a week his Government fell, the new king William IV sent for Earl Grey, and nearly 50 years of Tory rule was at an end.

Reform was a fever in the nation's blood which had to be cooled by some measure, however nominal or symbolic. Earl Grey's Government had to find a remedy: 'Peace, Retrenchment, Reform', was its slogan, 'to restore confidence and satisfaction upon the part of the people.' Grey's instruction to his drafting committee was conservative: the Bill must satisfy opinion and block further innovation. Grey's line with William IV was that the Bill was an aristocratic measure, to consolidate existing interests. There would be no clause for a secret ballot: Grey and the king were both opposed; 'it was inconsistent with the manly spirit and the free avowal of opinion which distinguish the people of England,' said the king. Besides, a secret ballot was unlikely to find favour in Parliament. In advance of the Bill's publication, political unions sprang up, and sent up to Parliament about 3000 petitions in six months.

In March 1831 the first Reform Bill was introduced. In the months before it finally received royal assent, the political nation was as gripped by the rise and fall of its fortunes as any mother during a first pregnancy. The hysteria of the time seems out of all proportion to the Bill's modest achievement: a reform of the unequal constituency system and a small extension of the franchise to

*'The Great Public Question of Reform', an allegorical representation
celebrating the proponents of reform castigating its opponents.*

just under 5 per cent of the population, but that reform should be
addressed at all was itself a wonder. Tory objections to it were that it
would open the floodgates to the overthrow of society. Peel was eloquent in the Commons: 'These are vulgar arts of government;
others will outbid you, not now, but at no remote period; they will
offer votes and power to a million of men . . . and will carry your
principles to their legitimate and natural consequences.' Macaulay
for the government argued that the Bill was a guarantee against revolution, by bringing over the middle classes to the side of security

and stability. Rejection of the Bill would entail 'the wreck of law, the confusion of ranks, the spoliation of property, and the dissolution of social order.'

In defiance of the evidence of massive popular support across the country, the first Bill passed the Commons by only one vote, 302–301. Macaulay was present, and his account is unsurpassed: 'It was like seeing Caesar stabbed in the Senate House, or seeing Oliver taking the mace from the Table, a sight to be seen only once and never forgotten. The ayes and the noes were like two volleys of cannon from opposite sides of a field of battle. The Opposition went out into the lobby, the ayes kept their seats and were counted in the chamber. At 300 there was a short cry of joy, at 302 another. 'The doors were thrown open, and in they came . . . we were all breathless when Charles Wood, who stood near the door, jumped on a bench and cried out, "They are only 301". We set up a shout that you might have heard to Charing Cross, waving our hats, stamping on the floor, and clapping our hands. The tellers scarcely got through the crowd, for the House was thronged up to the table and all the floor was fluctuating with heads like the pit of a theatre. The crowd overflowed the house in every part . . . you might have heard a pin drop as Duncannon read the numbers. Then again the shouts broke out, and many of us shed tears. And the jaw of Peel fell; and the face of Twiss was as the face of a damned soul; and Herries looked like Judas taking his necktie off for the last operation. We shook hands, and clapped each other on the back, and went out laughing and crying and huzzaing into the Lobby. All the passages and stairs into the waiting rooms were thronged with people who had waited till 4 o'clock in the morning to know the issue. We passed through a narrow lane between two thick masses of them, and all the way down they were shouting and waving their hats, till we got into the open air. I called a cabriolet, and the first thing the driver asked was, "Is the Bill carried?" "Yes, by one." "Thank God for it, sir!"'

But it was only the start of a tortuous journey. It was defeated on the second reading. Grey asked the king for a dissolution, and there were furious scenes in the Lords and the Commons. Grey called a Reform election and won handsomely; a second Bill was carried by 367–231 in the Commons in July 1831. Now the pressure was on the Lords. It was rejected there by 199–158, a majority of forty-one, twenty-one of them bishops ('199 versus 22,000,000' read a placard

The Duke of Wellington attacked by a mob,
because of his opposition to the Reform Bill.

in Bond Street). Mobs went on the rampage in Nottingham, Derby
and Bristol; there were riots countrywide, and Peel amassed arms
ready to defend his property in Staffordshire. A third Bill was introduced, with minor modifications: Grey would not waver from the
essentials – disfranchisement of decayed boroughs, representation
for large towns, and a uniform franchise for 10-pound freeholders.
He persuaded the king to threaten to appoint enough Whig peers to
secure its passage in the Lords. The mere threat was enough to carry

the second reading there by nine votes, but it was defeated at the committee stage. Grey then had to resign again. The king turned to the Tories; posters appeared across London: 'To Stop the Duke – Go for Gold.' A cobbled-together ministry collapsed on its first day; William renewed his assurances about the creation of peers, and the Whigs were back in government. After its roller-coaster journey, the Reform Bill finally received the royal assent in an almost empty Lords Chamber. The Duke of Sussex, eccentric brother of the king, announced that it was the happiest day of his life. An old Tory peer behind him raised his hands in horror and cried, 'Oh Christ!'

The Reform Bill was not so much the beginning of democracy as the beginning of the end of oligarchy. The Duke of Wellington was sure that there was not a man in England 'who does not think that this Reform must lead to the total extinction of the power and property of this country.' The Whigs had taken up the cause of reform belatedly, and without enthusiasm. Grey, a reluctant reformer, had espoused it only to head off radicalism. He recommended it to the Lords as 'a conservative principle', which arose from an over-whelmingly aristocratic Cabinet. Parliament after the Act was very much like any other, dominated by country gentlemen and aristo-cratic families. There were still nomination boroughs, bribery and corruption, and infrequent ballots. 'Interests' still counted for far more than population figures in elections. Yet for the first time, pop-ular opinion had communicated itself to the Commons and had forced the king and the Lords to accept a measure they disliked. The authority of the Commons in relation to the Crown and the Lords had been enhanced. It extended political rights to some of those thought capable of exercising them, and the criterion was the possession of property, believed by all parties to confer the qualities requisite for a voice in affairs. The detailed provisions of the Reform Bill may, in retrospect, seem insignificant, but the fact of its passing was immense. Change had become possible at last.

Women in Parliament

But not for women. In the eighteenth century, ladies and women were both attracted to Parliament, differentiated by wealth and dress, but not perhaps so much by motivation or conduct. Orange women thronged the lobbies, to provide for the needs of members for a very different fruit, in the taverns, alleys or coaches that abounded in the old Palace. The downright sexual honesty of the period has much to commend it. Charles James Fox, accused of complicity in the Gordon Riots, gave as his very proper excuse that his involvement was impossible since he was in bed with his mistress at the time. From the 1730s ladies began to appear in the Strangers' Gallery. But in 1743 some of them, for reasons we can only speculate about, urinated on members below: 'Some gentlewomen, in our gallery, not being able to hold their water, let it run on Mr Dodington, and a Scots member who sat under. The first had a white duffel frock spoiled, the latter almost blinded.' They continued to be admitted, but were usually cleared out when the galleries were emptied of strangers, despite chivalrous protests from some of the members. Fashionable ladies wished to see husbands and lovers in action, and, when husbands and lovers wished to exclude them, they stormed the galleries and occupied them by force of numbers. In 1778 a party led by Georgiana, Duchess of Devonshire, caused a riot by refusing to leave the gallery when ordered to do so and, in an anticipation of later suffragette protests, clung on to their seats, assisted by sympathetic members. The disturbance lasted two hours, and the consequence was that the gallery was closed altogether to ladies. From then until 1850 they had to view proceedings as best they could from the dark and dusty space above Wren's false ceiling, where they could glimpse the chamber through the grille above the Commons chandelier. From this curious vantage, representatives of half the nation tried to view politics. The novelist Maria Edgeworth was there in 1822: 'One lantern, with one farthing candle in it, all the light. In the middle of the garret is what seemed like a sentry box of deal boards, and old chairs placed around it; on these we got and stood, and peeped over the top of the boards. Saw large chandelier with lights blazing immediately below . . . we saw half the Table, and the Mace lying on it, and papers . . . but no eye could see the Speaker or his chair – only his feet; his voice and terrible "Order" was soon heard.' Here in this gloom one evening Daniel O'Connell, arriving for a meeting with his wife, mistook another for her and embraced the Dowager Duchess of Richmond. Or so his story ran. There was no joy for women in the controversy over the Reform Bill. The Dean of Gloucester published a pamphlet hostile to reform which argued that democratic logic must lead to votes for women, an idea which is 'an insult to common sense'.

The Press Gallery

Journalism was midwife to the changes of political perception which underlay the Reform Bill. In the opening years of the nineteenth century, urban concentration and rising literacy created all the conditions necessary for a wider public interest in the activities of Parliament. The term 'middle class' began to be used around 1812 to denote respectable town-dwellers who provided the market for newspapers.

But reporters had had to fight their way into Parliament. In the seventeenth century members had wished to keep their proceedings secret from the king and his ministers, and resolved in 1660 that 'no person whatever do presume at his peril to print votes and proceedings of this House.' Though orders of the House reiterated in 1705, 1711 and 1738 that it was 'a notorious breach of privilege to give any account of the debates', a blind eye was turned and reporters were unofficially admitted to the rear gallery, probably to the benefit of the doorkeepers' pockets. So by the 1730s the practice of members 'spying strangers' and having the gallery cleared was in general use, as if to signal that the rights to observe and report could not be taken for granted. Such rights were of no interest to Dr Johnson, who wrote parliamentary reports from 1741 to 1744 by embellishing an outline of information, such as the speakers' names, and inventing their speeches himself. His prejudices were so strong – 'the first Whig was the devil,' he told Boswell – that he preferred debate to match his own preconceptions. Johnson's friend David Garrick was on one occasion observed listening to debate. One member moved to clear the House, urging the impropriety of admitting players. Burke opposed the move: it would be neither decent nor liberal to exclude a man to whom they were all obliged, who was the great master of eloquence, and in whose school they had all imbibed the art of speaking and been taught the elements of rhetoric. He was seconded by Fox. But when Garrick was sought, like Hamlet's father's ghost, he had vanished. Some years before, in 1751, the House had indeed adjourned to go to Drury Lane to see Garrick's Othello.

Systematic reporting began in 1768, but reporters and printers who produced accounts of debates were still liable to punishment. In 1771 a member informed the Speaker that a city printer had reported his speech in the *Gentleman's Magazine*. The messenger of the serjeant-at-arms was sent to arrest the man. But the City Corporation claimed total jurisdiction over city affairs, and Lord Mayor Crosby put the serjeant-at-arms' messenger in prison for assault. The Commons, now a nest of hornets, summoned Crosby to the bar of the House, but he was attended by an angry crowd of tradesmen who halted carriages and dragged MPs out of them. The Prime Minister, Lord North, was struck with a baton as he stepped from his carriage. 'Gentlemen, do you call this liberty?' he cried. 'Yes, and great liberty too,' was the joyous reply. Crosby was committed to the Tower, but emerged triumphant when Parliament came to its senses. From then on reporters were freely – but still unofficially – admitted, usually by paying the doorkeeper a guinea to guarantee admission for the whole session.

In 1803 a speech by Pitt on the war with France went unreported because the general public had spilled over into the seats where reporters were accustomed to sit. Next day the Speaker ordered that the back row should be reserved for journalists. The Press Gallery had been legitimised, and William Cobbett made his name when he began reporting debates in that very first year. He was followed in 1812 by Luke Hansard, whose name and tradition live on. That the presence of reports was both accepted and valued was attested by Macaulay's celebrated observation in 1828 that 'There are three estates in Parliament, but, in the Reporters' Gallery yonder, there sits a fourth estate more important than them all.'

Coleridge and Hazlitt were both briefly parliamentary reporters in the early years, but neither took to it with the exuberant success of Dickens, who began reporting for the *Mirror of Parliament* in 1831, when he was only 19. He was in no time 'the rapidest and most accurate short-hand writer in the gallery', and his imagination seemed to relish the turbulent congestion of the Chambers and the murky decadence of the buildings. Conditions on the back bench of the Strangers' Gallery were cramped, dark and unventilated, but Dickens was undeterred: 'I have worn my knees by writing on them in the old gallery of the old House of Commons; and I have worn my feet by standing to write in a preposterous pen in the old House of Lords, where we used to be huddled together like so many sheep.' In 1834 he joined the *Morning Chronicle* as its parliamentary reporter, and in all worked in Westminster for four years. They were momentous ones: he saw the Reform Bill, the Poor Law and

Factory Acts, and the Abolition of Slavery; he wept at O'Connell's description of suffering Irish peasants oppressed by the soldiers when they protested against paying tithes; he disliked Lord Grey's manner – 'his fishy coldness, his uncongenial and unsympathetic politeness, his insufferable though most gentlemanly artificiality'. In the Palace of Westminster Dickens was gratified by extremes of sensation; the ancient buildings drew him back and possessed his imagination. One extreme is his glimpse into the Lords, from *Sketches by Boz*: 'all talking, laughing, lounging, coughing, oh-ing, questioning, or groaning; presenting a conglomeration of noise and confusion to be met with in no other place in existence, not even excepting Smithfield on a market day, or a cockpit in its glory.' But the place also offered escape and dark solitude. On finding his first sketch in print in the *Monthly Magazine*, he was so agitated that he escaped from the crowded streets into Westminster Hall and paced the stone floor, 'my eyes so dimmed with pride and joy that they could not bear the street, and were not fit to be seen.'

The Lords approved an exclusive Press Gallery in 1831; the Commons copied them in 1835 when they moved into the Lords as temporary quarters after the fire of 1834; not until 1852 when the Commons at last moved into their new Chamber was a dedicated Press Gallery provided.

The last word must be William Cobbett's, the first journalist to move from the bench of reporters to the Chamber when he became MP for Oldham in 1832, at the age of 69, three years before his death. The old curmudgeon was as fiery and outspoken as ever: 'Why 658 of us crammed into a space that allows to us no more than half a foot square? There we are, crammed into this little hole; squeezing one another, treading upon each other's toes, going to the House at 7 o'clock in the morning, as I do, to stick a bit of paper with my name on it on a bench to indicate that I mean to sit there for that day; then routed out of those places again after a division has taken place and running and scrambling for a seat in just the same manner as people do when they are let into a dining room at a public dinner at the Crown and Anchor.'

His ill-humour, and the spirit of reform, were about to be appeased and consummated by fire.

CHAPTER SIX

A Dream in Stone:
Fire and Rebuilding 1834–70

A S IF TO PROVE that reform was not confined to Lord Grey's Whig Government, the Almighty, with perfect timing, contrived to have the greater part of the old Palace of Westminster consumed by fire on 16 October 1834. The process of reform was extended by *force majeure*.

Demands for change had been reverberating for over 100 years. Conditions of work in the old Palace were wholly unsuited to the growing responsibilities of Parliament. A mass of new legislation required more rooms for committees – up to forty at once in 1824, for example – than could be made available. After the murder of Spencer Perceval members felt themselves at risk in the dark and tortuous passageways of the old buildings. In 1831 a committee was appointed to look into ways of improving the condition of the Commons. Many schemes were aired and no decisions taken, since the government was committed to economy, and thought it prudent to make do. But the Palace was ripe for combustion. A jumble of buildings, patched and extended with wood, tarred paper and sailcloth, riddled with fireplaces and flues, needed little help to blaze. And on 16 October 1834 it was encouraged to excess by tally sticks.

A new Court of Bankruptcy was needed, into which the Tally Office in New Palace Yard was to be incorporated. But it was choc-a-bloc with obsolete wooden tally sticks, stored there since 1826 when they ceased to be used as a method of government accounting. The wonder was that the practice had endured so long. On a medieval royal progress, purveyors were sent on ahead to secure

*Old Palace Yard, 1808. Westminster Hall is on
the left, the House of Lords is in the centre.*

provision. The promise of payment was a tally, a piece of wood split
lengthways, with notches cut in it to denote pounds, shillings and
pence. The matching of the two halves secured the money. Dickens
mocked the practice as a symbol of reactionary governments,
which kept accounts 'much as Robinson Crusoe kept his calendar
on the desert island . . . official routine inclined to these notched
sticks, as if they were pillars of the constitution.' Richard Whibley,
Clerk of the Works, was ordered to burn them in the Exchequer
Yard, but thought a blaze there might alarm the neighbourhood.
He preferred to use the furnaces of the House of Lords. So from 7
a.m. to 5 p.m. on 16 October, two labourers fed the stoves. The
flues had not been cleaned for a year, and the continually opening
doors created a fierce draught.

It was a quiet time of year. Neither the Lords nor Commons had
sat for three weeks and Mrs Wright was standing in for her daugh-
ter-in-law, the regular Lords Housekeeper, and earning a bit of
money by showing round any interested visitors. About 4 o'clock
Mr Snell and Mr Shuter asked to see the House of Lords, and Mrs
Wright took them in. They were disconcerted by the heat, which
they could feel through their boots, and the smoke, which obscured
the throne at the far end. Mrs Wright conceded that it was 'in a
smother', but explained that it always got hot like this, that work-

men were below, and that since it was a stone floor there was no danger. She locked up and complained to the labourers, who said they were only obeying orders. About 5 o'clock the men finished the job and went off for beer. An hour later Mrs Mullencamp, wife of the Lords doorkeeper, disturbed Mrs Wright's comfort by pounding on the door and crying out: 'Oh good God, the House of Lords is on fire.' Black Rod's wooden box was already in flames. Mrs Wright rushed about, met a terrified Whibley who did nothing, and ran into the street 'without bonnet and shawl' shouting for help. It was too late. The overheated flues had begun to devour the Palace, and the brisk south-west wind that blew until the early hours of the 17th was a perfect accomplice.

At 7.30 the fire engines arrived, led by Chance, the mongrel dog and mascot of the London Fire Engine Establishment, who was loudly cheered by the vast crowd that had quickly congregated for a spectacular street party. The Lords was already gutted, and the Commons too on fire. At 10 p.m. the walls of the Lords collapsed; each fall of masonry prompted a great cheer from the crowd who had to be restrained by the Grenadier and Coldstream Guards to keep a clear space for firefighters and officials. But the former were inadequate and the latter too plentiful. 'The firemen shouted their directions from above, to the numerous, busy, meddling people, whose rank embarrassed but whose wisdom afforded little guide from below. There was zealous interference on all sides but the great want of a Commander-in-Chief.' The Prime Minister, Lord Melbourne, was there, commandeering cabs to carry away loads of records and documents which an enterprising minor official of the House of Lords called Smith was throwing out of windows. When the Chancellor of the Exchequer, Lord Althrop, voiced the principal anxiety of the event: 'Damn the House of Commons, let it blaze away; but save, oh save the Hall', Melbourne directed the efforts to prevent the flames taking hold of the wooden roof by playing water over the beams from the interior. In the early hours of 17 October, when the wind had changed, and the tide had turned so that a floating fire engine could be towed up river by steamboat, the flames were brought under control and the firemen could stagger off to local taverns for refreshment.

It had been a good night out: no one was killed, and the crowd had been in good humour. In 1833 the radical MP Joseph Hume had tabled a motion for better accommodation. At the height of the

The Palace of Westminster on fire.

blaze a wag's remark that 'Mr Hume's motion for a new house was carried without a division' amused the crowd mightily. Pickpockets and boatmen had made a killing. The event had drawn in some interesting witnesses. Turner and Constable both watched the fire, and later painted their memories; Dickens, then a parliamentary reporter, observed an MP and the firemen's dog, 'both running up and down, and in and out, getting under people's feet, and into everybody's way, fully impressed with the belief that they were doing a great deal of good, and barking tremendously.' Charles Barry, a rising young architect, on his way back from Brighton by coach, saw 'a red glare on the London side of the horizon', made his way to Westminster and passed the whole night 'absorbed in the grandeur and terror of the sight' among the crowds. Augustus Welby Pugin, aged 22, a furniture designer, theatrical scene painter and devotee of Gothic architecture, was also in London and wrote to a friend: 'I was fortunate enough to witness [the great conflagration] from almost the beginning till the termination of all danger as the hall had been saved which is to me almost miraculous as it was surrounded by fire. There is nothing much to regret and much to rejoice in a vast quantity of Soane's mixtures and Wyatt's herasies [*sic*] having been effectually consigned to oblivion. Oh it was a glorious sight to see his composition mullions and cement pinnacles and battlements flying and cracking while his 2*s*. 6*d*. turrets were smoking like so many manufacturing chimnies [*sic*] till the heat shivered them into a thousand pieces.' Pugin's mood of exhilaration was widely shared. The fire was widely hailed as the culmination of the reform process; the old radical Cobbett cheered it as 'a great event'. The painter Benjamin Hayden reflected 'the comfort is there is now a better prospect of painting a House of Lords,' but the poor man committed suicide when he was later passed over. But first the melodrama of the fire had to yield to an appraisal of the remains, and a decision about what to do with them, and the immediate practical challenge of rehousing the Lords and Commons. Robert Smirke, official architect to the Board of Works, created temporary quarters for the Lords within the shell of the burned-out Painted Chamber, and for the Commons on the site of the Court of Requests, which the Lords had used from 1801 to the time of the fire. His speed was extraordinary: both were ready for use by February 1835.

The rumours of arson that briefly fuelled the popular imagination when it was discovered that one of Whibley's labourers was a jailbird and the other an Irish Papist were quickly displaced by a lively public debate. The weight of feeling was for a noble replacement on good reform principles. *The Times* and the *Spectator* came out strongly: 'no jobbing, precipitancy or secrecy'. Pugin feared the worst: 'that execrable designer Smirke has already been giving his opinions . . . a prelude to his selling his diabolical plans and detestable details.' The only area of agreement in the debate about the rebuilding was the importance of incorporating Westminster Hall, saved by a miracle: 'This most venerable relic of the olden time, the ruin of which could not be compensated for by as many modern trumpery structures that would suffice to cover a wilderness.' In 1835 a Commons committee was appointed, and quickly opted for an open competition for designs in either the Gothic or the Elizabethan style, in the belief that both were truly national. The aim was clear: to sweep away the medieval ruins, to abandon former ideas of a classical senate house, and to build a palace fit for the public affairs of the world's greatest nation.

The closing date for entries for the competition for the new Palace was 1 December 1835. Ninety-seven entries were submitted. On 29 February 1836 the winner was announced: entry number 64, denoted by a portcullis (the identification mark chosen by Charles Barry), 'bears throughout such evident marks of genius and superiority of talent as fully to entitle it to the preference we have given it.' A further unvoiced attraction was its cheapness – Barry's estimate was £724,986 – and its proposed time scale of six years, though the eventual cost was over £2 million, and the building time around 30 years.

As soon as Barry's victory was announced, there was an outcry. Ninety-six disappointed entrants were now free to carp and snipe, and challenge the outcome. Hostility was led by the *Morning Herald*: 'Though pretty to the uninformed eye, it is meretricious. The chaste and truly beautiful St Stephen's Chapel is completely sacrificed.' The gallery in the Commons is like 'one of the shilling galleries in one of our great theatres'. Supporters of classicism spread hysterical arguments: 'Gothic was a mere ecclesiastical style; the bishops had plotted to turn Parliament into a monastery, and its members were to wear habits, so why not use the Abbey and save the expense'. 'Gothic barbarism', fulminated the antiquary W. R. Hamilton, 'is again to be allowed to triumph over the masterpieces of Italy and Greece.' Contending factions flung adjectives at one another like squibs: manly, chaste, dignified, strong, gloomy, national, dangerously artistic. No one pointed out that a Gothic building was far more costly to build and maintain than a classical one.

But the committee stood its ground, and appointed a controlling commission to monitor progress and expense. Transcending all disputes about style and the intolerable working conditions Barry had to endure is the certainty that the new Palace of Westminster ushered in a new age, with a new sense of itself. Nothing on such a scale had ever been attempted before. The bravura of its lofty towers and elaborate ornamentation mark the new Victorian age. Though the fashion for Perpendicular Gothic was to be short-lived, the Palace remained a model for public buildings all over the world for decades after it was itself condemned as 'a metropolitan asylum for birds' nests and soot'. As the building slowly rose, praise began to be lavished. 'Un rêve en pierre,' said Tsar Nicholas I; 'a fairy palace, a marvel of the Thousand and One Nights,' said the French architect Lassus. And once on the London skyline, it exerted visual magnetism for many of Europe's great artists, enabling Lord Clark, a hundred years on, to hail it as 'a triumph of the picturesque'. Perhaps its eclecticism is part of its magic. Barry was an architect trained in classicism, and the symmetry of his great palace violates the strict canons of Gothic. 'All Grecian, sir,' was Pugin's mischievous comment on the river frontage, 'Tudor details on a classic body'. Yet from the moment the competition was won, Barry was to know scarcely any more satisfaction. The great enterprise destroyed the health of Barry and Pugin, its chief creators, and brought their lives to premature ends.

Charles Barry and Augustus Pugin

Barry was linked with the Palace of Westminster at birth: the home of his father, a humble stationer, was in Bridge Street. His great clock tower stands only a few yards from where he was born. His mother died when he was 3, his father when he was 10. At 15 he was articled to a small architects' and surveyors' practice in Lambeth; from 1817 to 1820 he used his small inheritance for a grand tour to study European architecture, and went as far as Egypt and Syria. Throughout his life working relationships were complicated by his sense of social inferiority and his pride in his humble origins. His manner was awkward, his speech often curt, even truculent.

Pugin's father had taken refuge in England from revolutionary France. He founded an architect's office where young Pugin worked briefly before being articled to a furniture designer. He also became involved in theatre design, worked at Covent Garden from 1830 to 1832, and was offered a job at a Paris opera house. But in 1833 he resolved 'to give up my theatrical connection altogether and to devote myself entirely to Gothic architecture', his father's great love. By 1834 he had compiled ten volumes of fantasy Gothic buildings. In 1834 he became a Catholic convert, for aesthetic rather than doctrinal reasons. Seen to cross himself in a railway carriage, the only other occupant, a lady, was appalled. 'You are a Catholic, sir! Guard, guard, let me out – I must get into another carriage.'

Barry first employed Pugin in 1834, to supply Tudor Gothic details for King Edward VI School, Birmingham. Barry visited him after the fire at Westminster, and Pugin's notebook reads, 'Worked

Photograph of Charles Barry.

all night Parlt. H.' In the autumn of 1835 he helped Barry with his competition entry, and throughout 1836 and 1837 he was hard at work on designs for ornaments: fireplaces, doors, lamps. Barry was delighted with the outcome: 'Nothing can be more satisfactory than the result of your labours hitherto.' From 1837 to 1844 Pugin was active elsewhere, but then Barry, under constant harassment from his employers about his slow progress, sought Pugin's help again: 'It is of vital importance to me that the fittings and decorations of the House of Lords should be finished with the utmost possible dispatch.' They entered into a permanent arrangement: Pugin's misleading title was Superintendent of the wood-carving. Barry called him 'my comet', and his demonic energy was indispensable to the hard-pressed architect. He not only filled many portfolios with designs, but brought with him to the Palace his associate artificers: Hardman for metal work, Crace for painting, Minton for encaustic tiles and Gillow for furniture. It was a team for which Barry had every reason to be thankful. The House of Lords was a triumph when it was finished and occupied in March 1847. Pugin's frenzied creativity allied to Barry's perfectionism (he

*Augustus Welby Pugin, painting
in the Palace of Westminster.*

constantly revised Pugin's designs) fashioned what neither could
have achieved alone. But the toll on Pugin was a terrible one: he
was already afflicted with the eye disease, perhaps linked to a brain
tumour and his working habits, which led to his insanity. His last
working days were spent designing inkwells and umbrella stands.
Then in the spring of 1852 he had an attack of 'nervous fever', was
straitjacketed and then confined to Bedlam, where he died, aged
only 40, on 14 September. His doctor observed that he had done
100 years' work.

Even before Pugin's death, controversy was being stirred. From
about 1845 rumours were rife that Barry was a charlatan, and that
Pugin had prepared the winning designs for the 1835 competition.
Barry's offhand behaviour after Pugin's early death fuelled speculation. In 1858 he borrowed from the Pugin family a series of letters
which he had written to the designer, and they were never seen
again. Not long after Barry himself was dead, in May 1860, of a
heart attack. Palmerston moved the adjournment of the House on
the day of Barry's funeral in the Abbey, but only so that he could go
to Epsom, where he had a horse running in the Derby.

The controversy was reopened in 1867 when Pugin's son published a polemic: 'Who was the art architect of the Houses of Parliament?', in which he claimed that his father rather than Barry was principally responsible for the building, but had received no recognition, whereas Barry had been knighted by Queen Victoria when she arrived at the Palace to open Parliament on 3 February 1852, just as Pugin was descending into insanity. Barry's sons joined battle on their father's behalf, but undoubtedly Barry's memory and reputation were tarnished.

Barry certainly owed more to Pugin than he or his sons were prepared to admit, and had not acknowledged his debt either while Pugin was alive or after his death. Yet Pugin had generously recognised Barry's role: 'Barry's grand plan was immeasurably superior to any that I could at any time have produced . . . Barry after all is the right man in the right place; what more could we wish?' Yet in Kenneth Clark's assessment, 'every visible foot of the houses of Parliament is the work of Pugin . . . every panel, every wallpaper, every chair sprang from Pugin's brain.' But he could never put his details together, and conceded that only Barry could pull everything into unity. It was a perfect match of two extremely dissimilar personalities and talents. Barry had a noble vision of the building which he stubbornly adhered to in the face of unremitting interference, and chose Pugin, whose prodigious talent matched Barry's conception, and with whom he had evolved a harmonious partnership. Barry was the anchor, ready to undertake the tedious business of administration, freed from which the cornucopia of Pugin's genius had its brief intense flourishing.

Before building could begin, the stone had to be chosen. An official party of scientists and architects, accompanied by Barry, enjoyed a £1300 jaunt around the quarries of England in 1838. Their first choice, Bolsover magnesian, yielded blocks of insufficient size, so they had to settle for stone from the Duke of Leeds' quarry at Anston, which proved to be full of flaws, often unmarked at the quarry and so wrongly laid on site. In September 1837 work began on the coffer dam to reclaim from the river the line of the terrace embankment, which was between 80 and 100 ft. beyond the line of the old wharves. The temporary dam took 16 months to construct, and cost £24,000. A 10-horsepower steam engine pumped out water round the clock, and the site was dry by New Year's Day 1839, when building work began. On 27 April 1840, in a private ceremony, Mrs Barry laid the foundation stone at the corner of the Speaker's House nearest Westminster Bridge. By 1844 700 men were at work. There was no room for more. Not the least of Barry's problems was a close-packed site on which the Lords and Commons also continued to meet. Canal barges brought 775,000 cu. ft. of Anston stone, bricks, girders and iron plates from Birmingham to the Thames wharves, now converted into the Victoria Tower Gardens. When the six years Barry had estimated were up, he was still working on the foundations. But after 1844 the pace quickened, and the Lords moved happily into their new Chamber in February 1847, and Barry was at last able to demolish the remains of the Painted Chamber. But in May 1850 when the Commons first occupied their new Chamber, there was nothing but umbrage, no doubt fuelled by envy of the Lords' magnificence. The Chamber was too high. The seating was insufficient. The lobbies were too small. The acoustics were impossible. Money enough had been spent to have provided golden seats. The admirable Peel defended Barry and blamed the House for limiting expenses and then complaining about the results they produced. Despite Barry's following their instructions to the letter, members were determined to find fault. 'Any schoolboy would be flogged for designing such a place,' declared the irascible Joseph Hume. 'Re-erect it in Hyde Park as a better home for the Great Exhibition than the Crystal Palace.' Disraeli waggishly suggested that the government might hang the architect to prevent such blunders in future. Barry was forced to make major alterations while the Commons retreated in a sulk to their temporary quarters. A new ceiling cut off the tops of his original windows, the division lobbies were enlarged and the galleries altered, at a cost of £15,000. Once the Commons reoccupied it, in February 1853, it is said that Barry never entered the Chamber again.

The clock tower gave Barry much difficulty (Pugin eventually proposed the projecting gables for the clock faces), but not as much difficulty as the clock and its attendant bells. Rivalry for the contract in the 1850s between Vulliamy, the Royal Clockmaker, and Dent was inflamed by the intervention of both the Astronomer Royal and an irascible amateur horologist, a barrister called E. B. Denison, who suspected Barry of being in league with Vulliamy. Denison commandeered the project, designed the clock, which was constructed by Dent, selected the foundry for the casting of the great bell (Warners of Stockton-on-Tees) and even supplied the formula

A proud announcement by the manufacturers of 'Big Ben'.

for the bell metal. It was cast in August 1856, and brought by schooner (which came close to foundering) from West Hartlepool to London. A team of sixteen horses was needed to haul it over Westminster Bridge; great crowds turned out, and London was en fête. The foundrymen had christened it 'Big Ben', either after Benjamin Hall, Commissioner of Works, whose name was on the bell, or, more probably, after Benjamin Caunt, a popular prizefighter and landlord of the Coach and Horses in St Martin's Lane. It was hung on a temporary frame at the foot of the tower for a year, to test it. But in October 1857 it cracked; Denison was probably to blame for insisting on too heavy a hammer. Recast at the Whitechapel Bell Foundry, it was raised up the central shaft in October 1858; the 200-ft. vertical lift took 18 hours. In July 1859 it began to tell London the time, but it cracked again in September. There was another outburst of public recrimination and court actions; *The Times* had to refuse to print any more of Denison's hysterical letters; people claimed they were being deafened by the bell. But everyone was satisfied by the simple expedient of turning the bell a fraction so that the hammer fell at a different point on its perimeter. In the clock room was hung a board with the prayer that matched the chimes:

> Lord through this hour
> Be thou my guide,
> That by thy power
> No foot shall slide.

The 4-ft. crack in the bell is still there.

There was no grand opening for the new Palace. Queen Victoria first used the royal porch below the Victoria Tower in 1852, the occasion on which Barry became Sir Charles. But his remaining years were unfulfilling. The Crimean War caused further retrenchment, and, despite the desperate need for still more space, his scheme for the enclosure of New Palace Yard was abandoned. A prisoner both of his own creation, and of the government, he could neither finish his work nor leave it alone. Endless minor revisions of the still incomplete Palace occupied all his time until his sudden death in 1860.

From the moment in 1836 when he was declared the winner of the competition, he had been subjected to 24 years of harassment. There was a protracted wrangle over his commission, symptomatic of the inability of 'gentlemen', especially in public life, to accord an architect the professional respect Barry felt he deserved. In consequence he was intolerably plagued by unanticipated interference by ignorant but self-important amateurs. At the start of the project both Houses set up meddlesome committees of enquiry, and as costs rose and time stretched, more and more of Barry's own time was consumed by appearances before them. Grilling the architect became a parliamentary sport, and each year he had to face hundreds of questions. 'I am in a towering rage,' he wrote to Pugin in 1848, 'and in the right humour for throwing up my appointment at the New Palace of Westminster, which I expect I shall be driven to do before long. All the arrangements of the new House of Commons are in abeyance, and awaiting the fiat of a Committee of the House of Commons, of all tribunals the most unfit to decide.' Embittered, he withheld all the drawings of the building as a protest.

A restive Commons had prompted the appointment of a Royal Commission in 1848 to superintend the completion of the new Palace, so burdening Barry with yet another tier of authority. Conflict continued even when the Palace was at last in use, and its querulous occupants quietened. He was persecuted by Benjamin Hall, Commissioner of Works, who articulated the establishment view: 'the difficulty of restraining architects must have been practically felt by any gentleman who ever employed one.' Barry must bear some responsibility for the impasse in relations with his employers. He was obsessively unable to leave his designs alone; he lacked graciousness with committees; he appointed George Allen, an accomplished but overbearing foreman, whose conduct caused a stonemasons' strike in 1841. But the chief fault lay with Parliament and its wrangles about accommodation. 'The entire plan and construction of the building has had to be modified and recast over and over again,' complained Barry. Petty territorial disputes about residences for parliamentary officials forced continual changes. Two hundred and eighty-one rooms were allotted for residential use; nine residences each had twenty or more rooms provided. Even the Speaker's train-bearer had four rooms. In consequence there were no rooms for members, and no space either for 'the gentlemen of the Press' who already comprised nearly four hundred. Such mismanagement of space led to the early and unhappy precedent of building into the courtyards, on to the roofs, and subdividing rooms, a practice which continues to the present day and violates Barry's noble conception. The Building Committee, another of the architect's many crosses, was appalled at the proposal to provide accommodation for ladies. It was 'contrary to the principle which ought to govern legislative proceedings'. Lord Brougham declared that ladies were better employed anywhere else than in listening to parliamentary debates. He liked to see them in their proper places. But eventually a small gallery was set aside for them, but enclosed by a metal grille, so that they could see but not be seen.

Not the least of Barry's troubles were caused by the cranks and charlatans appointed by Parliament to oversee particular services that the Palace required. Chief of these was 'the Great Ventilator', Dr David Boswell Reid. He had installed a ventilation system in the temporary Commons which 'had rendered rheumatism a Parliamentary complaint'. But the plausibility of his 'ventilating philosophy' led to his appointment as the ventilator of the new Palace, operating independently of Barry, in 1840. He was an impossible man. He was an easily offended megalomaniac and a theoretician unable to read or provide architectural plans. His ludicrous and ever-changing demands drove Barry to such distraction that after 1845 he would only deal with him by letter. He devised seven different ways of constructing the flues and the ventilation chambers in the roof; he demanded one-third of the cubic capacity of the building for ventilation cavities. He demanded the addition of the 300-ft.-high spire above Central Lobby, from which four hundred fires and furnaces were to expel 'vitiated air' from the whole Palace. It cost £32,000, and was never used. Barry was forced to reduce the height of the windows in the lobby to accommodate Reid's demand, and recommended the compensation of mosaics 'to give a general cheerfulness and lightness' instead. Barry was contemptuous of Reid's abilities. Questioned by yet another committee, he replied: 'To make such a novel system work, great mechanical skill, a thorough knowledge of the arts of construction, sound judgement and decision, and in fact the habits and methods of a man of business would be required, in all which attainments and qualities of mind, Dr Reid is, in my opinion, most certainly deficient.' So responsibility was divided: Barry provided ventilation in the Lords, and Reid was given free rein in the Commons. More grousing from the Commons: 'Like the unclaimed bodies of paupers, members were resigned to all the vicissitudes of scientific experiment.' There will be no remedy, said one, until some of the robust members on the Treasury Bench are ventilated into another place.

The problems were acute. Disraeli called the Thames 'a Stygian pool, reeking with ineffable and unbearable horrors'. 'The Great Stink' of raw sewage and industrial waste was feebly repelled by sheets of canvas soaked in chloride of lime hung across the riverside windows. By 1850 the clash of ventilators had become a national jest. *Punch* satirised both; *The Times* supported Barry and mocked Reid as 'an aerial Guy Fawkes capable of blowing up Parliament'. The Commons at last saw through him when they moved finally into their new Chamber to find it cold in winter, hot in summer, and beset all year round by river smells, kitchen smells and stable smells. In 1852 Reid petitioned Parliament about his authority, and they took the opportunity to dismiss him. One deluded fanatic was replaced by another. Goldsworthy Gurney let off gunpowder in the chambers to test the air, and nearly propelled the new Clock Tower into the air as a giant rocket by trying to flame off sewer gases from its spire. He reversed the prevailing system to draw in air at river level and expel it via the towers. The stench – of horse manure (one air inlet was by the door to the Ladies' Gallery, where coaches sometimes waited for hours, and horses passed the time in the usual way), sewage and the bone boilers of Lambeth – was now worse than ever. A hundred tons of lime were tipped into the river each day from the terrace, and between 4 and 6 p.m. many members were in a state of semi-asphyxia. Their condition was exacerbated by the 80 tons of coal a week burned on the Palace fires, adding their mite to London's pea-soupers, and by the gaslight chandeliers in the Chambers which had to be raised on pulleys because they made members too hot. Thus raised, they began to char the roof and turn beams into dust.

The Interior of the Palace

The public outcry against 'jobbery' after the fire nurtured an idealistic conception of a new Palace chronicling the story of the nation, and embellished with national art and craftsmanship. In 1841 a Select Committee chaired by Peel considered the promotion of the fine arts in connection with the rebuilding of the Houses of Parliament. William Dyce, director of the government-funded school of design in Somerset House, and Charles Eastlake, later President of the Royal Academy and Director of the National Gallery, both gave evidence and commended fresco as 'the noblest of the visual arts'.

Barry's own conception of the building was in harmony with the prevailing mood. He wished it to be 'a sculptured memorial of our national history'. The tradition of narrative and historical painting in the old Palace dated from the thirteenth and fourteenth centuries, and some of the draughts in the old House of Lords had been kept out by a great sequence of tapestries depicting the defeat of the Spanish Armada. Barry even proposed raising the roof of Westminster Hall to create 'an English Valhalla' with frescoes, statues, trophies and mosaics 'set in a profuse enrichment of colour'. Fortunately he was dissuaded from his atavistic desire to see the Hall as the depository for all trophies obtained in wars with foreign nations.

The non-parliamentary Royal Fine Arts Commission, chaired by Prince Albert, was convened in November 1841 to supervise the internal decoration of the new building. It was the product of an earnest campaign by radicals and utilitarians to use the Palace to elevate the moral, spiritual and intellectual state of the populace. The recording of English history in fresco painting, sculpture and craftsmanship rapidly evolved as its objective. But composed as it was of gentlemen amateurs, there was no place on it for either Barry or Pugin, and responsibility for the decoration became hopelessly divided.

In 1842 the Commission held a competition, followed by an exhibition of entries the following year in Westminster Hall, which attracted huge crowds. Cartoons were invited, either of subjects from British history, or of scenes from the works of Spenser, Shakespeare and Milton. The exhibition was the occasion for *Punch* to appropriate the word 'cartoon' and apply it for the first time to comic subjects, the magazine's own spoof entries. It was the first time that state patronage had been offered to artists.

'Sculpture without, sculpture, painting and stained glass within, are to preserve the memorials of the past and declare the date and object of the building,' declared Barry in evidence to the Commission. In general terms they were in agreement, but on every issue except painting tensions arose between architect and Commission; delays and suspicion grew. 'Every step Sir Charles takes requires careful watching,' the Prince Consort was heard to say. Barry felt that Pugin had provided him with all the craftsmen and manufacturers he needed, and resented the Commission's determination to select its own contributors. There were some unhappy mistakes with the sculpture: the marble statues of monarchs to line the Royal Gallery were found to be too big, and the seven completed were exiled first to Guildhall and then to the entrance hall of the Old Bailey. The sculptural centrepiece of the Prince's Chamber, of Queen Victoria flanked by Justice and Mercy created by John Gibson, has become one of the most highly esteemed of all Victorian sculptures, though between 1955 and 1976 it, too, was thought to be too big. Justice and Mercy were banished to storage for 20 years, and part of the scales of Justice were lost.

The division of responsibility meant, in practice, Barry's retention of control over sculpture, metalwork, stained glass and furniture, and the Commission taking charge of painting. Furniture and metalwork were Pugin's special pride. He designed furniture for all the public spaces and official residences, and provided in all over 1600 different patterns for metalwork, revealing an inexhaustible genius for everything from door furniture and letter boxes to calendars, stationery racks and name-card holders. He supplied, too, most of the designs for the heraldic stained glass, an important element in Barry's desire for 'a general spread of minute ornament' to give a sense of extreme richness. He supported Barry in his dispute with the Commission about the quality of the glass produced by the first manufacturer, and architect and designer won the argument.

The sequence of pictorial representation of national history began in the Royal Robing Room at the southern end of the Palace, with uplifting scenes from Arthurian legend, which was perceived by many Victorians as the wellspring of nationhood. In 1848 William Dyce was given the commission for the frescoes, though in the 16 years until his death, Dyce completed less than five of the seven planned. Despite setting up residence in the room for months at a time, and even giving it as his London address, he experienced difficulty from both unsuitable weather conditions and the quantity of chain mail he thought each image required. The Royal Gallery was reserved for subjects relating 'to the military history and glory of the country'. Daniel Maclise was commissioned in 1859 to paint the two enormous frescoes, of Waterloo and Trafalgar. One practical reason for choosing fresco was that its matt surface was non-reflecting, unlike painting in oils. But there was no established tradition of fresco painting in the British climate, and the damp atmosphere of the riverside allied with the dirt and dust of the building works in progress all around settled the fate of the early frescoes in the Palace. Maclise watched the colours of his Wellington and Blücher painting fade even as he painted its companion piece, and today they are virtually monochrome. Prince Albert had to cajole him into completing work of which he despaired. In the last year of the unhappy artist's life a brutal critic declared, 'we eagerly look forward to the removal of these unfortunate frescoes which year by year blacken on the wall.'

Challenged by the rapid deterioration of colour and paintings peeling from the walls, the Consort imported from Berlin the new waterglass technique of fixing fresco painting by spraying it with liquid silica, though it proved of little more use in preserving it than his earlier conviction that it could be cleaned by being rubbed with bread. The Clean Air Acts of 1956 and 1968, and better control of temperature and humidity within the building, have probably halted further decline.

But the allegories of Justice, Religion and Chivalry in the Lords Chamber, together with examples of them drawn from medieval history, the scenes from Stuart history in the Peers' Corridor and above all Maclise's ruined masterpieces in the Royal Gallery seem to have the sadness of their creators still hanging about them. All the chief authors of the Palace of Westminster seemed to have been cursed, inadequately rewarded and acknowledged, censured by Parliament and public opinion, their health and happiness destroyed and their lives foreshortened. The contrast between their distress, and the self-importance and complacency of their employers scarred the greatest English building project of the nineteenth century. One of them, Henry Hallam, who helped select the subjects from Stuart history, was in no doubt that 'no unbiased observer can fail to consider the long and uninterruptedly increasing prosperity of England as the most beautiful phenomenon in the history of mankind.'

The evil eye of authority had one more victim to fix, of the next generation of the Barry family. When Sir Charles died in May 1860, the Palace was substantially finished. Final details, it was supposed, would take at most a few months. Edward Barry, Sir Charles's second son, was appointed to complete the work. He had established his own reputation with Covent Garden Theatre and the adjacent Floral Hall. At Westminster he was efficient, decisive and always within budget. For ten years he worked diligently to complete his father's dream. Much remained to be done after all. The Royal Robing Room and Staircase had to be finished, the Chapel of St Mary Undercroft lovingly restored and decorated, the Cloister Walk in the New Palace Yard to be designed and built. He had to prepare plans for a new Chamber for the dissatisfied Commons, which were rejected on grounds of expense by Gladstone's Government in 1868. He had to field endless petty complaints from members and officials. The Palace had been designed as a grand club for an aristocratic group of part-timers with their own town houses near by, but the social range of members was changing, and demands on their time increasing. Under these new conditions, facilities were inadequate. The Commons was too small and the Lords too big. But governments would not contemplate further expenditure, so there was nothing to be done but grumble.

The exterior stonework had begun to decay before the building was even finished. The choice of Anston stone had been, and remains, a costly mistake; the 300 figures on the façades have had regularly to be replaced. Another committee in 1861 blamed London's sooty atmosphere. Barry's recommendations for the treatment of the stone were not acted on, so the disease spread. Then in 1867 came the controversy about the true creator of the Palace, and the name of Barry was tarnished. In 1870 Edward Barry was abruptly and insultingly dismissed, in a letter which, it was said in the Commons, 'no gentleman would have sent to his butler.' His courteous letters of enquiry were ignored, and he was ordered to surrender all the drawings of the Palace, which had been his father's chief bequest to him. The momentum for finishing the Palace had been lost, and 50 years were to pass before the completion of the mosaics of Saints Andrew and Patrick in Central Lobby in 1922–4, and the frescoes recording the building of Britain in St Stephen's Hall in 1927–8.

There was a comic echo of the remark about Barry's letter of dismissal in 1963, on Macmillan's Night of the Long Knives, when he dismissed over half his cabinet. Lord Kilmuir, the Lord Chancellor, complained that he was sacked in a letter no gentleman would send to his chef. 'Ah,' reflected Supermac, 'but a good chef is hard to find.'

CHAPTER SEVEN

Parliament and Politics

1832–1906

Parliament between the Reform Acts 1832–67

WELLINGTON'S APOCALYPTIC bodings at the time of the Great Reform Act were mollified when he surveyed the first gathering of Parliament after 1832. Asked what he thought of it, he replied that he had never seen so many bad hats in his life. Though headgear was not all that changed as a result of reform, the changes were not as radical as the establishment had feared and popular opinion had hoped. Opposition to reform had naturally come from those who were happily accustomed to the alliance of political power with wealth and property. It had taken systematic rioting between 1830 and 1832 to threaten such advantages and to nudge the reluctant into the 'aye' lobbies. 'The cry of alarm was raised,' said John Roebuck, 'to keep the House of Lords and the aristocracy generally in a state of wholesome terror.'

Electoral change did not portend the end of civilisation. Only the most glaring electoral inequalities were abolished. Fifty-six pocket boroughs with fewer than 2000 occupants, electing between them 111 members, were disfranchised. Ninety-seven new seats were created to improve the representation of large towns: over 30,000 new voters were added in Birmingham, Manchester, Leeds and Sheffield. The new £10 householder criterion for male franchise pushed up the electorate from 12 per cent of the male population to nearly 20 per cent: about 650,000 voters in all. But local electoral corruption still throve, because of patronage and open voting, with the result that many constituencies were still uncontested at elections: 240 in 1859 (over half the total), 188 in 1874, 109 in 1880. More significant reforms to the system had to wait until 1867 and 1884.

And despite the scare of the Reform Act, there was more continuity than change too, at least on the surface, in the control of political position and influence by the establishment: the aristocratic and landed interest. Throughout the nineteenth century, Parliament and cabinets were dominated by aristocrats and country gentlemen, and the social background of the Commons was overwhelmingly from the same stable. 217 members of the Commons were baronets or the sons of peers in 1833; 180 in 1860; 170 in 1880. Not until the 1885 election was a minority of gentry and relatives of the nobility returned to the Commons. The last political flourish of the old order was the aristocrat-dominated administration of Lord Salisbury in the 1890s, which contained so many of his relatives that it was popularly known as 'The Hotel Cecil'. Though the property qualification for members of the Commons was abolished in 1858, they were still mostly drawn, of necessity, from a level of society at which private incomes were assured, since no salaries were payable for MPs. There was no serious challenge during the century to the easy assumption that lives of privilege were justified by the responsibilities of rulers. Disraeli, an outsider, actively cultivated 'the aristocratic settlement of the country' because that class was the focus for his romantic patriotism.

The nobility clung on to a surprisingly large slice of power in the light of the revolutionary social and economic changes that were transforming Europe in the nineteenth century. The tenacity of the English landed interest after the Reform Act was as remarkable as the fact of the Reform Act itself. Only the policies of the Liberal Government of 1906 onwards, followed by the loss of so many sons and heirs in the First World War, uprooted the long tradition of aristocratic influence over political policy. By the 1930s only one in ten members of the Commons came from the class that had ruled politics in the nineteenth century.

A revealing measure of the conservative temper even of the reformed Parliament was its response to the People's Charter of 1838, which demanded universal manhood suffrage, a secret ballot, equal constituencies, annual elections, the abolition of property qualifications, and the introduction of salaries for MPs. Though such largely defensible ideas had been circulating for 50 years or more, they were perceived as presumptuous by an elite disinclined to appraise its right to govern. In 1839 the Commons refused to consider the Chartist petitions by a majority of 235 to 46. There was continuity, too, in habits of dress. Wellington might not have approved of the tailors or hatters, but frock coats and top hats continued to be worn by almost everyone until 1901. Lounge suits only arrived on the Treasury Bench with Asquith and Balfour.

Even the House of Lords, which should have lost both influence and prestige over its handling of the Reform Bill, rapidly re-established its confidence and importance in the late 1830s, though it had clearly learned a painful lesson. On two occasions when confrontation with government policy might have been regarded as certain, over the Repeal of the Corn Laws and the Disestablishment of the Irish Church, it was persuaded to vote prudently.

Yet there was a permanent change to political sensibility, even if as much symbolic as real. John Bright hailed 1832 as a vote for the middle classes, and the new Commons of 1833 was informed by a new radical spirit, exerting pressures for legal and social reform which abolished slavery, reformed local government, passed Factory Acts and the new Poor Law, and attacked unfettered commercial activity. Sir Robert Peel, who headed a short ministry in 1835, was the first Prime Minister from a manufacturing family, and his Government was seen at the time as a turning point in national politics: 'Not a single old family; how are the Aristocracy fallen!' Looking back, the Reform Act can be seen as the prelude to a distinguished – perhaps the most distinguished – phase of parliamentary life during which the colossal challenges posed by metropolitan and industrial life were faced with energy, optimism and public-spiritedness.

The bungling actions of William IV in the 1830s silenced the last echoes of the prerogative that the Hanoverian kings had expected to exercise over both ministries and Parliament. When Grey first withdrew the Reform Bill the king arrived at the Palace in person to dissolve Parliament. The king popped up again in the political confusions of 1834. Grey resigned, his ministry divided over Irish Coercion Acts. William disliked Melbourne, who succeeded Grey, and when the new prime minister sought a coalition by nominating Lord John Russell as Chancellor, the king dismissed the government on his own initiative, despite Melbourne's majority in the

Commons. This was the last occasion on which a monarch dared to do so. His final appearance in Parliament was a comic masterpiece. On a dark day, with poor lighting, he struggled to read the speech from the throne. He reached a difficult word and held out the paper to Melbourne, with 'Eh, what is it?' Eventually two wax candles were brought in, and he broke off: 'My Lords and Gentlemen, I have hitherto from want of light not been able to read this speech in the way its importance deserves, but as lights are now brought me I will now read it again from the commencement, and in a way which, I trust, will command your attention.' His death in 1837 was the last occasion on which the death of the monarch was followed automatically by a general election. Victoria, his successor, was in no position to meddle in politics in the way William had, and had to put up, year after year, with her 'dreadful old men', Palmerston, Lord John Russell and Gladstone.

From 'Interest' to 'Party'

There was a distinctive character to the politics between the 1832 Reform Act and its successor in 1867. Many unstable administrations served short terms: each of the six Parliaments elected between 1841 and 1865 brought down at least one administration. 'The Commons made and unmade Cabinets,' commented Bagehot; it was the height of parliamentary power. Many of the administrations had no reliable majority in Parliament, because it was still dominated by fluid groupings and allegiances. The idea of 'party' had not set hard: it was the ebbing of the eighteenth-century preference for coalitions. George III had been hostile to the emergence of 'party' and its attendant disciplines, and most of his ministers tried to humour his desire 'to root out the method of banding together' by choosing ministers from a variety of groups. Such a method of forming ministries was reliable when there was a broad assumption of common purpose, the landed interest. But Catholic Emancipation in 1829, the Reform Act in 1832, and the Repeal of the Corn Laws in 1846 delivered mortal blows to the assumption that policy would automatically defer to the aristocratic and agricultural interest. The period reflects a limbo in which interest-based politics was dying, and party-based politics still unformed. The contrast between Peel and Disraeli marks the change. Peel disliked 'party': 'To adopt the opinions of men who have not access to your knowledge, and could not profit by it if they had, who spend their time in eating and drinking and hunting, shooting and gambling, horseracing and so forth, would be an odious servitude, to which I will never submit.' Disraeli, Peel's tormentor within the Tory party in the 1840s, was as uncritically devoted to 'party' as Peel was in abhorring it: 'I believe that without Party, parliamentary government is impossible.' By the time Disraeli led a ministry, he was right: politics was required to be more professional. But the old habit of gentlemanly groupings lingered until the 1860s. The death of Palmerston in 1865 brought the era of fluid alliances to an end. 'The truce of parties is over,' declared Disraeli, 'I foresee tempestuous times, and great vicissitudes in public life.' Perhaps he was gazing into a mirror.

Activity in Parliament

Another notable characteristic of the period was the growth of interventionist legislation which largely transcended sectional interests. Between 1832 and 1850 most legislation became public, of general application. To initiate it, governments had to exercise increasing control over the parliamentary timetable. The volume of legislation considered was enormous, not only in the urgent addressing of social and economic problems such as public health, mines, the prison system, merchant shipping and factory inspection, but also in the explosion of railway building. In the 1840s, as many as forty different Bills a day were being scrutinised by committees. Standing committees were established; questions to ministers allowed; parliamentary sessions lengthened to cope with the workload. Parliament was changing from a club into a workplace, where earnest men such as Cobden and Bright turned politics into a high-principled vocation. Superior men were contemptuous. Greville, courtier and snob, far preferred the Conservatives, 'the rich and fashionable, constantly drawn away by one attraction or another, their habitual haunts the clubs and houses of the west end of town', to the Whig opposition, 'a dense body of fellows who have no vocation out of the walls of the House of Commons, who put up in the vicinity, either do not dine at all, or get their meals at some adjoining chop-house, throng the benches early, and never think of moving until everything is over.' *Plus ça change.*

The Duke of Wellington and Sir Robert Peel,
from a painting in the Palace of Westminster.

For most of the century, Parliament must have seemed like the centre of all things. The nation's destiny, and sometimes that of the whole world, seemed to turn on the issues debated there. Worthy newspapers devoted many pages to the reporting of proceedings. Such a place, keeping strange hours, clubbable and entirely masculine, in the eye of every storm, and where passions ran high, was certain to breed excess, of drama, rhetoric and character. The personalities of the great Victorian Parliamentarians still seem larger than life over 100 years on, and have already acquired mythic status. Peel, Palmerston and Russell preceded the watershed of Victorian politics in the 1860s; Gladstone and Disraeli, though members of the Commons much earlier, reached the summit of their achievements after it.

Peel was described by a successor, Lord Rosebery, as 'the model of all Prime Ministers'. A man of utmost integrity, he had the ability to transcend narrow factional interests and to put those of the whole nation first, to take a long-term view and, with hard work, shrewdness and administrative thoroughness, get business done speedily. Though hostile to party, ironically he produced in the 'Tamworth Manifesto' after the dissolution of Parliament in December 1834 the first electoral party platform. But its distinguished sentiments of justice and responsibility should be read as a model by all aspiring Prime Ministers, and serve as a lasting rebuke to the knee-jerk politics we have become familiar with. The manifesto refused to adopt the spirit of the Reform Bill if it compels us 'to live in a perpetual vortex of agitation; if public men can only support themselves in public estimation by adopting every popular impression of the day, by promising the instant redress of anything which anybody may call an abuse.'

Peel's first ministry in 1835 was short-lived. But Melbourne's Whig Government was brought down in 1841, and Peel came to power again in a heroic ministry which repealed the Corn Laws but destroyed his own leadership. He had magisterially scorned the previous administration in the debate which led to its defeat: 'Can there be a more lamentable picture than that of a Chancellor of Exchequer seated on an empty chest, by the pool of a bottomless deficiency, fishing for a Budget?' But a far greater crisis confronted him in 1845. Great rifts between landed and urban interests, aristocracy and middle classes, protectionists and free traders, English and Irish, rich and poor were opened up by Peel's determination to repeal the Corn Laws, which guaranteed minimum prices for wheat, and therefore kept the price of bread high. The trigger for repeal was famine in Ireland, the background the miseries of the urban poor. 'It was rotten potatoes did it all,' said the inimitable Wellington: 'it was that that put poor Peel into his damned fright.' Repeal was seen by the landed interest in the Conservative Party as a betrayal, but by John Bright as the victory of the middle classes over the great landowners. Peel's cabinet was divided: Peel resigned in December 1845. John Russell failed to form a government, and 'handed back the poisoned chalice to Sir Robert'. In May 1846 the Bill was carried, but 231 Conservatives voted against him. The party split. In the Lords the threat of rejection was headed off by the astute authority of Wellington, who formed a free-trade group of peers, and addressed the Lords as if he were their headmaster, relishing the drama of it. 'This night [is] probably the last on which I shall ever venture to address to you any advice again. This bill has

been passed by the Commons, recommended by the Crown. The
Lords cannot stand alone in rejecting this measure; it is a position in
which you cannot stand, because you are entirely powerless; without the House of Commons and the Crown, the House of Lords
can do nothing.'

Peel's party, led by the bloodhound Disraeli, took its full revenge
on him at the third reading of the Irish Coercion Bill. He lost the
vote and resigned, accusing the protectionists in his party of want-
ing high food prices for the poor in order to swell their own profits.
The conduct of the facile Disraeli in the debate was illuminating.
Five years before, full of ambition, he had written to Peel begging
for office. Peel refused, and Disraeli now took a personal revenge to
win a cheap popularity in the party. 'I find that for between thirty
and forty years the right hon. Gentleman has traded on the ideas
and intelligence of others. (Loud cheering.) His life has been a great
appropriation clause. (Shouts of laughter and cheers.) He is a bur-
glar of others' intellect. . . . There is no statesman who has
committed political petty larceny on so great a scale.' Peel, with
dignity, asked why Disraeli had been 'ready, as I think he was, to
unite his fortunes with mine in office?' Disraeli denied that he had
ever done so. Peel, who was thought to have Disraeli's begging letter in his pocket, did not produce it, and remained silent. His
farewell was also his epitaph: 'I shall leave a name execrated by
every monopolist who clamours for protection because it accrues to
his individual benefit, but it may be that I shall leave a name sometimes remembered with expressions of goodwill in the abodes of
those whose lot it is to labour . . . when they shall recruit their
exhausted strength with abundant and untaxed food, the sweeter
because it is no longer leavened by a sense of injustice.' When he
died in 1850 after a riding accident in Hyde Park, the outburst of
popular grief and sentiment was one that few politicians have ever
been accorded, and most would die for.

Peel's resignation and early death left the political field open to
Queen Victoria's two *bêtes noires*: Lord John Russell and Palmerston.
Both enjoyed long – too long for the Queen – and varied political
careers. Russell, as committed a free trader as Peel, was disinclined
to direct government, but preferred to seek consensus and coalition.
An adept tactician, he steered a shrewd course, in his ministry of
1846–52, though the Irish famine, financial crisis, resurgent Char-
tism, and a Europe in turmoil in 1848. Much of his legislation was

'Not so very unreasonable': a working man presents the Charter to Lord John Russell in a Punch *cartoon of 1848.*

humane: a new Poor Law Act, the Ten Hour Bill for factories, the Health of Towns Bill are examples. He devised the idea of life peerages 100 years ahead of its acceptance. Yet there were also curious inconsistencies about his conduct. In the 1847 election Baron de Rothschild, a practising Jew, was elected for the city of London. Because of his faith, he was disabled from taking his seat for 11 years. Russell brought forward a Bill to remove the civil exclusion of Jews, but the Commons rejected it. This was the occasion on which Disraeli, born a Jew but converted to Christianity in his youth, spoke out in defence of Judaism and was thought to have seriously jeopardised his political career. His argument, that Jews and Christians had a close affinity, provoked outrage. Yet in 1851, when the Catholic Church proposed a diocesan system in Britain, Russell's intemperate attack both on 'Papal Aggression' and on High Church Anglicans, both accused of 'mummeries of superstition', provoked a convulsion of anti-Catholic sentiment, alienated Peelite supporters, angered the Irish and brought down the government.

Palmerston had entered Parliament in 1807, and was a minister for 48 of his 58 years in the House, with long periods as Secretary for War ('Lord Pumice Stone') and Foreign Secretary. His cavalier conduct in defence of British interests around the world was never better displayed than in the 'Don Pacifico affair' of 1850, when he ordered the Mediterranean fleet to blockade Greece because of supposed loss of the property of a single British citizen in a riot. His parliamentary defence of his action won him great popular acclaim: 'As the Roman held himself free from indignity when he could say "Civis Romanus sum", so also a British subject shall feel England will protect him against injustice and wrong.' Palmerston's conduct was often outrageous. He was a martinet who worked from dawn to midnight, and expected those around him to do the same. He loved snooping in Foreign Office corridors. He was rude and habitually unpunctual. It was a London saying that 'the Palmerstons always miss the soup.' He was late for a dinner given by the Turkish ambassador, whom he scorned as 'a greasy, stupid old Turk, one of Bluebeard's attendants'. He even kept the Queen waiting, his offhand excuse being 'Public business must be attended to, Ma'am.' Victoria was unable to forgive him for an incident at Windsor Castle early in the reign when he blundered one night into the bedroom of one of the ladies-in-waiting. Victoria and Albert were certain it was a case of attempted rape; Palmerston's explanation was that he mistook the room for that of another lady who was joyfully expecting him. Carelessness over Foreign Office telegrams in 1851 gave Victoria the opportunity to demand his dismissal, and she vetoed his return to the Foreign Office in Aberdeen's ministry of 1853: 'Nothing will induce Her Majesty to have Palmerston.' So he served as Home Secretary in a government which drifted hopelessly into war in the Crimea, driven by public opinion, with forces totally unprepared and ill-equipped after 40 years of peace. More soldiers died from illness and malnutrition than at Russian hands. It was the newspaper age; reporters were on hand to record the debacle, and the popular indignation generated led to the fall of Aberdeen's Government. A resolution to set up a committee of enquiry into the handling of the war was passed by a majority of 305 to 148. John Bright's was again the passionate voice of radical protest against aristocratic ineptitude in public affairs. The House would fill up to listen to his rhetoric: 'The angel of death has been abroad throughout the land; you may almost hear the beating of his

Disraeli watches Palmerston speaking in the House of Commons, 1860.

wings.' Palmerston loyally defended the government, which had desperately needed his experience in the Foreign Office, but he could not save it. And when it fell, he was Aberdeen's only possible successor, despite Victoria's searching for any alternative. 'I am *l'inévitable,*' he reflected. His dominance was irrefutable, though he was often in trouble. When the Indian Mutiny broke out, the Queen told him that if she were an MP she would have denounced him in the Commons for incompetence. When churchmen asked him to declare a national day of prayer in the face of a cholera epidemic in Scotland his reply – that 'it is better to improve sanitation in Edinburgh' – caused him much trouble. The Church of England complained that he always treated Heaven like a foreign power.

He was defeated in 1858 after the attempt to assassinate the French Emperor in Paris with explosives made in Birmingham. In response to the French charge that England was providing sanctuary for terrorists, Palmerston brought in the Conspiracy to Murder Bill, which was denounced in the press and in the Commons as knuckling under to France. But after a brief Derby ministry in

1858–9, Palmerston was back again in 1859, heading a remarkable new coalition of Whigs, Peelites, Radicals and Irish Nationalists. At 80 he was still Prime Minister, still making passes at handsome women, still tucking into nine successive dishes of meat at a banquet. He could easily rise above royal disapproval, and the cheap contempt of Disraeli: 'only ginger beer and not champagne, and now an old painted pantaloon, very deaf, very blind, and with false teeth which would fall out of his mouth when speaking if he did not hesitate and halt so in his talk.' He may, like Churchill, have cultivated senility as a tactic. He seemed always asleep in Cabinet and the Commons, concealing it by wearing his hat over his eyes. What kept him going so long was his hatred of Gladstone, his obvious successor: 'Whenever he gets my place we shall have strange doings. He will wreck the Liberal Party, and end up in a madhouse.' Chalk and cheese they may have been, but distinguished companions in longevity.

Reform 1867–85

The bungled Crimean War, reported at first hand by William Russell of *The Times*, exposed the inadequacies of aristocratic amateurism in the conduct of affairs. Pressure for further political reforms had been building since the late 1830s, through the Chartist Movement's petitions and demonstrations, through the transformation of political consciousness by the rapid growth of railways and dense accumulations of population in industrial towns, the availability of cheap newspapers, and by the earthquake shocks of instability in mainland Europe.

A belated professionalism was entering Parliament. In 1866 the appointment of a Comptroller and Auditor-General and the setting up of the Public Accounts Committee provided increased scrutiny of government accounts. At the same time parties and their leaders were contending to seize the banner of reform. No act of larceny of which Disraeli accused Peel could have been as brazen as Disraeli's own seizure of the issue of Reform in 1866 and 1867. As in 1830, there was again strong popular pressure for change. In the 1860s John Bright was the leading popular politician, seeking to encourage workers and their unions into political participation. The electoral process continued to arouse discontent. Many seats were not contested at elections; there was much absenteeism from the

House by gentlemen who still saw politics as a part-time affair, and as late as the 1850s it was alleged that not one-tenth of the entire house had been legally elected when bribery laws were so generally disregarded.

Lord John Russell's Whig Government first put forward proposals for reform of the franchise in 1866, but they provoked deep divisions. Robert Lowe was their chief opponent. He argued that the franchise was 'a lever to raise men': it was open to citizens to strive for the privilege of voting through their industry, thrift and responsibility. The unity and property of England was linked to the limitation of the franchise to those who had succeeded. The rejection of Russell's proposals caused his resignation. Derby now headed a Conservative Government, but effective power lay with Disraeli, Chancellor and Leader in the Commons. Both were keen to take up the issue of reform in order to end the Liberal monopoly of popular causes: 'to dish the Whigs' was the phrase Disraeli filched from Derby and made his own. Disraeli's motives were purely pragmatic: to keep the Conservatives in power and gain personal acclaim. He displayed brilliant tactical management in steering through the Commons a much more radical Bill than that rejected the previous year. There was a great weight of opposition from the right of the party, who felt that the end of the world was upon them. Lord Cranborne (later, as Lord Salisbury, Prime Minister) opted for melodrama: 'The monarchical principle is dead, the aristocratic principle doomed and the democratic principle triumphant, all because of a political betrayal which has no parallel in our annals.' Property owners generally were deeply disquieted at the transfer of power to 'those who have no other property than the labours of their hands. The omnipotence of Parliament is theirs.' Disraeli's tactics cleverly included additional members for the industrial cities in order to secure Liberal support. In the House he aired his reasons for a wide extension of the franchise. He was opposed to admitting only 'a certain and favoured portion of the working classes as a form of Praetorial Guard, shutting out other portions of the working class from the pale of the constitution. There is greater peril in that than in appealing to the sympathies of the great body of the people. There is a better chance of touching the popular heart, of evoking the national sentiment, by embracing the great body of those men who occupy houses and fulfil the duties of citizenship by the payment of rates.'

In 1867 the Act was passed. The franchise was effectively doubled, to include about a million new voters, mostly from the industrial towns. Now 2,500,000 men had the vote, about 30 per cent of the adult male population. The *Manchester Examiner* declared that the people had been called in to redress the balance in the Commons: 'The nation decreed its own political organisation.' At the end of the parliamentary proceedings, the indignant General Peel, appalled by intimations of futurity, said he had learned that nothing had so little vitality as a vital point, nothing so insecure as a security, and nothing so elastic as the conscience of a Cabinet minister. The inclusion of all rate-paying households in the franchise may have been more than Disraeli intended: it was an idea he was juggling with, and the ball came down in his hand. Even he insisted that democracy was a form of government with which the Conservative Party had no sympathy.

Maybe the new voters believed him, for they voted him out of office in 1868, when Derby retired. Disraeli at last succeeded him and called an election. Gladstone's Liberal Government now resumed the crusade Disraeli had usurped, and raised the banner of further reform. The civil service was made attainable by open competition in 1868, and in 1871 army reform abolished the purchase of commissions. There was predictable outrage in the Commons from some who thought 'only gentlemen can command obedience'. In 1872 the secret ballot was made compulsory at elections, as a condition of John Bright's joining Gladstone's Cabinet. A third wave of reform followed in 1883 and 1884, first the Corrupt and Legal Practices Act, to remove major sources of electoral corruption, and then the Representation of the People Act, the third great Reform Act of the century, in which household suffrage was extended to the counties and the franchise to any householder or lodger who had been at his address for a year. Now nearly 60 per cent of adult men had the vote. The Lords, sensing the slackening of their grip on rural politics, refused to pass it until proposals for redistribution of seats had been agreed. Their intransigence fomented intense radical hostility to the Upper House. The outcome was the Redistribution of Seats Act of 1885, which made all parliamentary seats single-member constituencies of approximately equal populations.

An important consequence of political reform was the formation of local party organisations to proselytise among the large urban electorates. A popular manifesto, slogans and promises were necessary if politicians were to woo the allegiance of new voters. A much more clearly defined two-party system, with rules to secure the loyalty and discipline of parliamentary members, followed suit. Rewards for the nationwide organisation of the Conservatives came in the election of 1874, when big gains in the industrial towns brought Disraeli, at a late stage in his life, into the sweets of power.

The death of Palmerston in 1865, and the retirement of Derby and Russell in 1867 and 1868, brought face to face as party leaders those two talismen of Victorian England, Benjamin Disraeli and William Ewart Gladstone. Their extraordinary careers and personalities, more sharply etched by contrast, are rivalled only by those of Lloyd George and Churchill in political history.

Disraeli was, in J. A. Froude's phrase, 'a child of Parliament'. He had to endure both a weight of mistrust, and years of being marginalised before coming to power in old age. He had to struggle much longer than Gladstone to get into Parliament, shamelessly changing his convictions to suit each contest: 'The people have their passions, and it is even the duty of public men occasionally to adopt sentiments with which they do not agree, because the people must have leaders.' Such pragmatism was only one of several qualities Disraeli brought to political life which his contemporaries thought ungentlemanly. His professionalism made him the father of modern politics. He did not shy from unscrupulous personal attacks; in opposition he was the first leader to oppose everything irrespective of its merits, and he was adept at unprincipled manipulation. He was a cynosure of the Commons, in or out of office. When attacked, he sat with impassive self-control, arms folded, legs crossed, hat pulled down over his eyes, apparently dozing. But when he rose he smoothed his clothes over his hips with his hands, pulled his coat down at the front, threw his shoulders back, and struck. His stylishness, wit and self-confidence, his theatricality of language and manner were as distinctive as his habitual flowery waistcoat.

In December 1837 he made an unwise maiden speech on the controversial topic of Irish elections, and adopted an unusually swaggering and ornate manner of delivery. He was largely drowned by hisses, groans, hoots, catcalls, drumming of feet, loud conversation and animal imitations. 'My debut was a failure', he wrote to his sister, 'not occasioned by my breaking down or any incompetency on my part, but from the physical powers of my adversaries.' As he was forced to sit, he shouted: 'I will sit down now, but the time will come when you will hear me.' Peel's view was that he had done all that he could under the circumstances. 'I say anything but failure; he must make his way.' But Peel was not going to help him further. He was wounded by Peel's refusal to give him a place in his ministry in 1841, and thereafter harassed him with virulent personal hostility. He even sought from Peel a position for his brother. Peel thought it 'a good thing when such a man [puts] his shabbiness on record.' Peel's was the general view of him: an impudent upstart, not to be trusted.

But his instinctive political gifts could not be ignored. When Derby succeeded Russell in 1852 he wanted Disraeli as Chancellor. The Queen was deeply suspicious of him, and only accepted him as a minister on condition that Derby undertook responsibility for his behaviour. Again his debut was a disaster. His five-hour-long Budget speech in December 1852 revealed that he was not in command of his brief. Gladstone, for the opposition, broke with precedent in standing to speak last in the debate on it, censuring Disraeli's refusal to learn 'the limits of discretion, of moderation and forbearance that ought to restrain the conduct and language of every member of the House.' He then savaged the Budget proposals, 'fraudulent chimeras of enchanters and magicians'. This confrontation sowed the seeds of the long personal animosity between them. 'When roused,' noted Balfour, 'Mr Gladstone without any preparation could pulverise all his opponents, as his moral indignation was always more formidable than Disraeli's facile ridicule.' Yet the nimbleness and opportunism of Disraeli would sometimes leave Gladstone 'blundering and blustering'.

The 1852 Budget disaster forced the resignation of Derby's Government, and Disraeli was out of office, though Leader of the Opposition in the Commons, for five years. He advocated peace in the Crimea, and protested at English atrocities during the Indian Mutiny. He was Chancellor once more in the brief Derby Government of 1858–9, which was soon defeated over its policy on Italian reunification, and he found himself sidelined again for six more years of Palmerston's last Government, and largely reviled by his own party, who charged him with holding no principles except political advancement. But Conservatives can forgive everything for success, and after his skilful piloting of the Reform Bill through the

Benjamin Disraeli, c.1868.

Commons in 1867, he was cheered to the rafters at the Carlton Club. Returning home late in a fine humour he found the devoted Mrs Disraeli waiting up for him with his favourite pie and champagne. 'Why, my dear, you are more like a mistress than a wife.' This was from a man who held the theory that no one was regular in attending the Commons until he was married.

In 1868 Derby retired, and Disraeli succeeded him as Prime Minister. 'I have climbed to the top of the greasy pole.' There was much anxiety in the party. Lord Cranborne called him 'a mere political gamester, without principles and honesty'. But he had an unexpected devotee. As Leader of the House in the 1860s he had begun to cultivate the Queen, sending her an extravagant tribute on the death of the Consort, and through the regular reports on proceedings he had to write for her. Now she was entirely reconciled to him. He was 'her man risen from the people'. 'The present Man will do well,' she confided to her diary, 'and will be particularly loyal and anxious to please me in every way. He is vy. peculiar, but vy. clever and sensible, and vy. conciliatory . . . full of poetry, romance and chivalry. When he knelt down to kiss my hand wh. he took in both his – he said: "In loving loyalty and faith".' As he admitted, he laid it on with a trowel. After a short first ministry, he was lucky to survive one of the Conservative Party's typically ruthless lynchings of its leaders. He had become, for one backbencher, 'That hellish Jew'.

But in 1874 he had an election triumph, and held power until 1880. His ministry was dominated by the Eastern Question, when feelings in the country ran high for an interventionist war in the conflict between Russia and Turkey. The Queen and Disraeli were for the Turks, Gladstone for the Russians. 'Jingoism' was invented by anti-Russian feeling when European Turkey was invaded. Disraeli played his cards triumphantly at the Congress of Berlin in 1878, at which he signed himself 'Prime Minister', thus snatching a title from his imagination and bestowing it on himself and his successors. He received a hero's welcome back in England, where the glory of bringing 'Peace with Honour' was unsullied by a sour and envious minority, including Carlyle, who savaged him as 'a cursed Jew, not worth his weight in cold bacon'. He finished his Prime Ministership in the Lords, where the Queen persuaded him to go to ease his burden. Though old and ill, he was reluctant to leave the Commons for the Upper House. Earlier he had advised a young peer who wished to make an impression there to go and practise upon tombstones. He lost the 1880 election to an efficient Liberal Party organisation which had learned the lesson of constituency management from the Conservatives. The Queen was appalled at the return of Gladstone, 'that half-mad firebrand who wd. soon ruin everything and be a Dictator.'

A journalist observed Disraeli's last speech in the Lords in March 1881, late at night, when his final illness was upon him. He was sustained only by swallowing and inhaling drugs, and the 'impressive pallid face of this strange man of genius' haunted those present. In April he took to his bed. Victoria wanted to visit him, but he refused: 'No, it is better not. She would only ask me to take a message to Albert.'

Gladstone entered Parliament earlier than Disraeli, and outlived him by 15 years. He was elected for a pocket borough in 1833, and made his maiden speech in June, in the old St Stephen's before the fire. His subject was the Slavery Abolition Bill; even as a young man

Speaker's Procession, 1884: a painting in the House of Commons.

the moral fervour was there. He spoke for 50 minutes, and afterwards wrote in his diary: 'My leading desire was to benefit the cause of those who are now so sorely beset. The House heard me very kindly, and my friends were satisfied. Tea afterwards at the Carlton.' He was a junior minister in Peel's brief 1834 administration, and became a Cabinet minister for the first time in 1843. His authority as a Parliamentarian was sealed by his attack on Disraeli's inept first budget of 1852. He wrote to his wife just before the debate: 'I am sorry to say that I have a long speech fermenting in me and I feel as a loaf might in the oven.' His own first budget speech the following year lasted five hours, and was acclaimed. For three preceding nights he had been unable to sleep from excitement. He had a further notable triumph as Chancellor in 1861. His budget proposals thrust the government into conflict with the Lords. Gladstone, in a righteous fury, secured Cabinet backing to confront the Upper House by challenging them to reject the entire budget. The Lords gave way; the supremacy of the Commons in money bills was endorsed, and Gladstone won immense popularity. Palmerston's death and Russell's retirement handed him the party leadership. He led a government, energetic in pursuing reform, from 1868 to 1873, when he was defeated on Irish educational reform, and resigned. From this moment on the subject of Ireland was to haunt him for the last 20 years of his political life, bringing him his most bitter disappointments. In 1873 the wily Disraeli refused to form a government, and Gladstone had to return, though his popularity was waning. He fought the 1874 election on a platform dear to his heart, 'retrenchment and cheap government', though his desire to abolish income tax cut no ice with the many new electors enfranchised by reform who were not in the tax bracket. Disraeli triumphed; Gladstone retired: 'deeply desiring an interval between Parliament and the grave.'

But Parliament proved the more alluring option, and in 1880 he was Prime Minister again. His first response to the summons was quixotic: 'my mission is to pacify Ireland.' In the 1880s and 1890s he became obsessed with Irish Home Rule to the exclusion of almost everything else, but the defeat of his two Home Rule Bills, first by the Commons in 1886, and next by the Lords in 1893, cruelly destroyed his hopes. In 1886 most eyes in the Commons, when the result was announced, turned to Gladstone on the Treasury Bench. 'The noble head was brought low by the shock; the face grew ashen white. The formal motion which it was his duty to make had to be written for him and read, and the hand which held the written paper shook, and the voice shook, and the figure was the figure of a man who had suddenly aged. Not even the loyal greetings of loyal friends could bring back into his wearied face the light of delight in the battle, or the joy of the personal triumph he had won and of the political triumph he still expects to achieve.'

Such low moments were uncharacteristic. His fervour, his passion, his stamina (the latter fortified by his 'pomatum pot' of egg and sherry prepared for him each day by his wife) amazed all who witnessed him in the chamber. 'He had a wonderful eye,' wrote Lecky, 'a bird-of-prey eye, fierce, luminous and restless. When he differed from you, a great friend and admirer of his once said to me, "there were moments when he would give you a glance as if he would stab you to the heart." His own temper was visible and audible whenever he rose to speak; the mixture of anger and contempt in his voice almost painful to witness.' An irritable nature was his constitutional infirmity. At first he would essay control, putting his hands behind his back and folding them together, 'as if each were in the custody of the other'. But gradually the hands escaped, and expressive gestures began. His usual business was to excite one side

*Willam Ewart Gladstone in action: a sketch
portrait in the House of Commons.*

of the House against the other, and to achieve this aim he cut loose,
bending across the table with loud and denunciatory tones, thrusting his face as nearly as the space between the two Front Benches
allowed into the face of his antagonist, 'too much after the manner
of a provocative street scold'. When baited by an opponent he
would crouch like a tiger, 'jumping up with arms raised, or swept
wide, or with a finger stretched out in derision, eyes blazing, looking as if he might spring across the table.' Disraeli wore a habitual
expression of thankfulness for the solid furniture which separated
them, and which parried the many resounding blows that he was
unable to deliver direct to his opponent. Yet Gladstone also relished
playing to the Chamber in a lighter vein. In 1885 when he first
appeared in the Commons with a stick, he received a sympathetic
cheer; 'The old man could not conceal his delight; he paused for
several minutes, gave a profound bow after the manner of a prima
donna, with a simper in his face as if he were a member of a great
operatic or theatrical corps.' He found Parliament irresistible, and

Mourners file past Gladstone's coffin in Westminster Hall.

even in his eighties could be roused to youthful energy by run-of-the-mill issues. Lloyd George heard him in full flow in 1891, on the Roman Catholic Disabilities Bill, and wrote to his family: 'Give the old chap an ecclesiastical topic and he is happy. He bounced, whirled around, he flung his arms, he banged the brass box, he shouted until the corridors rang. Wonderful old boy. He was as agile as a child. Never heard his like.' It was characteristic that he should have been the first political leader to discover the delights of using railways for election campaigns. But the defeat of the Second Home Rule Bill in the Lords in 1893 was a blow too many. He made his last speech in the Commons in March, a nobly worded protest against the irresponsible power of the 'Nominated Chamber', and walked out, 'without ceremony or farewell, walking fast, with his dispatch box dangling from his right hand, as he passed the Speaker's Chair, and quitted the scene of his life's work for ever.' Two days later he resigned. There was much solemnity and ferocity about the Grand Old Man, qualities not greatly in fashion in modern parliamentary life. But his manner enabled him to get away with the statements that no satirist could better and any politician might envy. In 1882, when his Government engaged in a war to gain control of Egypt, he had authority enough to tell the Commons: 'We have carried out this war from a love of peace, and, I may say, on the principle of peace.' But by then he was, appropriately, sinking into the quicksands of Irish politics. In May 1898 Gladstone lay in state for two days in Westminster Hall after his death, and both Houses of Parliament accompanied his coffin from the Hall to the Abbey for his funeral.

One form of indulgence had been institutionalised in the Palace of Westminster in 1773 when John Bellamy was appointed Deputy Housekeeper of the Lords and Commons. From then until the fire in 1834 Bellamy, a wine merchant, and his son supplied meat pies and port to sustain and comfort members. Dickens portrayed Bellamy's in the *Evening Chronicle* as a place where honourable members proved their perfect independence by remaining during the whole of a heavy debate, summoned from it by whippers-in for a division, and 'to find a vent for the playful exuberance of their wine-inspired fancies, in boisterous shouts of "Divide" occasionally varied with a little howling, barking, crowing, or other ebullitions of senatorial pleasantry.' By the end of the eighteenth century, the dinner hour was greatly relished; bores were known as 'dinnerbells', and the Chamber emptied for them. Sometimes members returned in a merry mood: Sir George Rose, after a glass too many, asked the Speaker for a comic song. The Serjeant took him into custody and brought him to the Bar of the House to apologise. He said he would beg no man's pardon, not even King George's, and certainly not that of the little man in a big wig. He was locked up overnight. Mr Fuller, in 1810, audibly mistook the Speaker for an owl in an ivy bush, and was also handed over to the Serjeant.

Such alcoholic excesses seem mere dormitory japes when compared to 'the dry rot in the Commons'. From 1801 to 1921 one further indispensable ingredient for excess – of comedy, subversion and disorder – was present: the Irish members. Brought to Westminster against their will, to debate their affairs in what they considered a foreign nation, with no respect for the traditions of the Parliament in which they sat, they resolved to 'use every form of this house, every right, every privilege, every power which membership of this house gives us . . . just as it seems to be best for Ireland.' So effective were their tactics that British democracy came close to foundering in the turbulent 1880s, and one Cabinet minister declared that simply banishing the Irish members from Westminster would be enough to make Home Rule popular. If, over a century later, many of the issues and tactics seem familiar, the undying spirit of the Irish nation, and the intractable nature of its political legacy, a poisoned chalice which has destroyed more ministerial careers than any other, are sufficient to account for the sense of a time warp.

Resentment over the Act of Union was inflamed to revolutionary heat in the 1820s over the issue of Catholic Emancipation. Daniel O'Connell's inspired tactic of mass gatherings for non-violent disruptive protest has been imitated by repressed peoples worldwide, most notably in India and South Africa. By 1832, when there was a Bill before the House 'prohibiting those processions of Orangemen which have excited a good deal of irritation in Ireland', bitter Protestant fanatics tried to block its progress. The 1840s brought the potato famine and, in its harsh progress, the birth of the Young Ireland movement. The absence of any sign of political concessions provoked the outbreak of Fenian terrorism in the 1860s; a second modern political tactic was born. Gladstone's instinct, then and for the rest of his career, was to try to remedy grievances but the prevailing view was that terrorism should be suppressed rather than rewarded. The 1870 Irish Land Act brought more social distress to Ireland. Agricultural depression and the eviction of tenant farmers turned attention to the injustices of absentee landowners. The Land League was formed, and in 1877

The Chamber of the House of Commons, 1858.

Charles Stewart Parnell became leader of the Irish Home Rule party, which won 61 seats in the 1880 election, at which Gladstone replaced Disraeli. Now was their moment. To increase pressure on the government, obstruction of parliamentary business became a settled and accomplished tactic. It was first practised in 1879, in the debates on the Army Regulation Bill. Queen Victoria was alarmed, and wrote to Disraeli: 'Ought you not to come to some agreement with some of the sensible, and reasonable and not violent men on the other side, to put a stop to what clearly is a determination to force the disruption of the British Empire?' Disraeli replied that there were no sensible, and reasonable, and really not violent men on the other side.

The Parliament elected in 1880 was unusually stormy. Parnell and his Nationalists filibustered and obstructed and exploited every loophole in the rules of debate. In the session of 1881, fourteen Irish members delivered between them 3828 speeches, a daily average of twenty each. 'We are the laughing stock of Europe,' wrote Disraeli to Lady Bradford. Business ground to a halt; hours of work had to be extended. After a continuous sitting of 41 hours on the Protection of Persons and Property (Ireland) Bill, Speaker Brand used his own authority to end the debate at 9 a.m. on 2 February. 'An important measure is being arrested by the actions of an inconsiderable minority, the members of which have resorted to those methods of "obstruction" which have been recognised by the House as a Parliamentary offence.' His appeal to the 'sense of the House' to empower the Speaker to curtail discussion to prevent the paralysis of legislation established 'closure' as a recognised practice in the Commons. The Irish members were incensed, the rest triumphant. After the division on the first reading, the Nationalists stood up, shouted 'Privilege', bowed to the chair and marched single file out of the Chamber. Next day they returned in disorder: 28 were suspended, and had to be forcibly removed. 'We must show these gentlemen', declared Parnell, 'that if they won't do what we want they shall do nothing else.' Up to 1887 the average hour of adjournment was 2.20 a.m. Only the Speaker could then preside, and he was allowed only half an hour for his evening chop. So two further methods of curtailment were introduced: the guillotine, which ended debate at a pre-arranged time, and the right of any member to move that 'the question be now put'. Such devices for limiting debate, first introduced as emergency measures, proved far too useful for subsequent governments for them ever to be rescinded. Even less contentious rules were susceptible to an Irish gloss. Supplementary questions, then as now, are supposed to depend on the answer to the principal question. One Irish member, told by the Speaker that his supplementary was not in order, replied 'it distinctly arises out of an answer which the right honourable gentleman has not given.'

For decades control in Ireland had been maintained by regular 'Coercion Acts', giving authorities special powers to curb unrest. Gladstone tried to reinforce the stick with the carrot, and introduced both a Coercion Act and a Land Act in 1881. But Irish juries failed to convict, and emergency powers had to be applied. One consequence was the assassination of the Viceroy in Phoenix Park, Dublin; popular outrage fuelled yet more repressive legislation, and the familiar dismal cycle was set in motion. In February 1885 the

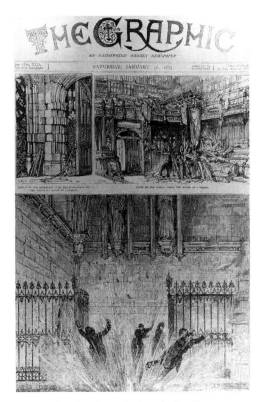

Fenian bomb explosions in Parliament.

Nationalists obstructed the proceedings of the House en masse, and thirty-seven had to be removed by the Serjeant-at-Arms. Later in the year Parnell and his party defected to the Conservatives in a Commons vote; Lord Salisbury briefly replaced Gladstone, but the Liberals were returned in the election. Parnell, now leading eighty-six Nationalists, held great sway. Gladstone brought in the first Home Rule Bill in 1886, but after a 16-day debate in April, the second reading was defeated. There were ninety-three Liberal defections, led by John Bright, who refused to accept a surrender to those responsible for violence. (Fenian bombs had exploded in Westminster Hall and the Commons Chamber in November 1885.) Home Rule split the Liberal Party. The 1886 election rejected Home Rule, and brought Salisbury to power. 'Politics are Ireland,' he declared as his ministry was launched. Lord Randolph Churchill shamelessly played 'the Orange card' at the election, claiming that Home Rule abandoned loyal Protestants. His prayer, 'Please God, it may turn out to be the ace of trumps and not the two', would be invoked by almost all Prime Ministers over the next

100 years. But in Ireland, the value of any card played seems to change the moment it is placed upon the table. In 1890 and 1891 the Parnell divorce case split the Nationalists and destroyed him. He ended his political career fighting other Irishmen. Gladstone returned as Prime Minister in 1892, and introduced his second Home Rule Bill, which again failed to address the dilemma of Ulster.

In July 1893 there were scenes of high drama at the moment of the guillotine on the Bill. Joseph Chamberlain split from Gladstone, and taunted his supporters. 'Judas,' cried T. P. O'Connor. The Unionists were outraged, and a mêlée broke out, in which the Irish predominated. Colonel Saunderson, stalwart and substantial Unionist, was the preferred target of the Nationalists, and happily struck out on all sides. Dr Tanner came up behind him, and battered his bald head, but the Colonel sent him flying with a sweep of his great arm. The scrimmage lasted around 20 minutes, and involved at least forty members – 'what is known in quieter times as a quorum' – while the aged Gladstone looked on in horror. 'Send for the Speaker,' someone cried out. The majestic Speaker Peel appeared like a terrible headmaster, and called 'Order, order'; the fighting subsided; the dust began to settle. Peel asked for an explanation; Gladstone, 'like the head boy of a class who has failed to keep order', gave it, with embarrassment, not helped by the repeating hissing of an Opposition member: 'All your fault! All your fault!' And suddenly, everyone began to laugh. The Bill passed the Commons with a majority of thirty-four, though all knew it was doomed in the Lords, where in September it was defeated by the appalling majority of 419 to 41. The second rejection of Home Rule had two consequences: the birth of the Sinn Fein movement, and a delay of 20 years before Asquith's Liberal Government had the courage to pick up the time bomb again.

Yet when Home Rule at last came, in 1921, a traditional Tory reflected that 'one of the disasters has been the loss inflicted on the vivacity and humour of the House of Commons.' Many individual Irish members were held in great affection for the delight they provided, either intentionally or unintentionally. Major Purcell O'Gormon, a Liberal Home Ruler of gargantuan stature, sat for Waterford from 1874 to 1880. He was an instant celebrity. 'Be in your place when O'Gormon speaks,' was Disraeli's advice to a member whose spirits were low, 'that will enliven you – if anything can.' 'O'Gormon is up,' was enough to empty dining and smoking rooms, and send a crowd rushing into the chamber to enjoy the brogue of his random cadences. His huge frame was beset by regular internal earthquakes that enlivened dull debates. Provoked once by Disraeli, he alarmingly heaved himself up and, with slow pace, 'like an East Indiaman with sails bellied with the summer breeze', he made straight for the Prime Minister as if he intended to tuck him under his arm and walk off with him. The House was apprehensive and hushed. At the crucial moment the Major turned sharply to sit on the benches immediately opposite Disraeli, the better to punctuate his speech with roaring. One evening, on a self-evident division, 433 members voted 'no', and one 'aye'. The 'aye' was Major O'Gormon. Asked afterwards why he had gone against his own party, he mopped at his sweating brow and replied, 'Bedad, it's a hot night, and I knew there would be more room in the "aye" Lobby.' The story was told of him that one night, when his cab door was opened by the hotel porter, the Major, hot and breathless, was standing upright. The bottom of the cab had fallen through under his weight, and so he had had to trot along at the same pace as the horse in order to get home safely.

J. P. Ronayne, MP for Cork, and an engineer by training, caused consternation for the government on a division in 1874, when he cut the wires of the newly installed electric division bells, so that those dining in St Stephen's Club, in Bridge St., missed the vote. Then there was Joseph Biggar, a small, extremely ugly but fearless member for Cavan who provoked Disraeli, when he first set eyes on him, into exclaiming, 'What is that? He seems to be what in Ireland you call a leprechaun.' On one occasion, he 'spied strangers' in order to have the Prince of Wales, whom he had spotted, turned out of the Gallery; on another, after a three-hour obstructive speech consisting mostly of extracts from Blue Books, the Speaker, hoping to halt him, said that he really couldn't hear what the Hon. Member was saying. 'Quite right, Mr Speaker,' said Biggar cheerfully. 'The acoustic properties of this House are something shocking. I will come nearer.' And gathering up all his materials, he trotted down to the front benches and began all over again. Sir Henry Havelock-Allen, Liberal Unionist, first hurled himself unprovoked on an unoffending member in 1889, then dogged another to the Library and back making such threats as: 'I'll do you in on your doorstep, where I will be at 2 a.m. and cut your liver out.' Asked by the Speaker to apologise, his excuse was that he was in great pain from pinching his finger while shutting a window the day before. He was so tickled by his explanation that he reduced all around to laughter. The Irish readiness to resort to physical expression when blarney failed continued into the new century. In 1912 Ronald M'Neill, a 7-ft.-tall Ulsterman, hurled a book at Churchill, who was walking out of the House, which struck him on the side of the face and opened up a gash, and as late as 1972 Bernadette Devlin, on the day after Bloody Sunday, assaulted the Home Secretary, Reginald Maudling, calling him a liar and a murdering hypocrite, and had to be removed from the Chamber by a couple of Whips.

The Irish monopoly of disorder was not total. There were dishonourable scenes in 1880 after the election for Northampton of Charles Bradlaugh, an atheist, radical, and advocate of birth control. The House, led by Gladstone, refused him permission to either affirm or take the oath of allegiance, and so take his seat. In desperation he tried to force his way in, and was dragged by the serjeant-at-arms and his assistants from the lobby to the courtyard, with his clothes torn. His supporters, gathered in the Hall, cried out: 'They are killing him,' and a dangerous riot was narrowly averted. Speaker Brand placed Bradlaugh in the custody of the Serjeant-at-Arms, and he was detained for one night in the prison room of the Clock Tower. After being elected three times for Northampton, he was begrudgingly allowed to affirm rather than swear on the Bible, and admitted to the Commons, where he showed himself so responsible a member that in January 1891 as he lay dying, the House made a belated apology and expunged from the *Journal* the resolution banning him from taking the oath.

Then there was 'Don Roberto' (R. C. Cunninghame Graham), a colourful maverick who had been a cattle rancher in South America. From 1886 to 1892 he was MP for North Lanarkshire, and often rode to Westminster on his mustang, called 'Pampa'. He made a controversial maiden speech in 1887 denouncing capitalist society ('Heaven for 30,000 and a Hell for 30,000,000'), and was repeatedly suspended for unparliamentary behaviour while seeking to air the plight of exploited labourers. On one occasion, 'named' by the Speaker for referring to 'shareholders in swindling companies', he protested: 'I am simply named for standing up for socialism in this House in the face of a swindling speech endeavouring to draw

House of Commons Chamber, 1878: a painting in the Palace of Westminster.

ridiculous distinctions. That is why I am named.' Secretary of State for Home Affairs: 'I beg to move, in the terms of the Standing Order, that the Honourable Member be suspended from the service of the House.' Don Roberto: 'Suspend away! I do not care a damn!' Cries of 'Order! Order!' as he strode out of the chamber.

The Last Flourish of the Aristocracy

The political landscape at the end of the nineteenth century was still dominated to a quite astonishing degree by the nobility. Gladstone's cabinet of 1885 contained seven Whig aristocrats; Lord Salisbury was Prime Minister for 14 of the 17 years from 1885 to 1902; the Lords threw out the second Home Rule Bill in 1893. The most magnetic and dangerous politician in the 1880s was Lord Randolph Churchill, who had risked the 'Ulster card' at the 1886 election and helped Salisbury's Conservatives to victory. Salisbury had felt obliged to make him Chancellor, yet when, in pursuit of spending cuts, he met opposition, he staged a dramatic resignation (written, to Queen Victoria's displeasure, on Windsor Castle notepaper). He had thought himself indispensable, and was surprised when Salisbury, with relief, accepted it. His meteoric career was over; he had contracted syphilis and his faculties rapidly declined, yet he carried on with his political life. Lord Rosebery described the pitiful process: 'There was no retirement, no concealment. He died by inches in public, sole mourner at his own protracted funeral.' And his son Winston's account: 'The crowds who were drawn by the old glamour of his name, departed sorrowful and shuddering at the spectacle of a dying man, and those who loved him were consumed with embarrassment and grief.' It is tempting to see his death as prophetic of the beginning of the end of aristocratic supremacy. In the same year the Earl of Rosebery, who had succeeded Gladstone as Prime Minister, abruptly resigned when he found his Cabinet divided. He was a man of great ability ('I feel that if I had his brains I would move mountains,' envied Churchill), but his taste spurned the rough house of political life. He had been known to leave an important debate in the Lords when his valet told him, 'Your grouse is done to a turn, my Lord.' But there was a still unresolved scandal hanging about him, the death the previous October, in suspicious circumstances, of Viscount Drumlanrig, his private secretary, elder brother of Lord Alfred Douglas, and perhaps Rosebery's lover.

Salisbury returned again, to head a Conservative–Liberal Unionist coalition. Salisbury, arrogant and outspoken, was 'a great master of gibes and flouts and jeers', according to Disraeli. His views were unreformed: he likened Irish terrorists to Hottentots, and declared that rural life would be rendered more interesting by a circus than a parish council. During his administration, Parliament voted in favour of a memorial to Cromwell, a statue to be placed in Westminster Hall. Conservatives and Irish Nationalists were deeply hostile. When it was at last erected on low-lying ground to the west of the Hall, Salisbury said a ditch was the perfect place for it. He was returned to power easily in the 'Khaki Election' of 1900 because of popular sentiment backing his Boer War policy. Lloyd George, who had opposed the war as 'an outrage perpetrated in the name of human freedom', was nearly torn apart by a Birmingham mob for attacking both the war and Joseph Chamberlain. But the exposure of military incompetence in South Africa quickly soured the mood and, as after the debacle in the Crimea, outrage led to calls for better political and military management. But when Salisbury retired in 1902, he was succeeded by his nephew, Balfour, rather than Chamberlain, whose political gifts were greater. Democracy was still more patrician than popular; it mattered that the right families led governments. Balfour, who was famous for never reading newspapers, and who was 'hampered by no passionate convictions', and Chamberlain would never be easy bedfellows; Chamberlain, who had split the Liberals in 1892 over Home Rule, now split the Conservatives. In 1903 he left the Cabinet for 'a raging tearing campaign' for Tariff Reform and Imperial Preference. Salisbury's mockery of his 'splendid isolation' could not halt his undermining of the government and uniting of the opposition: from 1902 until the election of 1906 Herbert Gladstone and Ramsay MacDonald made the first 'Lib–Lab pact'. Balfour resigned in 1905; his Conservative–Unionist government died, in Lloyd George's phrase, 'with their drawn salaries in their hands'. Conservative numbers were halved by the Liberal triumph at the election. The first great reforming modern government had been called to office, one that promptly accepted that old political and economic structures must give place to greater justice and equality.

'There are many rocks the young speaker in Parliament should avoid,' advised Trollope, 'but no rock requires such careful avoiding as the rock of eloquence.' Victorian rhetoric, like Victorian whiskers, was on the way out. A loan to India described as 'a flea-bite in the ocean'; declarations such as 'The pale face of the British soldier is the backbone of the Indian Army', and 'Things will never improve in Egypt until the Khedive is able to stand upon his own bottom', seem to belong, like the opposition in 1901 to the employment of waitresses on the Terrace for fear of scandal and flirtation, to an era of alien attitudes and language. In 1901 there was disorder when the new king opened Parliament, and there were injuries in the crush. In the same year the police were summoned to the Commons Chamber for the first time when Irish Nationalists, resenting the closure of the debate, refused to leave their seats and Speaker Gully had to seek police help to drag them struggling from the Chamber. Defiance of traditional authority; violence in centres of civilisation: soon these local inconveniences would blaze across the new century. And of the three immediate menaces to the order of things, war, workers and women, it was women who would strike first. And they were not to be waitresses on the Terrace.

CHAPTER EIGHT

Parliament in the
Twentieth Century 1906–2000

The Suffragette Movement

I N BARRY'S NEW House of Commons, a gallery for ladies had
been provided above the Speaker's chair. Diehards thought the
Commons a most unsuitable place for ladies, and even the radical Harriet Martineau felt that the gallery would attract the wrong
sort who would prove 'a nuisance to the legislature and a serious
disadvantage to the wiser of their own sex.' So, by a triumphant
British compromise, a metal grille had been fixed to the front of the
gallery, so that each side appeared to the other as if in a cage. Dis-
turbances in support of 'Votes for Women' began there in 1888,
but did not become orchestrated until a debate on women's
suffrage in April 1906. A white flag inscribed 'Justice for Women'
fluttered through the grille, and there were shouts and screams of
'Votes for Women' and, as the police and attendants cleared the
gallery on the Speaker's orders, taunts of 'You liberty-loving Liberals'. The disruptions increased. Some chained themselves to the
grille, so the gallery and Commons lobby were closed in 1908 to all
but the Speaker's guests after one suffragette rushed on to the floor
of the House shouting 'Votes for Women'. The militant response
was to charter a steam launch, and moor it close to the Terrace, to
harangue members taking tea. In 1909 the gallery was reopened,
under strict controls, but a bag of flour thrown from it one day
nearly hit Asquith. There were attacks on ministers outside Parliament, and stone throwing. One enterprising suffragette hid herself

Suffragettes in front of Parliament,
at the start of a new session in 1912.

in the Undercroft Chapel of St Mary on census night in 1910, was discovered by officials, and had her residence recorded as the Palace of Westminster. The 'Cat and Mouse Bill', which imprisoned militant suffragettes only to release them on the promise of good behaviour, caused passions to run high. George Lansbury, Labour member for Bow and Bromley, advanced on Asquith, shook his fist at him and hurled abuse: 'You are murdering, torturing and driving women mad. . . . It is the most disgraceful thing in the history of England. You will go down to history as the man who tortured innocent women!' The boil was lanced by the Great War. Women joined the workforce the war effort required. In 1917, on a free vote in the House, the franchise was extended to all women over thirty years of age. Asquith was among the converts: 'Some years ago I said "Let the women work out their own salvation". Well, they have worked it out during this war.' The absurd grille was at once removed, though for some years more it was the rule for the Ladies' Gallery to be cleared at 7.30 p.m. The emancipation of women became law in June 1918, and 8,500,000 new voters were enfranchised.

On 1 December 1919 Nancy Astor was the first woman MP to take her seat in the Commons. She was introduced by Balfour and Lloyd George, 'both of whom had said they believed in women but who would rather have had a rattlesnake in the House than me at the time.' Until she was joined by other women members she had an unfriendly time. Churchill said to her later: 'I felt like a woman had entered my bathroom and I had nothing to protect myself with except a sponge.' In 1928 'the flapper vote' was extended to women between 21 and 30, arousing much unregenerate mockery. Two final electoral anomalies (if the 'first past the post' system is discounted): university seats and a second vote for business premises were abolished in 1948. It had taken roughly 700 years for a broadly just democracy to flower.

The Liberal Government of 1906–15

The election of 1906 broke the mould of government dominance by Anglican landed interests. Balfour saw his defeat as part of a Europe-wide shift to the left, 'a faint echo of the same movement which has produced massacres in St Petersburg, riots in Vienna and Socialist processions in Berlin.' There were over two hundred new members, many from Nonconformist middle-class backgrounds. The formal dinner interval was abolished. The battered rump of Tory opposition could only make itself conspicuous with catcalls, cock crows, hee-haws, and other farmyard noises to prevent their opponents' arguments being heard. The new mood of purpose was embodied in Henry Campbell-Bannerman, who had emerged as Liberal leader before the election, 'creeping to the front inch by inch, no one exactly knows how.' In the debate on the Address in 1905, he had reminded the Commons that 'behind any Parliament or any majority in Parliament was the public conscience from which their power was derived.' Bolstered by his massive electoral victory, his own massive and forthright Scots presence brooked no elegant nonsense. In an early debate he silenced Balfour's attempt at witty repartee with 'enough of this foolery'. He vowed on taking office to make England 'less of a pleasure ground for the rich and more of a treasure house for the nation', and initiated a sweeping programme of social reform. The foundations of what was later called the Welfare State were quickly laid: the Pensions Act of 1908, and the introduction of a national insurance scheme in the 1909 budget. Diehard Unionists objected to pensions, because 'all drunkards, wife-deserters, pimps, procurers and criminals would get pensions at the expense of honest men.' The national insurance scheme provoked 'the revolt of duchesses', backed up by their servants and the *Daily Mail*, who refused to lick stamps for the 'bureaucratic and German' insurance cards. The partner in Campbell-Bannerman's crusade was his Chancellor, David Lloyd George, who introduced a series of 'People's Budgets'. His 1909 budget speech, which lasted five hours, was accused of declaring class war, and precipitated a constitutional crisis. He sought to finance old-age pensions and national insurance by 'robbing the hen roosts': raising income tax, and imposing supertax, death duties, a land values tax, and liquor duties. 'It is a war budget,' he declared. 'It is for raising money to wage implacable warfare against poverty and squalidness.' It was denounced by the opposition as 'spoliation and socialism'. A Tory whip accused the Chancellor of repealing the Eighth and Tenth Commandments. The predictable rejection of the Finance Bill by the Lords plunged democracy into crisis.

It was a crisis waiting to happen. A rising tide of radicalism in the 1890s, preaching social justice and anti-imperialism, was set to collide with traditional aristocratic interests which sensed the gradual dwindling of their authority. Agricultural depression in the 1870s, and the importing of cheap food from America and Australia had reduced profits; hostility to absentee landlords in Ireland had spread to Scotland and Wales; electoral reform had reduced their power of patronage; the creation of county councils in 1888 had undermined 'the rural House of Lords' which had always run the shires; death duties, first levied in 1894, were steadily rising. And the new breed of politician was keen to attack the aristocracy, in and out of politics. 'The lilies of the field, who toil not, neither do they spin,' mocked Chamberlain the industrialist. 'Aristocracy is like cheese – the older it gets, the higher it becomes,' teased Lloyd George, the solicitor's son, who also described the House of Lords as 'Five hundred men, chosen randomly from among the ranks of the unemployed.' Of the 602 members of the House in 1906, only 88 defined their allegiance as Liberal. They were ready for battle.

Their rejection of the 1909 budget asserted the Lords' right to amend money bills and challenged established practice. Asquith, Prime Minister after Campbell-Bannerman's death in 10 Downing Street in 1908, rightly took the matter to the country in January 1910. The Liberals were returned, and the budget proposals now passed both Houses. Asquith then brought forward a Parliament Bill which proposed that the Commons should have exclusive powers over money bills, that the Lords should be able only to delay legislation for a maximum of two years, and that the life of any Parliament should be reduced from seven years to five. A second election in December 1910 confirmed Asquith in power and launched the bitter constitutional crisis of 1911. Tory backwoodsmen, led by Lord Willoughby de Broke, fought a near-treasonable rearguard action against Asquith and Lloyd George. A Tory backbencher claimed that the Lords was the watchdog of the constitution. 'You mean it is Mr Balfour's poodle,' retorted Lloyd George. 'They are forcing a revolution. The Peers may decree a revolution, but the People will direct it.' By 'the People' Lloyd George usually meant himself. In a repeat of Grey's tactics over the Reform Bill, Asquith asked the new king, George V, should it become necessary, to create enough Liberal peers to steer the Bill through the Lords. On 24 July 1911 Asquith went to the Commons to announce that the government was not prepared to accept the Lords' amendments to the Bill, but intended to push it through in its original form. Between 3 p.m. and 5 p.m., when the Speaker was forced to adjourn the House, some of the most extraordinary and dishonourable scenes the Chamber ever witnessed were acted out. When Asquith entered, to the cheers of his own side, the opposition began to chant 'Traitor, traitor, traitor'. The outrage was so profound it was at first hard to realise it. When he rose to speak he was assailed by a storm of abuse. For half an hour he stood at the box, attempts to speak alternating with appeals from Speaker Lowther for the House to observe the courtesies of debate. 'Traitor, traitor', 'He has degraded Parliament', 'Trickster', 'Constitution-breaker', 'Traitor'. The Tories, led by Lord Hugh Cecil and F. E. Smith, 'behaved like mad baboons', screaming and writhing frenziedly. 'The king is in duress,' howled Lord Hugh Cecil. Asquith managed a reference to the death of Edward VII. 'Who killed the king?' they roared, 'who killed the king?' 'For the first time it came upon many that Mr Asquith was an old man. The ruddiness of strong manhood had left him, his hair was snow white, his delicate white hand holding the unspoken speech was trembling.' He gave up the attempt. 'I will not degrade myself further –' 'You could not,' someone bellowed back, 'you are a disgrace.' In a couple of sentences, he shouted out the government's intentions and sat down. Balfour rose to speak. The government benches, which might have been expected to take its revenge, did so, but by falling into the politest silence. 'These politicians, including a generous sprinkling of Labour men who had worked with their hands, had set themselves, with clenched teeth, to give a lesson in courtesy to the noisiest spirits of the party which claimed to represent the gentlemen of England.' And the gentlemen of England were nonplussed. Balfour improvised indignation: what was the reason for the government's amazing and unqualifiable proceeding? Asquith rose: 'The right honourable gentleman has not heard the reason because I was not allowed to state it. I was prevented by the right honourable gentleman's friends from doing so. He has had an advantage of a courtesy which has been denied to me.' Many were ashamed of the conduct of the House; some were unrepentant. It was as if Parliament had caught the miasma of violence and hatred that the new century seemed to have spawned. Faced with the inexorable, the Lords passed the Parliament Act by a majority of 17; its preamble read, 'It is intended to substitute for the House of Lords as it at present exists a second Chamber constituted on a popular instead of hereditary basis.' The principle was supported by Conservatives also. Balfour, speaking on the Bill in 1911, might easily have been speaking in 1999: 'If the House of Lords is to be merely an ornamental part of the constitution, reminding us of our long history, connected with many ancient and picturesque ceremonies, if it is to be classed with the beautiful armour in the Tower, as something ancient and valuable, but wholly useless for any modern purpose, well, then, I say, I care as little for the House of Lords as any honourable gentleman opposite. I want a second chamber.' The long stagnation of the intention to reform the Upper House until 1999 can be explained by the urgency of higher priorities, the tenacity of the existing social system, the distraction of short-term crises, the inability of anyone to find an acceptable alternative, or all four in concert.

As if disheartened by the conduct of his party, Balfour unexpectedly resigned the Conservative leadership in 1911, and, to much surprise, the unknown Bonar Law was chosen to succeed him. 'Lord have mercy upon us, and incline our hearts to Bonar Law,' was the prayer of one Tory backbencher; Asquith was more damning about him: 'I never wrestle with a chimney sweep, a good saying which I sometimes call to mind when I am confronting Bonar Law.' Hitting the nail on the head was a Yorkshire quality of which Asquith was proud. He had a fine clear intellect, and economy of expression, except after dinner, when he was sometimes the worse for drink. Churchill observed him in April 1911 and wrote to his wife Clementine: 'On Thursday night the PM was vy bad: and I squirmed with embarrassment. He could hardly speak, and many people noticed his condition. Only the persistent freemasonry of the House of Commons prevents a scandal. I like the old boy and admire both his intellect and his character. But what risks to run.' Prime Minister for nearly nine years from 1908 until the war exposed his limitations as a leader for a crisis, he was a reserved, aloof and sensitive man with little imagination or moral fervour. He was 'as incapable of histrionics as a ploughman'; as for battling, he could leave that to Lloyd George and Churchill. He was incapable of raising the pitch of his politics to the frenzy of energy and passion war required. However, one long overdue act of imagination which he supported in 1911 was the provision of salaries for Members of Parliament, demanded by the Chartists as early as 1838. The level was set at £400 a year; in 1936 it was raised to £600. There were many who opposed their introduction on the ground that it lowered the dignity of Parliament.

The running sore of Ireland quickly proved itself to have unlimited mileage for the new century. Between 1911 and 1914 it 'engulfed and embittered all the feuds of Britain.' The Liberals were convinced that Home Rule was essential, and had been since 1870; the Unionists championed the cause of Ulster, and were convinced that the break-up of the United Kingdom would lead to the break-up of the Empire. In April 1912 the Liberals produced the third Home Rule Bill, which looked, then as in the 1990s, to a devolutionary settlement, proposing separate Parliaments for England, Ireland, Scotland and Wales, with a federal Imperial Parliament at Westminster. For the next two years, as war approached, the Irish question was inflammatory. The Unionists were indignant at the prospect of the Bill's being forced through the Lords by the

Parliament Act, and Bonar Law's Blenheim Pledge of July 1912, echoing Carson's 'Ulster will fight and Ulster will be right' of 1886, came perilously close to sedition. 'He could imagine no length of resistance to which Ulster would go which he would not be ready to support.' Asquith denounced this as 'a complete grammar of anarchy'. In July 1914 George V called an emergency constitutional conference which broke down, as Irish conferences are prone to do, but on the same day that the news broke of the Austro-Hungarian ultimatum to Serbia. The civil war that was threatening Ireland was averted only by the declaration of war on Germany in August 1914. John Redmond, leader of the Irish Nationalists, made a courageous speech in support of the government, and accepted postponement of the Bill until the end of the war. In September 1914 the Home Rule Bill was carried, without the consent of the Lords, but its implementation suspended. There was another bitter confrontation between Asquith and the Unionists, who wanted Ulster excluded from the Bill. Asquith refused them because he was faced with a Nationalist rebellion. So the Unionists walked out of the Commons en masse on 15 September by way of protest. Yet Asquith did give assurances that the use of force for the coercion of Ulster was unthinkable, thus implicitly recognising the probability of eventual partition. After the Dublin Easter Rising in 1916, Nationalist MPs largely quit the Westminster Parliament, and all did so in 1918 when Lloyd George, faced with Ludendorf's late offensive along the Somme, extended conscription to Ireland, but added an undertaking not to apply it until Home Rule was granted. The outrage in Ireland led to a general strike; in practice it was the end of the Union. By the time of the first post-war election, in December 1918, violence in Ireland was running at such a level that the galleries of the Commons were closed as a security measure. Seventy-three Sinn Fein members were elected, but refused to come to Westminster and set themselves up as the Dáil in Dublin. Only after the savagery of the Troubles was a treaty with Ireland accepting partition concluded in December 1921. All sections of Irish opinion were angered by it, though it is hard to see what alternatives were to hand. Lloyd George's magical opportunism conjured up partition in order to get shot of a problem which it in fact perpetuated. And in the shorter term it helped to seal Lloyd George's political fate, like those of Peel and Gladstone before him.

War 1914–18

Viewed from the end of the twentieth century, the problem of Ireland suggested that history stands still. Other features of the same decade suggested that it goes round in circles: the manner of selecting and later rejecting an inspirational war leader; the readiness to go to war to aid small nations menaced by larger ones: Belgium, Poland, Kuwait, the Balkans. Sir Edward Grey, Foreign Secretary in 1914, argued the necessity of war in general terms, lest Britain 'should be isolated, discredited and hated; and there would be before us nothing but a miserable and ignoble future.' Lloyd George, at his best always as a warrior, was more specific. On 21 September 1914 he glorified going to war on behalf of Serbia. The history of Serbia is not unblotted, he began. But she is a small nation being bullied by a ramshackle empire, and Russia, her Slav big brother, has rallied to her defence. 'The world owes much to little nations and to little men.' Germany, who will only allow six foot two nations to stand in the ranks, must be taught a lesson. 'It is a great opportunity. It only comes once in many centuries to the children of men. For most generations sacrifice comes in drab meanness of spirit to men. It has come today to you, it has come today to us all, in the form of the glow and thrill of a great movement for liberty. . . . We have been living in a sheltered valley for generations. We have been too comfortable, too indulgent, perhaps too selfish. And the stern hand of fate has scourged us to an elevation where we can see the great everlasting things that matter for a nation, the great peaks of honour we had forgotten, duty and patriotism, and, clad in glittering white, the great pinnacle of sacrifice pointing like a rugged finger to heaven.' With his preacher's hwyl well tuned, Lloyd George was already bidding for war leadership. Yet between September 1914 and the formation of a coalition in May 1915, the Commons did not once discuss the war. Perhaps the gulf of culture and assumptions between Westminster and the front line was unbridgeable. The First War was not accompanied by the episodes of high drama in Parliament which were characteristic of the Second.

Asquith drifted into coalition in May 1915, and the last exclusively Liberal Government came to an end. Lloyd George was Minister of Munitions, and his demonic energy turned around the war effort. Wartime conditions made his rise inexorable. He was a one-man act, 'a master of improvisation', but with few political friends, and no colleagues who trusted him. He was aggressive and vengeful. 'Saki' observed the Commons engaged in the futile occupation of bringing Lloyd George to book for his offensive attacks on individuals. 'One might as well lecture a mole on colour-blindness. The Chancellor is one of those very vain men to whom all opposition is a personal offence calling for reciprocal outbursts of offensiveness.' But both Lloyd George and Bonar Law, outside the patrician circle of traditional leaders, were able to rise to the demands of a crisis; Bonar Law, visiting Asquith out of London, was shocked to find him playing bridge with three ladies on a Monday morning (though it was a Bank Holiday). The mire of the war deepened; the Military Service Act in January 1916 introduced conscription for unmarried men between 18 and 41. Then, in December, Lloyd George proposed a War Council chaired by himself. Asquith demurred: he must be chairman, and all decisions must be subject to Cabinet approval. Lloyd George appealed to Bonar Law: 'The life of the country depends on resolute action by you now.' Law supported Lloyd George. Asquith, obtusely failing to read the signs, first agreed to the War Council and then withdrew his agreement. Lloyd George resigned, forcing Asquith to do likewise. He challenged either Lloyd George or Law to form an alternative government: 'Then they will have to come in on my terms.' The king sent for Law, who agreed to form a government on condition that Asquith was in it. He refused, out of pique. 'What is the proposal? That I who have held first place for eight years should be asked to take a subordinate position?' Law advised the king to send for Lloyd George who appealed to Labour members to join him. As a man of the people he won over most of them, and so the first 'ordinary man' became Prime Minister by extraordinarily devious means, with the support of backbenchers and the press rather than by an aristocratic conclave. 'If he wants to be a dictator, let him be. If he thinks that he can run the war, I'm all for his having a try,' observed the noble Balfour. And he did. He set the Cabinet for the first time on a professional footing, with agendas, minutes and a secretariat, but then, characteristically, took almost all the advice he listened to from his cronies in 'The Garden Suburb', the huts built in St James's Park to extend the government machine. He nearly destroyed his Government by bringing in Churchill, which enraged the Tories. Curzon was apoplectic; the news put Bonar Law's pipe out; the *Morning*

Lloyd George at the Front, 1915.

Chronicle protested at the return of 'the floating kidney in the body politic'. Churchill laughed and asked the Prime Minister not to leave him alone with his new colleagues in case they ate him.

But however dubious Lloyd George's character and methods, he fought against a sinister alliance of king and military brass hats who thought they knew better, sacked Jellicoe (who wouldn't support the tactic of naval convoys) and saw the war through to victory. On Armistice Day in 1918 he read the terms to the Commons, and concluded: 'I hope we may say that thus, this fateful morning, come to an end all wars.' He wanted the war coalition to stay in power, but the Labour members refused and most ministers resigned. Within a month of the Armistice came the 'Coupon election', because of the bargain made between the Unionists and

Liberal whips that 150 Liberals would not be opposed by Unionist candidates. War sentiments strongly influenced the voting; 'Hang the Kaiser', and 'Make Germany pay' were among the slogans of government candidates. The Liberal candidates were not seriously at risk: Lloyd George's war record and his long association with social reform were enough to carry them to victory. His promise to make 'a fit country for heroes to live in' seemed golden. The new Parliament had 260 new members, and nearly 500 backed the Liberal–Unionist coalition. They did not impress: 'a selfish, swollen lot,' said Austen Chamberlain; 'a lot of hard-faced men, who look as if they had done very well out of the war,' observed Keynes. At first all went well. Lloyd George returned from Versailles in triumph, and the Commons rose to honour him and sang the National Anthem. There were only four votes against the Treaty. But the bitter feelings nourished by many Liberals because of Asquith's overthrow surfaced when the dictatorial manner of his war leadership persisted. Attitudes quickly changed. He failed to get to grips with the vast post-war social and economic problems; there was no rapid return of prosperity, so his election promise was hollow; there was industrial unrest, wages fell, and Labour made steady gains in by-elections. He was further discredited when, on reflection, left and right blamed him for having been too lenient with Germany in the Versailles Treaty. Discontent with the Irish Treaty undermined him; the final blow was a muddle over a military confrontation with Turkey which alienated the Dominions and came near to a humiliating evacuation. In October 1922, after a dramatic meeting at the Carlton Club, the Conservatives withdrew from the coalition. The reassuringly solid and English figure of Stanley Baldwin won great acclaim when he described Lloyd George as 'a great dynamic force – a very terrible thing'. He had destroyed his own party; the 'Squiffites', or Independent Liberals, were heading for extinction, and the Conservatives wanted to unhitch their boat before Lloyd George scuttled that too. Lloyd George resigned the same day, and party allegiances were resumed. 'I am sorry he is going,' said the king, 'but some day he will be Prime Minister again.' But he was to spend the remaining 22 years of his life in the political wilderness, still widely mistrusted. Like Churchill later, the great war leader lost his bearings in peacetime. Churchill understandably appreciated his qualities: 'He has more true insight and courage than anyone else.' He was the first

Prime Minister for 150 years to live openly with his mistress, and the first since Walpole to leave office a rich man. The Lloyd George fund, administered by Lloyd George, had been swelled by the clandestine sale of honours.

Lloyd George's departure was followed by an unstable time which saw three elections in two years. It was a transitional period in which, for the first time, three parties were in equal contention for power. Like buckets in a well, rising Labour was on a level with falling Liberal. The 1922 election was 'a plebiscite against Lloyd George' whose 'man of the people' tag had become tarnished by the rising fortunes of the people's party and by the financial crises which had prevented him from providing the longed-for post-war Utopia. Bonar Law became Prime Minister, with six peers in his Cabinet, derided by Churchill as 'a government of the second eleven'. But Law was already stricken with cancer, and had to resign in May 1923. The great George Curzon of Kedleston, Marquis, former Viceroy of India, Tory grandee for 30 years, was certain his hour had come. He was at Montacute, where there was no telephone. He waited impatiently for the telegram from Lord Stamfordham, the king's private secretary, which arrived in the evening, inviting him to return to London at once. Next day he travelled back. 'I shall use Number Ten only for official purposes. We shall still live and entertain at Carlton House Terrace.' The press were out in force to meet him. There was a long wait for Stamfordham. He arrived in some unease to report that the king had decided to send for Baldwin. Curzon insisted that the absurd decision be reversed. Stamfordham said that Baldwin was already at the Palace. Curzon collapsed into a chair and sobbed like a child. 'Not even a public figure! A man of no experience. And of the utmost insignificance!' A week after he became Prime Minister, Baldwin was elected leader of his party. Curzon proposed him, consoling himself with the thought that 'at least he was not one of nature's rats'. Baldwin, though a successful industrialist, cultivated the image of a country squire, as Walpole had done. His seeming amateurism was part of his appeal. He read few documents, and no newspapers. But his manner was misleading; after his death Churchill described him as 'the most formidable politician I have ever known in public life'. He was also the first Prime Minister to use Christian names in Cabinet meetings. Curzon's prejudice was confirmed in December

The cabinet of the first Labour Government.

1923 when Baldwin unwisely called an election to give him a mandate for his policy of protection. But the election produced a hung Parliament, and, despite much feverish backstairs confabulation, the likelihood of a minority Labour Government under Ramsay MacDonald. Asquith was acquiescent, believing that his party could throw the government out whenever it chose, and then he would be Prime Minister again. So when Baldwin's Government was defeated by 72 votes in the Commons in January 1924, George V sent for MacDonald, but confided to his diary: 'Today 23 years ago dear Grandmama died. I wonder what she would have thought of a Labour Government!' A policeman on duty at Buckingham Palace thought little enough of it. Emmanuel Shinwell, appointed a minister in MacDonald's Government, had to walk to the Palace in the absence of such benefits as ministers' cars. He reached the gates and announced: 'I am Emmanuel Shinwell. I am the Parliamentary Under-Secretary for Mines in the new Labour Government. I have come to kiss hands with the Sovereign.' 'Fuck off,' said the constable.

The Rise of the Labour Movement

The road to power had been a long one. It had begun in dear Grandmama's time. The Labour Party's roots were in the Social Democratic Foundation formed in 1881 by Harry Hyndman, the Fabian Society of 1884, and Keir Hardie's Independent Labour Party of 1893. Keir Hardie had been returned for West Ham in 1892. He arrived at Westminster to take his seat in style, in a wag-gonette, wearing a deerstalker and tweed suit, and accompanied by a cornet player. His little revolt against top hats and frock coats affronted traditionalists. In the 1895 elections, all 28 I.L.P. candi-dates, including Hardie, were defeated, but in the little revolution of 1906, 29 out of 51 Labour candidates were elected, including Ramsay MacDonald. 'The cottage', he said in the Queen's Hall celebrations, 'had arrived to fight and legislate for itself, since the palace had always neglected to do so.' Working men had received office earlier: Henry Broadhurst, a stonemason who had helped build the new Palace, was in Gladstone's 1886 Government, and Thomas Burt, a miner, was Secretary to the Board of Trade in 1892. But in 1906 John Burns was the first working man to reach the Cabinet, when Campbell-Bannerman offered him the Local Gov-ernment Board. 'Sir 'Enery,' said Burns, 'you never did a more popular thing in your life.' Palace and cottage liked the prospect of the brave new world: there was not a man in the 19-strong cabinet who did not feel that 'the ministry is stronger, more popular and more efficient because the Battersea engineer is sitting cheek by jowl with marquises and belted knights in the inner councils of the king.' Most Labour members had supported the war and con-tributed to Lloyd George's wartime coalition. MacDonald had very courageously opposed it, bringing opprobrium on his head. The 1922 election had returned 142 Labour members, about half of them union nominees, the rest from the professional middle classes. It had the potential for becoming a national party, though its I.L.P. hotheads from Glasgow could still raise alarms. David Kirkwood greeted the crowd who saw him off to Westminster: 'When we come back, this station, this railway will belong to the people.' The first Government belonging to the people, led by the formerly reviled MacDonald, was only in office a short time, though long enough to convince the country that such a revolution could be both possible and peaceful. 'England does not like coalitions,'

Keir Hardie addressing a peace meeting in Trafalgar Square, c.1914.

observed Disraeli, and a short-lived minority Labour Government was an interesting experiment preferable to the kind of coalition over which Lloyd George had so recently presided. MacDonald's tenuous Government lost a vote of censure in September 1924, and Baldwin, who had now decided to jettison his protectionist policy, was returned with a large majority. The Labour vote increased; the unhappy Liberals, who lost 100 seats, plunged into terminal decline as a party of government.

The Locust Years

With the reassuring Baldwin at the head of a stable Conservative Government, most of the country could settle contentedly into 'the years of gold', which saw little serious political disagreement. Baldwin and MacDonald could easily have changed places, as they were to do during the National Government of 1931. The 'Ten Years Rule', stating that there was no prospect of a major war, was adopted in 1925 and not revoked until 1932. Harold Macmillan first entered the Commons after the 1924 election, and noted that many members of his party had no desire for political advancement, but had entered public life because they felt it was the right way to serve their country and their locality. MPs still received only a nominal salary, and most did not consider it a full-time job. Arrangements in the Palace also signalled this: there were no offices, desks or secretaries for members. Nor did there seem great need for them. Baldwin's contemptuous dismissal of a backbench Bill to abolish the political levy in the unions, in March 1925, gave his Government the slogan the whole nation longed to hear: 'Give peace in our time, O Lord!' The embodiment of gentlemanly decorum in the Commons between the wars was Austen Chamberlain. With his frock coat, monocle and silk top hat, which he raised whenever he was mentioned, he embodied the old traditions of gentility and courtesy. Perhaps that is why, like R. A. Butler after the war, he never attained the highest office. There was a sad dignity about his last years in the Commons. On one occasion he showed A. P. Herbert the notes for a speech he had just delivered, with something written in very large letters in the centre. 'But you didn't mention that; Sir.' 'No,' replied Sir Austen. 'It was the one thing I wanted to say. So I wrote it large like that. But you know how it is. I forgot.'

Baldwin's Government hoped to disengage from Europe by means of the facile assurances of the Locarno Pact in 1925. 'The Polish corridor', declared Austen Chamberlain in a prophecy which he would not live to see overthrown, 'is something for which no British government ever will or can risk the bones of a British grenadier.' Attention was focused on domestic life. Heavy taxation of the wealthy was retained after the war, and was used to develop a programme of social reform which included public housing and contributory old-age pensions. Baldwin's inertia was more than compensated for by the passionate commitment of his Minister of Health, Neville Chamberlain, who steered twenty-one Bills through Parliament and secured Cabinet agreement that poverty was best tackled by government initiatives. He and Baldwin were closely linked politically: both were West Midlanders, and both had an obsessional mistrust of Lloyd George. Much party politicking was devoted to 'Dishing the Goat', as Baldwin had christened him.

'The Golden Years' were interrupted in 1926 by the brief General Strike, which was dangerously inflamed by the conduct of Churchill, whose eagerness to do battle with the workers won him

Armoured car in Oxford Street during the General Strike.

the lifelong distrust of the Labour Party. In the *British Gazette*, the official government newspaper which he edited, he denounced the strikers as 'the enemy' and demanded 'unconditional surrender'. He tried to provoke conflict by ordering armoured cars on to the streets. No doubt it was all useful practice for the war years.

May 1929 brought the only balanced three-cornered election in British history. The parties each had about 500 candidates, and fought as equals. 'Safety first', was Baldwin's characteristic slogan; there were no divisive issues. The irrepressible Lloyd George, to whom no one much listened, was full of bright ideas ahead of their time: a 'New Deal' involving a large public works programme and a deliberate budget deficit. The outcome was indecisive: MacDonald headed another minority Labour Government, and Margaret Bondfield, Minister of Labour, became the first woman member of the Cabinet. Baldwin was close to being a casualty of his poor election showing. The press lords Beaverbrook and Rothermere hounded him, and he agreed to resign. Chamberlain, confident of

*Neville Chamberlain and Stanley Baldwin arriving at
10 Downing Street for the Economic Conference, August 1931.*

the leadership, resigned as chairman of the party. But Baldwin
changed his mind and went on the attack. Borrowing a phrase from
his cousin Rudyard Kipling, he accused the press barons of want-
ing power without responsibility, 'the prerogative of the harlot
throughout the ages'.

No one in Parliament, except possibly Lloyd George, knew what
to do when the Great Depression gathered pace from October 1929
onwards. MacDonald explained it as the failure of capitalism.
Oswald Mosley's bold solutions were rejected by the Cabinet in
May 1930. He resigned and founded the New Party in February
1931, but was supported by only four MPs. A miscalculation as
great as Lord Randolph Churchill's in 1886 drove him out of mainstream politics and into the perilous waters of the British Union of
Fascists.

In the summer of 1931 a run on the pound induced a sense of
national crisis. The idea of a National Government to confront it
was all the more appealing because Lloyd George was temporarily
incapacitated by an operation. Baldwin, and Samuel for the Liberals, were both in favour. So it was formed on 24 August, led by

MacDonald , 'to deal with the national emergency that now exists.' The Labour Party execrated him as a traitor for ending the Labour Government, and he was expelled from the party. For a month the new Government strove to maintain the value of sterling, but the policy was torpedoed by sailors of the Atlantic Fleet at Invergordon who 'mutinied' against pay cuts. On 21 September the gold standard was suspended, and the value of the pound fell by 25 per cent. The process was unexpectedly painless: the modern notion of a managed currency had arrived by accident. The muddle-headedness of politics in the early 1930s was never better displayed than when the National Government, formed to save the pound but failed in less than a month, then asked for 'a doctor's mandate' in an election, and were hailed by the electorate as their saviours. The coalition won 521 seats, and Labour was down to 52. Lloyd George Liberals only had four, all members of his own family. There were fewer members on the Opposition benches than at any time since the French wars at the beginning of the nineteenth century. And so the drift continued. For years to come Parliament abdicated its responsibilities. The erosion of two-party government by the monolith of the coalition was partly to blame; there were not enough healthy growls from the backbenches. Party leaders were inadequate: Baldwin idle, Lloyd George unprincipled, MacDonald increasingly woolly-minded and infatuated with high society. 'His failing powers were an embarrassment to the government and himself.' Churchill observed that he had the gift of compressing the largest number of words into the smallest amount of thought. MacDonald's own diary entries are full of pathos: 'Trying to get something clear into my head for the H. of C. tomorrow. Cannot be done. Like man flying in mist: can fly all right but cannot see the course.' And, after the debate: 'Thoroughly bad speech. Could not get my way at all. The Creator might have devised more humane means of punishing me for overdrive and reckless use of body.' He resigned as Prime Minister in June 1935, but was already discredited, and a scapegoat for all sections of his coalition.

Now Britain had to face up to developments in Europe to which many blind eyes had been turned. Baldwin replaced MacDonald, and in the 1935 election sought a mandate for the National Government on a dishonest League of Nations/Collective Security platform, and had a majority of 250 for the National Government. Labour gained 100 seats. It was to be the last election for ten years.

Baldwin later admitted that if at the election he had said 'Germany is rearming, and we must rearm too', he would have lost. So he disguised the problem by arguing for a degree of rearmament to compensate for past deficiencies: 'I give you my word that there will be no great armaments.' The climate of the mid-1930s was intensely hostile to rearmament: the Covenant of the League of Nations obliged signatory states to seek arms limitation; the Labour and Liberal parties were passionately opposed to rearmament, even when Germany was known to be rearming: popular opinion recorded its views in the Peace Ballot and a by-election in Fulham which stole 20,000 Tory votes to elect a disarmament candidate, and the celebrated Oxford Union vote in 1933 in favour of not fighting for King and Country signalled youthful idealism for world peace in preference to the national interest. Baldwin was the perfect man for soothing a nervous nation. He had a measured, mellifluous manner of speech and charmed his audiences. He embodied gentlemanly reasonableness. Harold Balfour recalled a speech on India to a packed Commons, which began with a wide philosophical sweep of the tendencies and changes in distant lands. 'He gave us a few minutes of his favourite Mary Webb. There was never an interruption. It was a superb achievement. He sat down to general cheers including my own. I went out to the lobby saying to a friend that I had not heard such a moving speech. Suddenly it hit me. What had he said about India? Absolutely nothing. That was oratory – that was.' Harold Nicolson noted his unpleasant habit of sniffing at his notes (he liked the smell of paper), and licking the edges slightly as if they were the flap of an envelope. He scratched himself continuously 'like some tortoise half-awake smelling the air'.

The dominoes began to fall in 1935. Italy invaded Abyssinia. The Cabinet sought appeasement, and approved the Hoare–Laval Pact on the partition of Abyssinia. Public and political feeling was outraged, and the next domino in line was Hoare himself. The poor man had to make his resignation speech with his nose in plaster after a winter sports accident. Abandoned by his colleagues, he walked out of the House sobbing. Sanctions against Italy were abandoned as impracticable. 'There are the cowards,' cried Lloyd George, sweeping his arms towards the ministers on the Treasury bench. In March 1936 Germany reoccupied the Rhineland in breach of the Treaty of Versailles. The mood of the House was one of fear, noted Nicolson. 'Anything to keep out of war.' Baldwin warned his colleagues against the notion of concerted action with France. Germany might be crushed (!), but would then turn Bolshevik. 'If there is any fighting in Europe to be done, I should like to see the Bolshies and the Nazis doing it.' So a general election had been won on the promise of collective security which Baldwin then failed to achieve. He survived because he seemed more trustworthy than any alternative. In March 1936 he appointed a civil servant, Thomas Inskip, as Minister for Coordination of Defence, described as the most extraordinary promotion since Caligula made his horse a consul. Neither government nor people had the heart for gearing up the war machine. Europe was polarising between two unattractive ideologies, and to many, Fascism seemed less of a menace than Communism. The dilemma of mid-1930s politics was crystallised in the Spanish Civil War of 1936–9.

There was one Cassandra who was sure he knew which way the world was turning, and how Britain should make itself ready, a man who seemed through the 1930s to be as politically expended as Lloyd George. Winston Churchill had first been elected for Oldham in 1900. His experience of the Boer War, his lineage and his combative personality soon brought him to the notice of the House. He was never far from controversy. In 1905 he crossed the floor on the issue of Free Trade. His attack on the Tories made him famous: 'A party of great vested interests, bonded together in a formidable confederation, corruption at home, aggression to cover it up abroad, sentiment by the basketful, patriotism by the imperial pint . . . dear food for the millions, cheap labour for the millionaire.' He joined Lloyd George on the Liberal side. It was a timely move, and he was Under-Secretary for the Colonies in the 1906 Liberal Government, promoted in 1908 to the Board of Trade. Sir Edward Grey in 1905 reflected, 'It is probable he will be one day Prime Minister.' At the outbreak of the Great War he was First Lord of the Admiralty, but resigned after the military disaster in the Dardanelles in 1915, for which Kitchener was more to blame than Churchill. Characteristically, he then went off to command a battalion in Flanders. He was impatient and angry, and, on returning from the front in May 1916, he tried to knock sense into complacent heads in the Commons: 'What is going on while we are here, while we go away to dinner, or home to bed? Nearly one thousand men of our own race are knocked into bundles of bloody rags every 24 hours.' He was Minister for Munitions and Secretary for War in Lloyd George's wartime coalition and, late one night in 1917, took his P.P.S. into the darkened Commons: 'Look at it,' he said. 'This little place is what makes the difference between us and Germany. It is in virtue of this that we shall muddle through to success and for lack of this Germany's brilliant efficiency leads her to final disaster. This little room is the shrine of the world's liberties.' Parliament was already his religion.

In 1924 he crossed the floor again, and returned to Tory ranks as a 'constitutional candidate': Baldwin offered him the Exchequer. Would he take it? 'Would a bloody duck swim?' He was not a successful Chancellor, and in the 1930s his career went off the rails. In January 1931 he resigned from the Shadow Cabinet over the conciliation of the Indian Congress Party. He was a romantic champion of Empire, and 'always responded to the glittering words of history'. His disproportionate obsession with India and his instinctive aggressiveness cast him into the political wilderness. He was a 'sabre rattler' who alienated everybody, and discredited on every issue he chose to address. During the National Government he retired sulking, like Achilles, to his tent. By 1935 he was a man with no future, and contemptuous of the pussy-footing policies adopted by the Government to maintain a semblance of unity.

But he still loved Parliament. Harold Nicolson walked into the Smoking Room for the first time after the 1935 election. There were shouts and laughter and an almost complete absence of decorum. 'Winston rose tubbily and stretched out great arms. "Welcome! Welcome!" he yelled.' From 1935 onwards he dedicated himself to a courageous and unpopular crusade to warn the Commons about the German war machine. He ridiculed the Government's reluctance to rearm on the ground that there was no electoral mandate for it: 'The responsibility of Ministers for the public safety is absolute, and requires no mandate. It is in fact the prime object for which governments come into existence.' The Government Front Bench, noted Macmillan, put on that look of shocked disapproval which so often makes ministers look like supercilious camels. In November 1936 he shook the House with his denunciation of policy: 'The government cannot make up their minds, or they cannot get the Prime Minister to make up his mind. So they go on, in strange paradox, decided only to be undecided, resolved to be irresolute, adamant for drift, solid for fluidity, all-powerful to be impotent. So we go on, preparing more months and years for the locusts to eat.' But his warnings were widely dismissed by the easy-lifers as just more panic-mongering. Baldwin and Churchill had fallen out over India, and he was still out of office after the 1935 election. But Baldwin appreciated his character, and wrote to Lord Davidson to explain his exclusion from the government: 'Anything he undertakes he puts heart and soul into. If there is going to be war – and no one can say that there is not – we must keep him fresh to be our war Prime Minister.' They met one day side by side in a Commons lavatory. Baldwin turned towards him with, 'At last, my dear Winston, we meet on a common platform for a common purpose.'

Baldwin emerged from the Abdication crisis of December 1936 with his stature enhanced, while Churchill made a fool of himself. He made every mistake possible, misjudging public opinion, the king and the mood of the Commons, where he was booed into silence when he unwisely intervened on behalf of the king. 'Winston was behaving', recorded Robert Boothby, 'like a dog about to be sick on the carpet. He holds it for three days. Comes up to the House, and is sick right across the floor.' Baldwin entered, arranging his flimsy sheets of 'bromo'. The Speaker read the Abdication message. 'I have never known in any assemblage such accumulation of pity and terror,' noted Nicolson. Baldwin's simple and factual account was 'Sophoclean and almost unbearable'.

Baldwin chose May 1937, the time of the new king's Coronation, for his retirement. He so contrived it that his final words were to announce a £200 increase in MPs' salaries. 'No man has ever left in such a blaze of affection,' wrote Nicolson. Yet after the outbreak of war his name was so execrated that he was advised not to go to London in case he was attacked. Chamberlain's moment had come at last. But his personality was cold and unsympathetic, and misgivings were aroused by his apparent narrowness of mind and culture. 'Not a bad Lord Mayor of Birmingham in a lean year,' was the wicked verdict of Lloyd George. 'He always looks at foreign affairs through the wrong end of a municipal sewage pipe.' He had supported Inskip over Churchill for defence co-ordination: 'he would excite no enthusiasm, but he would involve us in no fresh perplexities.' As Prime Minister he was efficient, industrious, uncharismatic. His Cabinet was full of old faces reshuffled in an uninspired government. From the moment he took office, he was possessed by a mystical belief in his mission to save world peace. His imaginative failure led him to appalling misjudgements of Hitler and Mussolini, whom he assumed to be reasonable men who believed in promise-keeping. So certain was he of his own rightness that he picked Horace Wilson, who reflected his own views as a mirror might, and undermined his Foreign Secretary, Eden, who had no alternative but to resign. 'I wrote a letter to Mussolini on friendly terms,' wrote Chamberlain in his diary, 'and this was followed by a very cordial reply from him. I did not show my letter to the Foreign Secretary, for I had the feeling that he would object to it.' He insulated himself from opinion, and rarely visited the Smoking Room in the Commons. Macmillan observed that the successful Prime Ministers of the century were those who were clubbable and relished the camaraderie of the House: Churchill, Attlee, Wilson; not so Chamberlain, Douglas-Home, Heath. Mr Blair, take note.

In Eden's place he appointed the Earl of Halifax, who added to the Government's air of amateurism. A journalist asked him if he was worn out by the late nights. 'Not exactly,' he replied, 'but it spoils one's eye for the high birds.' His first reaction to Mussolini's invasion of Albania in 1939 was 'And on Good Friday too'. 1938 was the nadir of British foreign policy. Hitler had no hesitation in invading Austria in March. Churchill addressed the Commons in sombre tones. 'For five years I have talked to this House on these matters – not with very great success. I have watched this famous island descending, incontinently, fecklessly, the stairway which leads to a dark gulf. It is a fine broad stairway at the beginning, but after a bit the carpet ends. A little farther on there are only flag-stones, and a little farther on still these break beneath your feet. If catastrophe overtakes us, historians of the future will be baffled by how a victorious nation suffered itself to cast away all that they had gained by sacrifice and victory – "gone with the wind!".' Over tea a leading Tory dismissed it as 'the usual Churchillian filibuster; he likes to rattle the sabre and he does it jolly well, but you always have to take it with a grain of salt.' Chamberlain pursued his fantasy of a personal friendship with Mussolini and, 'with the mind and manner of a clothes brush', famously dismissed the German threat to Czechoslovakia, and surrendered British treaty rights to strategic ports in Eire. Churchill saw the danger of a neutral Irish Republic: 'You are casting away real and important means of security and survival for vain shadows and for ease.'

September 1938. The Munich crisis, and Chamberlain's long-awaited period of glory. A message was passed along the Treasury bench to him. He adjusted his pince-nez and read it. His whole face and body seemed to change. He raised his face so that the light from the ceiling fell full upon it. All the lines of weariness and anxiety seemed suddenly to have been smoothed out; he appeared ten years younger, and triumphant. When he announced the Munich meeting there was a second of absolute silence, and then a roar of cheering. The House rose, except Harold Nicolson. Liddall, a Tory, hissed. 'Stand up, you brute.' Nicolson was ashamed of the House, which he likened to a Welsh Revivalist meeting, and was sure that Chamberlain thought Mussolini had made the concession out of friendship for the Chamberlain family. He returned from Munich to a near-hysterical welcome. On a Labour-prompted division on the agreement, 30 Conservatives abstained and none voted against the Government despite widespread anxieties about Chamberlain's less than manly stand. Only Duff Cooper resigned from the Government: 'War should have been accepted to save Europe from brute domination by one aggressor.' Even Chamberlain admitted later that the phrase 'peace in our time' was coined under the stress of emotion. There was a period of brittle optimism. Malcolm MacDonald, Colonial Secretary, reached the climax of a speech about Palestine – 'I cannot remember a time when I was not told stories about Nazareth and Galilee, about Jerusalem and Bethlehem, where the Prince of Peace was born' – and paused for effect. Churchill's stage whisper filled the crowded House: 'Good heavens! I never knew Neville was born in Bethlehem,' and it fell about with laughter.

The hopelessly impracticable guarantee to Poland cheered people up. Chamberlain enjoyed another brief popularity. One Tory backbencher was overheard to say to another: 'I suppose we shall be able to get out of this beastly guarantee business.' 'Oh, of course, thank God we have Neville.' But in the summer of 1939 the introduction of peacetime conscription set Liberals and Labour like hounds upon the Government. The decision was scorned as a surrender to militarism. 'We have lost, and Hitler has won,' cried Bevan, and Attlee said that it was very dangerous to give generals all they wanted. The Grand Alliance with France and Russia never materialised because of suspicions of Stalin. 'If we are going in without the help of Russia we are walking into a trap,' warned Churchill and Lloyd George. But many still thought Hitler's Germany less unattractive. In August, out of the blue, came the Nazi–Soviet Pact, followed rapidly by the German invasion of Poland.

The Second World War

The Commons met on Saturday 2 September expecting to hear the declaration of war. But Chamberlain stalled, holding out vague prospects of further negotiations. The House gasped in disbelief. Attlee was ill, and Arthur Greenwood rose to speak for the Opposition. Someone, either Leo Amery or Bob Boothby, from the Tory benches called out 'Speak for England, Arthur' and he did: 'Every minute's delay now means the loss of life, imperilling our national interests, and the very foundation of our national honour.' The House dispersed in confusion. Greenwood went at once to Chamberlain and said that unless war were declared next day, it would be impossible to hold the House. The Commons forced an unwilling Government to war, and, in its wake, the still more unwilling French. Parliament met on a Sunday, 3 September, for the first time since the Reform Bill crisis of 1831. An air-raid siren sounded as Eden, Amery and Nicolson walked to the House, and they scrambled into the air-raid refuge. People swore they heard gunfire and bombs dropping, but it was only carpenters nailing asbestos linings to the windows. Chamberlain was in despair at the declaration of war: 'Everything that I have worked for, everything that I have believed in during my public life, has crashed in ruins.' He had neither the gift nor the heart to inspire the nation for a war he had gone to the limit to avoid. Nicolson heard him in the Commons later in September, and thought he was like the secretary of a firm of undertakers reading the minutes of the last meeting. Churchill sat hunched beside him, 'looking like the Chinese God of Plenty suffering from acute indigestion'. His first speech after his appointment as First Lord of the Admiralty contrasted so powerfully with the lacklustre Chamberlain that afterwards even Chamberlain supporters were saying in the lobbies, 'We have now found our leader.' Chamberlain should have resigned with his policy in ruins, but he clung to office, 'like a limpet on a coffin sunk in the sea', unable to articulate the moral argument for the war. The 'phoney war' made it an unreal time. A blockade of Germany was seen by Chamberlain as the main military tactic until the spring of 1940, and his colleagues were equally out of touch. Kingsley Wood, the Chancellor, responded to a proposal to burn down German forests with, 'Are you aware it is private property? Why, you will be asking me to bomb Essen next!'

The fall of Norway in May 1940 sealed Chamberlain's fate too. On 8 May the Commons were feverish. The Prime Minister entered to be greeted with shouts of 'Missed the bus', reversing his foolish taunt of the previous month against Hitler. 'Little Neville seemed heart-broken and shrivelled,' noted Henry Channon, one of his uncritical supporters. The House was a 'mad arena where the lions were out for blood'. Amery quoted Cromwell's words to the Long Parliament: 'You have sat here too long for any good you have been doing. . . . In the name of God, go.' Churchill energetically defended the action in Norway; Lloyd George urged him not to be converted into an air-raid shelter to keep the splinters from hitting his colleagues. Then he struck devastatingly at Chamberlain, whom he despised, and who had somewhat pathetically declared that he had his friends in the Chamber. 'It is not a question of who are the Prime Minister's friends. It is a far larger issue. . . . He has asked for sacrifice. The nation is prepared for every sacrifice so long as it has leadership. I say solemnly that the Prime Minister should give an example of sacrifice, because there is nothing which can contribute more to victory than that he should sacrifice the seals of office.' The Opposition challenged the Government to a division. Feelings were inflamed in the lobbies: 'Quislings! Rats!' shouted Chamberlain's men; 'Yes-men' was the return taunt. The Government's majority of 240 fell to 81, 41 supporters voting with the Opposition and 60 abstaining. There were shouts of 'Resign, resign', and 'Go, go'. 'That old ape Josh Wedgwood began to wave his arms about and sing "Rule Britannia". Harold Macmillan joined in, but they were howled down.' Chamberlain left the House: 'No crowds tonight to cheer him, as there had been before and after Munich; only a solitary little man, who had done his best for England.' The next day came a crucial meeting of Chamberlain, Churchill, Halifax and Margesson, the Chief Whip. The rebels wouldn't support Chamberlain, but the party as a whole, including Margesson, preferred Halifax to Churchill, who had promised to serve under anyone. But would Churchill serve under Halifax? One of the most pregnant silences in political history. Halifax broke it by observing that it would be difficult for a peer to be Prime Minister 'in such a war as this'. Attlee and Greenwood refused to join Chamberlain's Government. However, at this moment the Cabinet Secretary failed to tell Halifax that R. A. Butler was waiting outside with the message that Labour was prepared to serve in a coalition led by Halifax. Halifax left by another door to go to a dentist's appointment. The same day Germany invaded the Low Countries. On 10 May an improbably optimistic Chamberlain had to be told to resign by his Cabinet colleagues, and Churchill became Prime Minister. As he had observed of Lloyd George in 1916, 'he seized power. Perhaps the power was his to take.' If so, it was because he had the backing of popular opinion and the press against the hostility of 'the decayed serving men'. When the House met on 13 May, it was Chamberlain who was cheered by the Conservatives, and only the Labour members cheered Churchill. His speech of dedication confirmed the suspicions of his inveterate opponents, who saw him only as a romantic aggressor. But Lloyd George, describing it as a graver moment of jeopardy than had confronted a British minister for all time, gave him his blessing: 'We all, from the bottom of our hearts, wish him well. The friends of freedom and of human right throughout the world will wish him Godspeed.' 'Winston cries slightly, and mops his eyes,' noted Nicolson. Perhaps he knew that Lloyd George had also said of him, 'He would make a drum out of the skin of his mother in order to sound his own praises.' But the bond between the two men was strong enough for Churchill to invite Lloyd George to join his War Cabinet, but he declined, saying that he couldn't serve alongside Chamberlain, whom Churchill had kindly appointed Lord President of the Council. But Lloyd George, a lonely ghost, continued to haunt the Commons. Robert Boothby found him once in the Chamber on a Friday afternoon, when it was empty, and asked what he was doing. He replied: 'To anyone with politics in his blood, this place is like a pub to a drunkard.'

VE day came five years to the day after the Commons vote that brought Churchill to power. Those five years of war leadership have become the stuff of political legend. Particularly in the first two years, until Alamein, when the war picture showed nothing but reverses, and Britain was substantially alone, Churchill's manner and language, and his consummate skill as a parliamentary actor, somehow contrived to make everyone feel better even at bad news. Yet the controversy that had been his lifelong political companion never left him. Though he breathed the very air of Parliament, he often seemed to treat it with arrogance. 'He usurps a position in the House,' said George Lansbury, 'as if he had a right to walk in, make his speech, walk out, and leave the whole place as if God Almighty had spoken. . . . He never listens to any other man's speech but his own.' Sir Stafford Cripps, during the war, thought to bring Churchill's disregard of Parliament to his attention. 'Two things I put above everything in my life,' said Churchill, 'God and the House of Commons.' 'Well,' said Cripps, 'I hope you treat God better than you do the House of Commons.' He was deeply sentimental, often in tears in the House, and had an insatiable need to be loved. His appeal to the Commons in 1915 after the Dardanelles fiasco, when he resigned from the Admiralty, had been scorned by Violet Bonham-Carter: 'His plea to the House of Commons like saying "Do you love me?" – quite useless.' In the Second War she thought the tactic less useless: 'There is nothing more popular in the House than to blame yourself. "I have killed my mother. I will never do it again" is certain to raise a cheer. Mr Churchill has never been afraid of taking blame upon himself . . . a sort of genial self-censure.' Often he was able to transform a grim moment by such a device. During a vote of confidence debate (only ever moved by Conservatives, never by Labour members), he was questioned about the problems of the Churchill tank. 'It has many defects and teething troubles,' he said, 'and when these became apparent it was appropriately rechristened "The Churchill". These defects have now been largely overcome. I am sure that this tank will prove, in the end, a powerful, massive and serviceable weapon of war.' War, as it always had, brought out the best in him and raised him to an extraordinary peak of intensity. He was the only Prime Minister to wear military uniform while in office. He was a man in his element. Three characteristic moments are recorded in the early months of his leadership. In July 1940, when he announced that the Royal Navy had had to destroy the French fleet at Oran to prevent it falling into German hands, he sat with tears pouring down his cheeks. In October he was found in the Smoking Room, 'sipping a glass of port, and welcoming anyone who comes in. "How are you?" he calls gaily to the most obscure member. Not a pose: he likes to get away from being P.M. He reads the *Evening News* intently, as if it were the only source of information available to him.' In November the ruined Chamberlain died, and Churchill was generous in his tribute in the House, referring to 'the noble instincts of the human heart he strove to gratify, the love of peace, the pursuit of peace even at great peril and certainly to the bitter disdain of popularity or clamour.'

It took great courage to carry the burden of the bleak years of the war, and the support of Parliament was crucial. In December 1940 an I.L.P. motion for a negotiated peace was rejected by 341 votes to 4. After the losses in North Africa Churchill asked for a vote of confidence in May 1941, which was passed by 477 votes to 3, and he was given 'an ovation such as he had never yet received'. Then on 22 June 1941 Germany invaded Russia, and Churchill, with pressure relieved, was able to affirm a common cause: 'if Hitler invaded Hell I would make at least a favourable reference to the Devil in the House of Commons.' There was a habitual reassurance about his physical presence. Nicolson watched him standing there 'very stout and black, smoothing his palms down across his frame, beginning by patting his chest, then smoothing his stomach, and ending down at the groin. . . . He thrusts both his hands deep into his trouser pockets, and turns his tummy now to the right, now to the left, in evident enjoyment of his mastery of the position . . . he quotes Kipling's lines about the minesweepers, "Dusk off the Foreland – the last light going/ And the traffic crowding through,/ And five damned trawlers with their syreens blowing/ Heading the whole review!/ Sweep completed in the fairway./ No more mines remain", and is so moved by them that he chokes and cannot continue.' 1942 was a precarious year for the war and for his leadership. He won a vote of confidence by 464 votes to 1 in January, was cheered, and then, arm in arm with his wife, pushed through the crowds in Central Lobby, but then came a series of disasters that should have brought him down: Singapore, Malaya, Burma, Tobruk. Not a victory anywhere. His popularity was undermined, and he knew it: 'I am like a bomber pilot. I go out night after night, and I know that one night I shall not return.' The strain began to show. Southby, the Tory member for Epsom, implied that Churchill's son Randolph was not a fighting soldier. He approached Winston in the corridor afterwards to find a fist shaken in his face: 'Do not speak to me. You called my son a coward. You are my enemy. Do not speak to me.' But he survived because there was no one to replace him, and because he alone could tell the House of disasters and increase rather than diminish confidence. Four by-elections were lost to Independents, and he faced a vote of no confidence in July 1942. There was swelling resentment of Churchill's dictatorial manner, but one of his leading critics, Wardlaw-Milne, destroyed his case by proposing the Duke of Gloucester as Commander-in-Chief. The Commons burst out laughing, and the motion was defeated by 476 votes to 25, with 50 abstentions.

The hazards of war disrupted parliamentary life and placed members in the front line. On fourteen different occasions the Palace of Westminster suffered bomb damage. In November 1940 a bomb in New Palace Yard blew out many windows and fractured the sword of Richard the Lionheart. From November 1940 Church House, in Dean's Yard, was sometimes used for meetings of both Houses. There was an A.R.P. staff of around 700 on duty in the Palace, and members were assigned to fire-watching duties. It was a new democracy: Nicolson noted a bad night in Committee Room 9 in January 1942 when two stokers spat and snored all night. There was a munitions factory in the basement beneath Central Lobby, echoing the Gunpowder Plot, where members were also expected to lend a hand. Ruin arrived from the sky on the brilliantly clear night of 10 May 1941. A rain of incendiary bombs set the Palace alight. There was great derring-do. Police Sergeant Forbes climbed 350 ft. up the ladders on the scaffolded Victoria Tower carrying a sandbag to extinguish a dangerously flaming incendiary. The Commons Chamber and Westminster Hall were both alight, and the choice of the overstretched firefighters settled by Colonel Walter Elliot, a member on duty. 'Let the pseudo-Gothic go. We must save the Hall,' he cried, rushing with them to the north door. It was locked, and time was lost as he seized a fireman's axe and smashed his way in, forgetting that the side door had been left open for just such an emergency. But by saturating the beams with water from inside, the Hall roof was saved. The Commons was abandoned; high explosives followed the incendiaries, and it burned for two days, and was gutted. Five days later Nicolson went to see the ruins. The Members' Lobby was blocked by a mass of twisted girders. He went up the staircase to the Ladies' Gallery, turned the corner, and then, suddenly, 'there was the open air and a sort of Tintern Abbey gaping before me.' From June 1941 the Lords moved to the Royal Robing Room to allow the Commons to move in to the Lords

Chamber, which they occupied until 1950, when the rebuilt Commons was ready for use. Churchill's views on the rebuilding of the Chamber overruled all alternatives. 'We shape our buildings and afterwards our buildings shape us.' Like Disraeli before him, he was passionate for the two-party system and the intimacy of a small Chamber. His objection to the semi-circular assembly was that it admits 'various shades of pink according as the weather changes'.

After Alamein the tide of war at last began to turn, though moments of eloquent helpless despair recurred, as in December 1942 when a statement was sought on German plans to deport Jews from the occupied countries and put them to death in Eastern Europe, and the House rose and stood in silent witness to express its loathing of German barbarism. And fire-watching again in October 1943, Harold Nicolson climbed up to the Victoria Tower platform and was cold for three hours while Big Ben chimed 9 and 10 and 11. 'The guns spit and fire all round us, the river lies milkily in the misty moon, the searchlights sweep and cluster, and suddenly converge to a cone, and there high above our heads is a little white gadfly which is a German bomber.'

The landmarks of eventual victory began to be lit likewise. The collapse of Italy in September 1943: Lloyd George walked out towards the bar of the House, and Churchill scurried after him for a word. The eyes of all present were held by two fathers of victory. January 1944: Churchill returned to the Commons after convalescence at Marrakesh. Members jumped to their feet with cheer after cheer while Winston, 'very pink, rather shy, beaming with mischief, crept along the front bench and flung himself in to his accustomed seat. He had hardly sat down when two large tears began to trickle down his cheeks. He mopped at them clumsily with a huge white handkerchief.' Baldwin was invited to lunch with Churchill, and reported that 'the furnace of the war has smelted all base metals out of him'; Winston's dismissal of parliamentary dissenters as 'little folk who frolic alongside the juggernaut of war to see what fun or notoriety they can extract from the proceedings' confirmed Baldwin's insight. 6 June 1944: D-Day, and his announcement of the Normandy landings, 'the liberating assault with an immense armada of upwards of 4000 ships' which silenced those who had been complaining of delay. 'Everything is proceeding according to plan – and what a plan!' October 1944: Churchill returned from the Moscow conference. He made a statement in the

Winston Churchill surveys the ruins of
the House of Commons, May 1941.

House, and repaired to the Smoking Room. 'Collins, I should like a whisky and soda – single.' He sat down, and then stood up and went back to the bar. 'Collins, delete the word "single" and insert the word "double".' Then, grinning at everyone like a schoolboy, he returned to his seat. 8 May 1945: VE day, 3.23 p.m. Churchill, looking coy and cheerful, came in to a burst of ecstatic cheering and waving of order papers. He responded with an odd shy jerk of the head and a wide grin. He read the statement he had just broadcast, put the paper aside, and with wide gestures thanked and blessed the House for all its noble support. As Lloyd George had done in 1918, he proposed that 'this House do now attend at the Church of St Margaret's Westminster, to give humble and reverend thanks to Almighty God for our deliverance from the threat of German domination.' The Serjeant-at-Arms with the mace on his shoulder, the Speaker and all streamed through Central Lobby, through St Stephen's and out into the sunshine of Parliament Square. Back in the Palace Churchill made a dash for the Smoking Room. The crowd in Central Lobby broke into loud clapping. 'A little boy dashed out; "Please sir, may I have your autograph?" Churchill took a long time getting out his glasses and wiping them. Then he ruffled the little boy's hair and gave him back his beastly little album: "That will remind you of a glorious day".'

Labour Government 1945–51

The long coalition had been in power since 1935, though in two totally antithetical phases, the first trying and failing to preserve the peace, the second succeeding, as much by luck as by judgement, in winning the war. Now it began to dissolve. Labour offered to extend the coalition only until October; Churchill resigned on 23 May 1945, and was reappointed to head a caretaker government only until the General Election on 5 July. Everyone wanted to look forward, to peaceful home life, housing, employment, a new start. Led by Churchill, the Conservatives fought a clumsy scare campaign against Labour: 'an executive dictatorship backed by a Gestapo, and savings worthless.' The electorate would have none of it. Churchill, improbably, was booed at a political meeting in Walthamstow, and, when the results were declared at the end of July, found that he had been booted out. The Conservatives seemed to be set in pre-war attitudes, and in addition, there were

Clement Attlee celebrates election victory, in 1945, in the East End of London with his wife, Violet, MP for Limehouse. Wallie Edwards, MP for Whitechapel, is front row to the left and Phil Piratin, Communist MP for Mile End, behind and just to the right of Attlee.

sharp memories of the disappointments after 1918: 'Lloyd George brought ruin to Churchill from the grave.' Labour was elected for the first time as a majority government, and what a majority: 183 over all parties. It was indeed a new era: one good old Tory, survey-ing the gathering, exclaimed: 'Who are these people? They look like a lot of damned constituents.' Churchill came in as Leader of the Opposition, and Tory cheers modulated into a round of 'For he's a jolly good fellow', but the new Labour members faced with a challenge both musical and cultural, drowned them by standing to sing two verses of 'The Red Flag'. 'I wondered', said Speaker Clifton Brown, 'whether I was going to be elected Speaker of the House or director of a musical show.'

It was an altogether new political landscape. Parliament was the focus of national renewal. Clement Attlee's Government initiated a quite astonishing amount of radical legislation: the National

Health Service Bill in 1946, brilliantly presented by Aneurin Bevan, whom Baldwin had described in 1933 as 'the most dangerous man on that side'; the nationalisation of the country's chief industries and services; the granting of independence to India and Pakistan in 1947. The radical tide stopped short, though, of reforming the House of Lords, a scheme that was in the air, and there remained, as one sacred cow too many. Herbert Morrison cautiously observed to Clement Davies: 'We should not set up something new and different from the past.' The duties of members of the Commons, however, were revolutionised by Attlee's invention of the 'constituency surgery'. Before 1945 there was no expectation that a member should be ombudsman and agony aunt to his constituents. Burke scorned the notion in Bristol at the end of the eighteenth century: 'At the end of a session I come to my own house, fatigued in body and mind, to a little repose, and to a very little attention to my family and private concerns. I could hardly serve you as I have done, and court you too.' But now all is changed, and though Macmillan, of the old school, disparagingly remarked that the only quality needed to be an MP is the ability to write a good letter, some Members still find more job satisfaction in helping a constituent in need than in serving as lobby fodder.

Attlee's triumph was not only to transform the social and economic landscape, but to hold his volatile party together while doing so. The former Mayor of Stepney had proved his qualities during the war when, as Deputy Prime Minister, he had run both the country and Parliament while Churchill conducted the war. He was an admirable foil to the Prime Minister. 'The trouble with Winston', he told the Cabinet, 'is that he nails his trousers to the mast and he can't climb down.' An indignity Attlee was careful to avoid. He was a man of clear mind and few, undemonstrative words. 'Democracy means government by discussion,' he famously observed, 'but it is only effective if you can stop people talking.' He was a man of his word, notably laconic with his colleagues. A junior minister was summoned to Number Ten. 'I want your job,' said Attlee. 'But – why, Prime Minister?' 'Afraid you're not up to it.' The meeting was over. Again, to an older colleague; 'Well, you had a good innings. Time to put your bat up in the pavilion.'

Yet his Government rapidly lost favour. Austerity was its shibboleth; perhaps it had to be, after the Pyrrhic victory of the war, which had left the country ruined. But it was also puritanical, and retained rationing as a form of social engineering at a time when the electorate was longing for a reward for its wartime sacrifices. Between 1945 and 1950 Britain echoed the drab workers' states being set up in Eastern Europe. The public would have none of it, and in the 1950 election Labour's majority all but vanished. Aneurin Bevan's dramatic resignation in April 1951 split the party and dispatched it into a political wilderness for 13 years. Bevan, always a turbulent politician, felt that the true path of democratic socialism was being rejected in Gaitskell's budget, which made a large provision for armaments and introduced Health Service charges. At a stormy meeting of the P.L.P. in the Grand Committee Room Bevan rose, shook with rage and screamed, 'I have been martyred by the platform.' Charles Pannell asked Bevan's wife, Jennie Lee, to be quiet while Gaitskell was speaking, but Bevan turned on him: 'I'll take you outside and knock you down.' Harold Wilson and John Freeman resigned with Bevan, and the split between Bevanites and Labour mainstream lost the party the elections of both 1951 and 1955. 'I could not help but feel that a party unable to coexist with itself was really unfit to govern,' noted young Tony Benn in his diary. Attlee retired as leader in December 1955, and went to the Lords, doubtless feeling that he had earned some civilised respite after 20 years' leadership of such hysterical associates.

Conservative Government 1951–64

Churchill was Prime Minister again from 1951 to 1955, but apart from one visionary Commons speech about world government, the energies for leadership had gone. His decline was masked by a respectful press, and by the euphoria of the 1953 Coronation and his own eightieth birthday in November 1954, when Parliament honoured him in Westminster Hall. Party leaders tend to leave retirement too late, and in 1955 Churchill had to be nudged on his way by 'the consummate terminal expertise of the Conservative Party'. He returned to the backbenches, where he had spent the 1930s, for a further ten fitful years. He contributed little, but was always capable, by his presence alone, of upstaging other proceedings. He moved in and out of the House 'in pitiable slow motion, like a giant volcano refusing to accept that it was extinct.' He sat for an hour or two, 'hunched like a premature statue of himself,' sometimes ostentatiously switching off his hearing aid during a speech. He was present when a Secretary of State was presenting his Service Estimates, and the minister felt flattered. As he sat down, Churchill turned to him and said: 'I came to test a new hearing aid. It does not work.' On another occasion, during an interminable speech, he slumped in his seat with eyes closed. 'Must you fall asleep when I am speaking?' demanded the exasperated member. Dreamily, in a clear voice, without opening his eyes, came the reply: 'No, it is purely voluntary.' There was a celebrated search for a cough sweet during a major speech by Gaitskell, called by one correspondent 'The Fall of the Pastille'. He had ten thumbs, and a waistcoat with a hundred pockets, and the performance went on and on. 'I was only looking for my jujube,' he explained innocently. He still enjoyed repartee with men of his own stamp, such as Shinwell and Bevan, and he sometimes paid a nostalgic visit to the Smoking Room. 'That's Winston over there – they say he's in his dotage now.' 'Yes,' came the voice from the leather armchair, 'and they also say he's deaf.' At his death, in January 1965, Harold Wilson was, for once in his life, stirred in his Commons tribute to Churchillian rhetoric: 'For now the noise of hooves thundering over the veldt, the clamour of the hustings in a score of contests, the shots in Sidney Street, the angry guns of Gallipoli and Flanders, the sullen feet of the marching men in Tonypandy, the urgent warnings of the Nazi threat, the whine of the sirens and the dawn bombardment of the Normandy beaches; all these are silent.'

Anthony Eden, his elegant and experienced successor, who had resigned as Foreign Secretary in 1938 over Chamberlain's attempts to appease Mussolini, came quickly to grief over his refusal to attempt to appease Colonel Nasser, a man he mistakenly saw as a simulacrum of the dictators of the 1930s. The invasion of Egypt by French, British and Israeli forces 'to protect the Suez Canal' but without declaring war roused Labour to fury. Eden's gung-ho actions had damaged relations with the USA and Commonwealth, and violated the principles of the United Nations. One sitting was suspended in uproar; Eden was booed out of the Chamber, members were virtually at blows inside the House, and actually at blows outside it. George Wigg 'walloped' a Tory, Leslie Thomas; Thomas said: 'Gaitskell's a bloody traitor.' Wigg replied that he'd rather be led by a bloody traitor than a fucking murderer. Thomas asked him 'to come outside' where he hit Wigg. 'So I gave him one in the belly and two or three more, and he went down like a felled ox.' Off trotted Wigg to the Speaker to apologise. Labour made much of the analogy between Khrushchev's invasion of Hungary and the Anglo-French invasion of Egypt. The young Denis Healey made his Commons reputation by asking whether Eden had exchanged congratulations with Khruschev and by proposing, after the ceasefire on 6 November, that the Prime Minister should be recommended for the Nobel Peace Prize for demonstrating that aggression does not pay. He had to change his tune a few months later during the crisis in Oman in July 1957, and found himself agreeing with Tony Benn that you must close your eyes while British jets do their dirty work, and hope to God they do it quickly so that you can open them again and pretend you haven't seen anything nasty going on.

Crushed by his misadventure, Eden resigned in January 1957, and was succeeded by Harold Macmillan rather than R. A. Butler, whom many thought more suitable. Churchill later said to Macmillan that but for Hitler, neither of them would have got to the top. The shadow of the 1930s again fell across events 20 years later: Macmillan had opposed appeasement, Butler supported it. Macmillan's personality brought 'a little artistry to the business of the House of Commons'; Butler's intellectual subtlety, often perceived as deviousness, recommended itself less to Tory stalwarts. Knights of the shires still abounded in the Conservative Party under Macmillan. Sir Walter Davenport booted the Belgian ambassador in the backside, believing him to be a renegade backbencher; Sir Jocelyn Lucas bore down upon the newly elected Julian Critchley waiting in a crowded lobby to vote on a three-line whip. He grasped Critchley's arm and hissed: 'You're wearin' suede shoes,' and disappeared, never to speak to him again. Some of the old guard would be taken into custody by the Life Peerages Act, which Macmillan introduced in 1958, over 100 years after Lord John Russell had first proposed it. The House of Lords began to enter its long chrysalis stage.

Macmillan enjoyed the statesman's role; he pursued security in relations with the Soviet Union and heralded the post-colonial order that was imminent in Africa. His unflappable patrician manner, avuncular reassurance and stylish wit earned him much approval; they were also handy disguises for a Tory leader for, like Churchill, he was more of a traditional Liberal than a true-blue

Harold Macmillan and Edward Heath
in Brussels, early 1970s.

Tory. Asked what was the most difficult aspect of being Prime Minister, he replied, 'Events, dear boy, events'. His sleepy manner too was a disguise for sharp repartee in debate. Accused by Woodrow Wyatt of talking mumbo-jumbo, he demurred; 'I don't understand the Hampstead tribal language.' But his seeming impregnability vanished with the Profumo sex and spy scandal in June 1963, when he was exposed as hopelessly out of touch. It was the first of many such banana skins of personal conduct on which the Tory Party, disproportionately it seems, was firmly to set its collective foot between the 1960s and the 1990s. Perhaps a party espousing traditional values is more vulnerable to tabloid inquiry. Macmillan visibly sagged in the Commons when Nigel Birch quoted at him Browning's 'The Lost Leader': 'Let him never come back to us . . . never glad confident morning again.' Macmillan turned towards him, his face contorted with pain and anger. But a few weeks later he made a brilliant exit. He came into the Commons late at night on 26 July 1963 to make a statement. Everyone understood that he and his Government were finished, but he was going to go in style. He announced an international nuclear test ban treaty, and then

Harold Wilson and Barbara Castle applaud Michael Foot
at the Labour Party conference, 1975.

revelling in the prolonged cheers from all parts of the House, walked slowly past the Treasury bench and, on reaching the Speaker's Chair, turned and bowed twice to the House: 'This success is deeply moving to us all.' His subsequent resignation, and the mysterious inner workings of Tory grandees in the choice of his successor, brought together for a short time in the Commons the unlikely combination of the fourteenth Earl of Home, downgraded to Sir Alec, and the fourteenth Mr Wilson, who had been elected Leader of the Labour Party on the premature death of Hugh Gaitskell. It was easy to deride Home's administration as a 'lame duck' Government; as in 1945 and 1951, the electorate was ready for change, and in 1964 Wilson led Labour back into power, but with a majority of only two.

Palace and Parliament at the end of the Twentieth Century

Parsimony and failure of nerve have not served the Palace well in the twentieth century. The austere rebuilt Commons Chamber was opened in October 1950 with a ceremony in Westminster Hall where the Speakers of the Commonwealth Parliaments assembled. The Members' Lobby, which contains the war-ravaged Churchill arch as the entrance to the Chamber and as a memory of battle, is still incomplete: there are two vacant plinths for statues of former Prime Ministers. But there was much post-war discontent with working conditions. Members had no offices, typewriters, telephones, or space for files. They had to dictate to secretaries in corridors and broom cupboards. In 1950 Willie Hamilton was given a key to a locker no bigger than the one he had possessed at school. After 12 years' seniority he had graduated to a little desk in a dark attic shared with seven other members, access to which was by an antiquated lift.

Offices and secretaries had not been in Barry's brief: the first steel filing cabinet only arrived in 1931, the first young woman typist, a Miss Smith, in 1932. But grand living spaces for officials were, and after the war those in possession of space were fiercely tenacious of it. The Serjeant-at-Arms had forty rooms at his disposal; the Clerk of the Parliaments had a house with twelve principal bedrooms. There were fine plans to solve the problem of space. One was to build a new Commons between Bridge Street and Richmond Terrace. Another was to complete Barry's original scheme to enclose New Palace Yard, but all that materialised was a five-storey underground car park which cost ten times its estimate. There were two consequences: the lime trees planted above it withered and died, and the difficulty of distinguishing between a bag of cement and a bag of gelignite led to an explosion in the Westminster Hall cafeteria in 1974 which again threatened the ancient roof. A third scheme was for a new building in Bridge Street. In 1970 there was a competition, as in 1836, and a winner declared, but inflation, and opposition from the GLC scuppered it, and it was only at the turn of the century that Portcullis House, parsimony thrown to the winds, was completed on the Bridge Street site. For well over 100 years the cheap and short-term solutions to accommodation in the Palace have disfigured Barry's noble building with shabby excrescences. Windows have been blocked by huts perched on roofs, handsome rooms divided and subdivided, courtyards intended to provide light and air encroached upon by quick-fix extensions. In 1970 a prefabricated hut for Hansard staff even blocked the windows along one side of the Commons Chamber. The occupation of Portcullis House will, it is hoped, be followed by a thorough cleansing of Barry's much-defaced Palace. There is, understandably, some opposition to the isolation of members in their own offices on the grounds that the sense of community will be lost. Many attempts to provide improved accommodation for peers and MPs have foundered because of the magnetism of the overcrowded Palace. 'This place is all about gossiping with those who pass' is a view not to be derided, not least because passing the time of day is an antidote to one of the hazards of life at Westminster, overwork. The death of John Smith, Labour leader, in May 1994, was only the latest in a line of great talents prematurely snuffed out – Hugh Gaitskell, Ian Macleod, Tony Crosland – whose survival might have altered the whole trajectory of politics in the latter part of the century.

'A man's institution', said Mrs Baldwin of Parliament, 'evolved through centuries by men to deal with men's affairs in a man's way.' Both the Lords and the Commons are still overwhelmingly masculine places. Although the workforce in the Palace of Westminster as a whole has for some decades been predominantly female, the scales seemed to be tilted to make it difficult for women to become Members of Parliament. When Margaret Thatcher entered the Commons in 1959, she was one of only 17 women MPs; Betty Boothroyd stood for 17 years in losing seats before winning West Bromwich in 1973, when there were 27 women members. In 1993 there were 60, a number which doubled in 1997.

When the Palace was rebuilt in the mid-nineteenth century Mrs Baldwin's appraisal was entirely right. 'We shape our buildings, and then our buildings shape us,' Churchill had said of the Commons Chamber. His words are equally true of the whole building. Charles Barry also built London clubs (the Reform and the Travellers), and the Palace looks like a club on a grand scale. 'Genuine toffs' like Alan Clark loved its clubbable quality: 'The swinging studded Pugin doors which exclude those unentitled; the abundance of facilities, the deeply comfortable leather chairs at the "Silent" end of the Library where one can have a deep and refreshing sleep. There is constant access to snacks, "nips", and gossip.' Sometimes it seems very close to the world of Bertie Wooster. Harold Balfour arrived at Westminster as a new member to receive this advice from an old hand: 'Well my boy, remember two things. If you are a little drunk after dinner follow the white waistcoats and you'll be in the right lobby, and always leave the Chamber when a Liberal speaks.' Robert Maxwell was briefly put in charge of the wine cellar, and sold off much of the prize stock to himself and his friends. Perhaps the last refuge of the old club tie is the Smoking Room, now in decline, and populated only by 'soaks, traditionalists and memory-lane buffers'.

The Palace also evokes a grand Victorian boarding school. Sometimes conduct is capable of being nudged towards the sillier sides of schooliness, where again men feel at home. Poor behaviour in the Commons during Prime Minister's Question Time transforms it from the council of the nation to a rowdy class over which even an experienced teacher has to be watchful. The stale old joke which rechristened the chairman of the Kitchen Committee the 'Minister of the Interior' was straight from prep school. Members have sometimes erupted like adolescents letting off steam. Tony Benn, in 1971, at the end of a long night of divisions when members spent hours in the lobby, persuaded a few people to start singing 'The Red Flag', followed by 'Cwm Rhondda' and 'We Shall Overcome' as they trooped back into the Chamber and threw their order papers in the air when Harold Wilson arrived. One of the effects of a strident and puritanical woman leader on some of the men in the Commons between 1979 and 1990 was to reduce them to adolescents revelling in smut behind Matron's back. Frank Dobson and Alan Clark swapped stories, but Dobson's were 'unusable even at a rugby club dinner'. When John Wakeham, as Leader of the House, explained Mrs Thatcher's absence by announcing that 'she was making herself available for Mr Gorbachev', the ripe chuckles from the benches would have disgraced the fourth form. In recent Lords terminology, life peers were 'day boys' and hereditary ones 'boarders'. Memories of school, if not all school habits, seem to linger long with some layers of British society. The character of former inhabitants of the Whips' Office was captured by one of their victims as 'Fieldsport enthusiasts whose last and only fulfilment period had been bullying (and in some cases buggering) Lower Boys at Eton.'

'Unparliamentary language' is often taken straight from Billy Bunter's Greyfriars glossary. The characteristics of parliamentary language were described by Erskine May as 'good temper and moderation', but many fall short of the ideal. Neil Kinnock escaped censure when he called another member a 'jerk', but Dennis Skinner was 'named' for calling John Gummer 'this little squirt of a minister', and refusing to withdraw it. Tony Banks asked Mr

Margaret Thatcher celebrates her first general election victory, 4 May 1979.

Speaker to order 'the fat bounder [Nigel Lawson] to be dragged here from the dinner table.' Called to order, he substituted 'corpulent bounder', but the Speaker replied, 'That is almost as bad.' Banks was in trouble again in 1994 when he proposed that a condom machine should be installed in the Commons: 'I realise the installation would come rather too late for some Tory MPs; the more circumspect among us would welcome it.' His remarks were halted by the Speaker on the grounds of 'extremely bad taste'. In general the language of the Commons seems to have become more cautious in the last 20 years, as if members are uneasy with rhetoric, and what is remembered is not so much the noble statement of principle but the inspired insult. Mrs Thatcher provoked Denis Healey into mastery of the genre: she was 'the Catherine the Great of Finchley', 'Florence Nightingale with a blowtorch', and her Cabinet were the prisoners in *Fidelio*.

   In such a milieu, the women who rose tended to adopt the manner of their male colleagues. Mrs Thatcher said, on gaining power in 1979, 'I did not get here by being stridently female.' And Ann Widdecombe in 1997 corrected the stereotype: 'The idea that women civilise the House is wrong. Some of the greatest hecklers in this place are women.' But into this masculine domain surged 'Blair's Babes' in 1997. They were immediately disapproving, not least of Jane Shilling's fashion column in *The Times* which described the mass gathering of the Babes as 'an exceptionally nasty example of municipal planting'. They also turned their noses up at almost everything they found in Parliament: 'a cross between an Oxford college and a girls' boarding school.' 'The behaviour sometimes is still public school dormitory stuff. It really disgusts me. Some of the members putting their feet up on the Dispatch Box.' They envied, or resented, the men's networking skills as 'team players', seen by one critic as 'gangs in the school playground'. They fell foul of existing rules (they were not supposed to clap Mr Blair in the Chamber). They were impatient at the slow allocation of space – in order of seniority – so that some had to operate for a month in a corridor, with telephones and laptops on a window ledge. There was no discernible tide of reciprocal disapproval. Lord Mason's mock alarm when infants appeared with their mothers at the tea tables: 'They're breeding on the Terrace', did not suggest that the masculine hegemony of the Palace yet felt seriously challenged. But in the future an army of nature's nannies may arrive to sweep dirty feet from the Dispatch Box and smutty stories from the backbenches to safeguard democracy and restore family values.

Other institutions are sometimes invoked for comparison with the Palace. Fenner Brockway wrote that he had spent three years in prison and three years in Parliament and that he saw character deteriorate in Parliament more than in prison. 'The only lunatic asylum in the country which is run by the inmates,' Dudley Smith called it, and for Dennis Skinner it is 'sometimes like a church, and sometimes like a zoo'. A member first elected in 1997 likens it to a cruise liner, hermetically sealed, where all the needs of the affluent are provided for in function rooms, with the terraces serving as decks. These analogies all envisage the occupants as being in detention, and one aspect of the community shaped by the Palace is an obsessiveness that makes it hard to leave the building. It is enclosed, with few vistas of life outside itself. Its rhythm is centripetal. The Chinese whispers of gossip ripple through the echoing corridors; wit and indiscretion are quickly common knowledge; everyday conduct is felt to harbour some deeper meaning: a persistent craving for refreshment in the tearoom, for example, is interpreted as a symptom of leadership aspirations. Somewhere in the maze something sensational has just happened, is happening, or is about to, but no one knows where, and no one dares leave the place for fear of missing out. The compulsiveness of the building, supported by its sometimes eccentric hours, make alcohol and adultery the twin hazards of life at Westminster. 'Maze' suggests another quality of the community. 'It is a splendid place for a game of hide and seek.' There are secret passages, winding staircases, strange galleries and mysterious corridors. Members set forth to explore the labyrinth and never meet again. For the unwary there are dangerous territories, where officers bar their way. The Palace disposes its occupants towards the playing of games, composed, like the imagination of childhood, both of terror and delight. It is as well for the nation that members leave for their constituencies at weekends to have their noses rubbed in real life.

The Palace of Westminster is also a stage set, where there is no boundary line between audience and actors. Its theatrical atmosphere has proved a challenging test of character, with surprising successes and failures, some struck down by stage fright, others inspired by 'the beloved magical electric aura of the Chamber'. 'I have made my maiden speech,' wrote Belloc in 1906; 'after it I was sick.' A. P. Herbert found that addressing the Commons was like making a speech in a beehive. But in 1935 he was bold enough, in his maiden speech, to attack the Baldwin Government for usurping private members' time. A delighted Churchill sought him out afterwards: 'Call that a maiden speech? It was a brazen hussy of a speech, a painted lady paraded before a modest Parliament.' But the theatrical pressures of the place can also unsettle judgements and destroy careers. Lloyd George, Mosley, Powell, Jenkins and Owen form a lineage of men of authority and vision who marginalised themselves in Parliament by their misreading of circumstances.

At the beginning of a new millennium, Parliament seems in some disarray. The House of Lords has proved an easy target for a government which wanted to convince the electorate that 'modernisation' would rebrand the nation. It is changing irrevocably, and is in a fretful limbo between the exit of the hereditary peers and the implementation of stage two and the Government's response to the Royal Commission chaired by Lord Wakeham. But even if the vice of cronyism is averted, there will be a price to pay.

'Thanks to English snobbery,' wrote Enoch Powell, 'we enjoy the blessing of inexpensive patronage.' Cheapness was not the only usefulness, however, of a House containing both hereditary and life peers: there was a greater mix of age and experience than other criteria for appointment could easily supply. The ideal of public service was embodied in the attitude of many hereditary peers who, beholden to no one but their ancestors, could be entirely independent. The survival of some of the best features of the former House of Lords is important for Parliament and the nation. A Chamber characterised by self-regulation and largely civilised exchange is an admirable foil to the Commons cockpit, and its lesser defensibility confirms the clear priority of the elected House. It is not widely known that it has to carry much of the burden of legislative scrutiny. And it has also been a convenient scapegoat for, and sometimes opponent of, radical, or would-be radical, governments which threaten to get carried away by their own ideologies.

In the Commons, the major parties are in process of redefinition, both in some ways reeling from the delayed aftershocks of Margaret Thatcher's ideological governments. In the 1980s and 1990s, because of Europe, party splits ceased to be a Labour monopoly. John Major, though a pragmatist in the mould of Macmillan and Wilson, still failed to hold his party together. Is it possible both to keep a government unified and to follow a clear and determined set of policies? Mrs Thatcher followed her policies but divided her party. The subsequent flight from ideology has left the principal parties struggling to find coherent and acceptable political philosophies which confer identity and unify policy. Regular ritual Dutch auctions of tax cuts are no substitute for party platforms; they only demean politics and insult the electorate. Political correctness surfaces in its most literal form when the major parties seek to be all things to all men, and shun any suggestion of ideology which might alienate sections of the electorate. The danger of so pragmatic an approach is that governments are tempted into gesture politics, and are seen not as leading the nation but only responding to the currents of outrage and sentimentality stirred up by the popular press as a result of those 'events' so dreaded by Macmillan. New Labour has been redefined into electoral success, but perhaps at the cost of clear identity. The preservation of party unity from Millbank, and the sight of New Labour MPs, each 'on message', with a pager bearing the party logo and a red rose, may be a lesson learned from the disarray of the preceding governments, but is not self-evidently part of a healthy democracy. 'It is no mean thing to have the letters MP after one's name,' declared Trollope in the nineteenth century. But a continuing esteem for Parliament may depend on the willingness of members of both Houses to fight the cause of representative democracy against the pressures that threaten to subvert it. Otherwise they may dwindle into the childlike delight registered by one New Labour member elected in 1997 as he savoured the pleasures of the Palace: 'Being an MP is better than working.' But that was before he got his pager. Willingness to fight the cause of representative democracy presupposes too a willingness to make sacrifices to do a proper job. Responsibility for the affairs of a great nation cannot also be, as many members seem to think, a 9 to 5 activity. The Speaker, in her resignation statement of July 2000, passionate in defence of Parliament, reminded the House that 'the requirements of effective scrutiny and the democratic process must take priority over the convenience of members.'

Most judgements about Parliament in the recent past are likely to be premature. Yet it is hard to dismiss the impression that all is not well, both with parliamentary activity and public attitudes to it. Esteem for Parliament and politicians has receded in the last 40 years, particularly among the young, and, were that movement to continue, the prospects for representative democracy would be unhappy.

The foundations of politics have shifted in the last quarter of the twentieth century. At the heart of the process are the media, which have transformed public attitudes and radically altered the ways in which politicians behave. Executive government has also changed its character, towards a more presidential model, and there is a sense that Parliament has become marginalised, left behind under the burden of traditions and protocol it is unable to throw off.

The watershed of political life in the twentieth century appears to have been located in the 1960s. Macmillan's resignation, the defeat of the 14th Earl of Home by Harold Wilson, 'the cheekie chappie of politics', in the 1964 election, and the death of Churchill, marked the end of the pre-war, characteristically patrician, political lineage. The Profumo scandal, in which a Cabinet minister linked with call-girls and a Russian spy, was forced to admit that he had lied to Parliament, offered the nation a view of politicians which broke with convention. 'Government in Baldwin's day', wrote Edward Pearce, 'possessed mystique and a mantle of natural authority even if the generality of dithering stuffed shirts then in government did not deserve either.' A new climate of irreverence was marked by 'That Was The Week That Was', a joyously anarchic and popular television programme which ran for two years from November 1961, and set out to debag embodiments of stuffy establishment authority. Politicians provided material generously.

Since then, the impact of media power upon Parliament has been enormous. Its ubiquity, its appetite and its intrusiveness have unsettled confidence and judgement in ways previously unthinkable, and it has changed the rules by which politics is conducted. Its insatiability for news round the clock is partly responsible for the rise of spin in place of substance, for governmental obsession with news control, and for the impression that Downing Street and Fleet Street give of two cannibals trying to eat each other. In a media-dominated age, perceptions of Parliament have come to displace its essence, and public perceptions, however irrationally formed, have often been unflattering. Tony Benn, a passionate and committed Parliamentarian, argues that the communication lines between the electorate and Parliament have become disrupted. If he is right, some of the causes are identifiable.

Responsible newspaper coverage of Parliament, even in the broadsheets, has dwindled into snappy headlines, scandals, sound-bites and photo-opportunities, which tend to turn Parliament into political soap opera, a somewhat amateurish branch of the entertainment industry. And, ironically, the introduction of television cameras into the Commons in 1989 after a free vote in the House, was counter-balanced by the steady shift of the centre of political gravity to the television studio, where Parliamentarians could command a larger audience. The clips of Commons debate shown on news bulletins tend to feature the confrontational rituals that fire up tribal loyalties; the game of catcalls between rival supporters from the Commons terraces does not seem to commend Parliament to the rest of the nation, yet is unrepresentative of the serious work invisibly carried on in committee rooms.

Just as the calibration of political discourse to the level of tabloid man does disservice to issues of policy, the fascination of the popular press with public figures who may have skeletons in their cupboards does disservice to that great majority of Parliamentarians motivated by public service. It is of course healthy that politicians are scrutinised, but the handful of members of both Houses caught out in doubtful practices over 40 years has, on the rotten apple principle, tended to foster in the electorate the presupposition that most politicians must be 'on the make' or 'up to no good'. 'Sleaze' has entered the language of politics, and will not easily be dispelled. Indeed the appointment of the Nolan Committee and the Commissioner for Parliamentary Standards to ensure the continuing integrity of public life, have managed to reinforce the public idea that corruption must be widespread. Politicians are also the unfortunate victims of the peculiarly British hypocrisy of demanding very different standards from their elected representatives from those they accept in their private lives. Who, indeed, would have the courage to enter politics at all, knowing that at any time the pack might hunt them down and tear their reputation to pieces? Increasing cynicism about politicians is paradoxically accompanied by rising expectations of them: every year their postbags grow larger. Members of Parliament are more to be pitied than envied.

Parliament used to be 'the chief forum of the nation', in Betty Boothroyd's phrase; it is no longer so, except on the rare big occasion. Its supremacy has been eroded by a number of interrelated factors.

The powers of the Crown, vested in the government of the day, 'have increased, are increasing', and are not always accountable to the power of the people, vested in Parliament. 'The excessive power of the executive', observes Earl Russell, 'is the greatest single constitutional evil.' Ministers show disrespect for Parliament by reserving important announcements for other audiences. It is generally desirable that the people's representatives are the first to hear government policy, and the first to ask questions about it. Churchill regarded himself as 'the servant of the House'; but not all his successors have appeared to hold the Commons in such regard, and some have treated it with arrogance in their pursuit of a quasi-presidential role for the executive. All governments tend to acquire 'kitchen cabinets', but the practice appears to be waxing. Like 'sleaze', 'cronyism' has entered the language of politics. There is legitimate concern at the personal or financial influences that might be wielded upon policy, or to secure recognition, by individuals who are unelected and unaccountable to Parliament. 'Government from the top', or 'management democracy', challenges the legislature to exercise the checks and balances appropriate for a mighty executive. 'We are here', said Tony Benn in a speech in the Commons in 1999, 'to scrutinise and challenge the executive; we can table parliamentary questions and motions, hold debates and serve on Select Committees. We can accept, amend or reject government legislation.'

But the exercising of these admirable responsibilities is far from easy. Politics has become more professional, at least in terms of careerism. Many, if not most members of the Commons cherish hopes of eventual promotion to government; fewer than in the past are content to be good legislators and good representatives of their constituencies. If the Commons is seen as a waiting room for advancement, the healthy independence of legislature from executive is undermined.

There has also been a centralisation of power in all parties, which further inhibits the independence of members. Party discipline, intolerant of dissent, has devised means of deselecting mavericks, or of not selecting them in the first place; the crusader is under pressure to become pliant lobby fodder. 'Our duty', continued Benn, 'is to speak and vote as we believe to be right, within the framework of loyalty to our party, to our constituents and to our conscience.' He makes a case for more cross-party activity, of a kind that proved so stimulating at the time of the referendum on Europe in 1975, and for more free votes in the House. But the tendency is in the other direction. Party whips have claimed appointments to Select Committees for their empire, so that disinterested cross-party scrutiny and enquiry have become charged with party antagonisms, or conflict between the executive and the rest. The threat to democracy, and to the standing of Parliament, is a serious one, recognised by the backbench revolt in the summer of 2001 which rejected government placement for the chairmanship of the Foreign Affairs and Transport Committees.

Within the Commons Chamber the accountability of the executive can be subverted at question times. The former Speaker's impatience at political point-scoring which obscures the real issues, and long-windedness which reduces the number of questions that can be answered was sometimes palpable. But the spirit of her own chosen motto, 'I speak to serve', did not always prevail with members, and her powers over ministers were not always sufficient to remedy the abuse of time and procedures.

The Modernisation Committee, appointed to look at ways of reforming the work of Parliament, moves at a snail's pace, for perfectly intelligible reasons. The volume of legislation passing through Parliament has more than doubled in recent years from 1175 pages a year in 1971 to 2581 pages in 1989 and still rising, as governments try to push through ever more ambitious programmes. Statutory instruments, government orders that are scrutinised only in an abbreviated form of the legislative process, if at all, have increased in the same period from about 70 a year to over 1200. Even if it worked 24 hours a day, the Commons could not give adequate scrutiny to such a volume of legislative business, and up to now it has had to leave to the House of Lords to do so. Never has it been more necessary for the Lords not to be the poodle of any government.

The function of Parliament has also been undermined, and its clear legitimacy muddied, by devolution in its many forms. The European Commission and Parliament, the International Monetary Fund and other multinational organisations, public and commercial, have limited the remit of Westminster's authority. Devolution to the Scottish Parliament and the Welsh Assembly has removed further sectors of responsibility from Parliament's direct control. The electoral proliferation that has accompanied not only devolution, but also local votes for the Mayor of London and the future of grammar schools, has blurred the representative authority of a House of Commons chosen at a general election.

The product of these tendencies is a Parliament uncertain about how to use its power and its freedom, and one that appears to be sinking both in public esteem and under the burden of legislative work it is asked to undertake. Representative democracy needs its champions, both within and beyond Parliament. It has to adapt to a world in which the nation state is no longer the primary unit. It needs to attract the most talented men and women, with an independence nourished by wide experience, to serve it. The long and often tortuous evolution of Parliament in the Palace of Westminster is clearly unending.

Epilogue

11.30 p.m. Central Lobby. The Commons have risen, earlier than predicted, but the Lords remain in session until nearly midnight. The place is eerily silent. A postal worker makes a last collection from the box in the Lobby, the rattle of keys and the grating of hinges echoing around the gilded mosaic vault. A sudden sneeze from a late secretary seems to shake the whole building. The policemen on night duty are specially friendly.

11.45 p.m. The Police Room, adjacent to New Palace Yard and Westminster Hall. A Duty Inspector, about to end his day, and a duty sergeant, on for the night. Officers out of uniform stop by in little groups to clock off. No problems tonight. The Lords have risen, and the Ayrton light in the Clock Tower is turned off.

1.00 a.m. A long walk round the whole Palace, corridors, roofs, courtyards. All the lights are on until an hour after the last House rises. Late peers are being picked up by taxi at the Peers' Entrance, or collecting their cars in Old Palace Yard. Everywhere there are hidden knots of people, mostly still working. The Palace never closes. About a dozen staff are still busy in the Lords Hansard offices, transcribing and checking and editing the last hour of debate before it goes off to the printers. In the Committee Corridor two stone cleaners have just come on duty, a pair of Midases turning the grimy stone window frames to gold. There are two telephonists on night duty in the Commons Switch Room and three all-night sorters in the Post Room, distributing postbags which arrive every hour into wire racks labelled with the names of the 659 MPs. Engineers' Control is staffed all night by a small team monitoring fire, water, electricity, temperature, humidity. A white Stationery Office van drives through the courtyard every fifteen minutes or so to collect copy or deliver matter for the new day. The Press Gallery bar has closed. The Commons Chamber is in darkness, except for a spotlight picking out the Speaker's Chair, almost as if the Speaker might wish to practise 'Order, order' to an empty House to cure a sleepless night. And, at the far end of the Lords Library corridor, just before the lights go out, a door to the Lord Chancellor's study stands ajar, and there on his wig stand is the wig he discarded at the end of the sitting, not neatly positioned, but dissolutely lop-sided, as if the day had been too long for further effort.

Palace of Westminster

PRINCIPAL FLOOR PLAN

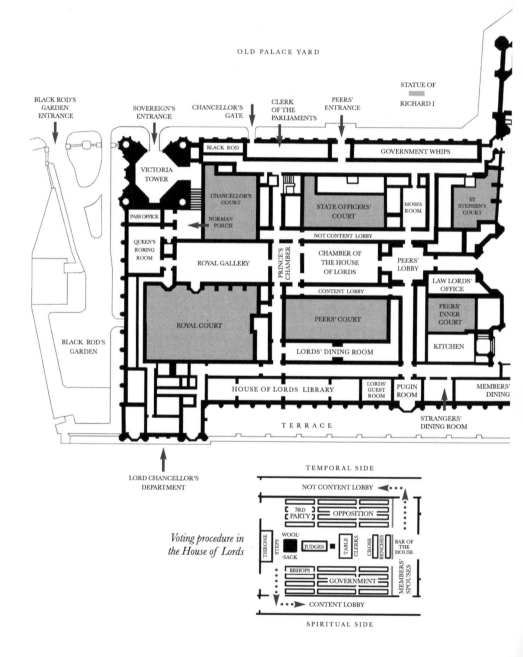

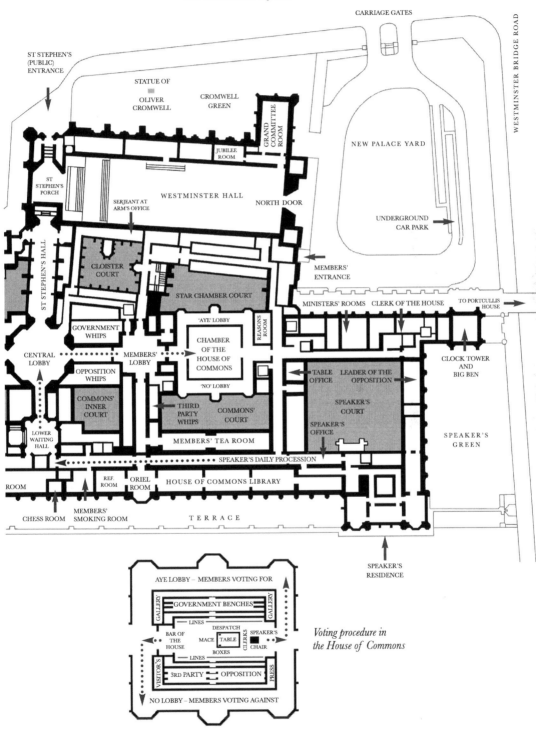

Voting procedure in
the House of Commons

Stages of a Bill in Parliament

The Bill is here assumed to have started in the Commons.
It might equally have been first introduced in the Lords.

P/R *the Bill is here printed or, if amended at this point, reprinted.*

* *Indicates where procedure differs between the Houses.*

House of Commons

FIRST READING

- The short title of the Bill is read out, by the Clerk.

- There is no debate and no vote.

- The Bill is then published in print form and on the internet. **P**

SECOND READING

- A date for this is announced after the First Reading.

- The principle of the Bill is debated without amendments and a vote may be taken.

* A Programme Motion is usually passed to limit time for debate at later stages.

- The debate is printed in Hansard and published on the Internet at: www.parliament.the-stationery-office.co.uk./pa/cm/cmhansrd.htm

COMMITTEE STAGE

- Usually starts two weeks after Second Reading and can take anything from one sitting to several months.

* Bills usually go to Standing Committee but sometimes to the floor of the House.

- The Bill is considered, and can be amended, clause by clause.

* Amendments may be moved subject to the chairman's selection.

- Votes may be taken on each clause and amendment. **R**

REPORT STAGE

- Usually two weeks after the end of the Committee Stage.

- There is a detailed review of the Bill, as amended, on the floor of the House.

- Further changes may be proposed, debated and voted on.

THIRD READING

- An overview by House of the Bill as amended, usually immediately after Report stage.

* Substantive amendments cannot be made.

- A vote may be taken. If the Bill passes its Third Reading it is then sent to the Lords.

House of Lords

FIRST READING

- Formal announcement.

- The Bill is reprinted in the form finally agreed in the Commons. **R**

SECOND READING

- Two weeks after the First Reading.

- There is a debate on the general principle of the Bill.

- * Government Bills included in the election manifesto are, by convention, not opposed at Second Reading, but 'reasoned' amendments, indicating dissent, may be tabled and voted on.

COMMITTEE STAGE

- Fourteen days after Second Reading and often spread over several days.

- * Bills usually go to a Committee of the whole House; but sometimes to Committees off the floor.

- Line by line examination.

- * There is no selection of amendments – all can be considered.

- * There is no guillotine; debate on amendments is unrestricted. **R**

REPORT STAGE

- Fourteen days after the Committee Stage for lengthy or complex Bills.

- Further chance to amend Bill.

- May be spread over several days. **R**

THIRD READING and PASSING

- * Amendments can be made provided that the issue has not been voted on at an earlier stage.

- * Passing: the final opportunity for peers to comment on the Bill.

Both Houses

- In this example the Commons now considers the Lords amendments; unless it accepts them all the Bill returns to the Lords and continues to pass between the two Houses until agreement is reached.

- If either House insists on its amendments, the Bill is normally lost.

If an impasse remains between the Houses the Parliament Act 1949 provides that the will of the Commons can prevail, basically after one year's delay.

ROYAL ASSENT

- When the Queen's assent is formally notified to both Houses the Bill becomes an Act.

- Royal assent has not been withheld since 1707.

All Bills, Acts, amendments and Hansard reports are published on the internet at www.parliament.uk

Committees of the House of Lords

COMMITTEES ON LEGISLATION
and
Delegated Legislation

Most committee stages of Bills are considered in the Chamber: a **COMMITTEE OF THE WHOLE HOUSE**. However individual Bills may be committed to various kinds of select committee. Public Bills may be considered by a **SELECT COMMITTEE**, a **PUBLIC BILL COMMITTEE** or a **SPECIAL PUBLIC BILL COMMITTEE**. These committees are separately appointed for each Bill. The committee stage of a public Bill may also be taken in a **GRAND COMMITTEE**, not a select committee because all Lords may take part; amendments considered in the same manner as a Committee of the whole House, but no division may take place.

The **CONSOLIDATION BILLS JOINT COMMITTEE** has 12 members from each House. The Lords members are nominated by the Lord Chancellor. The committee examines Consolidation Bills to ensure that they do not alter the law.

The **DELEGATED POWERS AND**

REGULATORY REFORM COMMITTEE has 9 members. It has two separate functions: (1) to examine whether the provisions of any Bill inappropriately delegate legislative power, and whether they subject the exercise of delegated power to an appropriate degree of legislative scrutiny; and (2) to examine draft orders and other documents laid before the House under the Regulatory Reform Act, 2001. The first of the functions is not paralleled by any Commons Committee.

Private Bills against which petitions have been deposited are committed to a **SELECT COMMITTEE** of five Lords which hears Counsel and witnesses for the promoters and petitioners. Such a committee meets morning and afternoon, and may meet for several days or even weeks in the case of a controversial Bill.

INVESTIGATIVE SELECT COMMITTEES

The **EUROPEAN UNION COMMITTEE** has 19 members. It scrutinises European Union legislative proposals and may report on other EU matters. Its work is largely undertaken through six sub-committees on which a total of about 70 Lords serve. They are:

A: Economic and Financial Affairs, Trade and External Relations;
B: Energy, Industry and Transport;
C: Common Foreign and Security Policy;
D: Environment, Agriculture, Public Health and Consumer Protection;
E: Law and Institutions;
F: Social, Education and Home Affairs.

The **SCIENCE AND TECHNOLOGY COMMITTEE** has 14 members. It examines issues within the fields of science and technology. Its work is largely undertaken through sub-committees, normally two, reconstituted for each new inquiry.

The **CONSTITUTION COMMITTEE** has 12 members. Its role is 'to examine the constitutional implications of all public Bills coming before the House; and to keep under review the operation of the constitution'.

The **JOINT COMMITTEE ON HUMAN RIGHTS** has six Members from each House. Its role is to consider 'matters relating to human rights in the United Kingdom (but excluding individual cases)' and to undertake functions in relation to remedial orders under the Human Rights Act, 1998.

The **ECONOMIC AFFAIRS COMMITTEE** has 12 members.

The above are sessional committees. In addition, **AD HOC COMMITTEES** may be appointed. In 2001 there were three: *Stem Cell Research, Animals in Scientific Procedures, the Chinook ZD 576 Helicopter Crash.*

SPECIAL COMMITTEES

The **APPEAL AND APPELLATE COMMITTEES** perform judicial functions and membership is restricted to the Law Lords. The Appeal Committees consider applications for leave to appeal, and the Appellate Committees conduct hearings of appeals. Normally three Lords sit on Appeal Committees and five on an Appellate Committee.

Committees of the House of Commons

COMMITTEES ON LEGISLATION
and Delegated Legislation

Most Bills after second reading are committed to a **STANDING COMMITTEE** for detailed examination and amendment. A different group of Members (usually about 18) is appointed for each Bill.

A few Bills, usually of constitutional importance but also including the annual Finance Bill, are committed in whole or part to the **COMMITTEE OF THE WHOLE HOUSE**. This consists of the entire House, sitting in the Chamber, and is a committee in a technical sense only.

Some other types of committee are used occasionally for Bills: **SPECIAL STANDING COMMITTEES**, which can take oral evidence as well as going through the Bill; **GRAND COMMITTEES**, which can consider Scottish, Welsh and Northern Ireland Bills at second reading and (except in the Welsh case) report stage; and **SECOND READING COMMITTEES,** which replace the second reading stage in the House.

There are also **STANDING**

COMMITTEES ON DELEGATED LEGISLATION and **EUROPEAN STANDING COMMITTEES**; the latter consider EU documents recommended for debate by the European Scrutiny Committee. In both cases Members are appointed (for each item of business in the case of delegated legislation), but any other Member may attend and speak (but not vote).

Private Bills against which petitions have been deposited are committed to an **OPPOSED BILL COMMITTEE** of four Members who sit in a quasi-judicial capacity hearing Counsel and witnesses.

SELECT COMMITTEES

There is (broadly) one committee per government department, with the role of examining 'the expenditure, administration and policy' of the relevant department and its 'associated public bodies' (e.g. regulators and quangos). Most have 11 Members appointed by the House for the duration of a Parliament. Some have sub-committees. They determine their own subjects for inquiry, collect evidence in writing and through oral evidence sessions, and make reports to the House, to which the Government subsequently replies.

Other investigative select committees are the **COMMITTEE OF PUBLIC ACCOUNTS**, the **SCIENCE AND TECHNOLOGY COMMITTEE**, scrutinising the Office of Science and Technology, the **SELECT COMMITTEE ON PUBLIC ADMINISTRATION**, examining the work of the ombudsmen and Civil Service matters, and the **ENVIRONMENTAL AUDIT COMMITTEE**, with a cross-cutting remit relating to environmental protection and sustainable development.

Other select committees perform tasks on behalf of the House: these include the **COMMITTEE ON STANDARDS AND PRIVILEGES**, whose most prominent task is assessing complaints against Members, the three scrutiny committees (**STATUTORY INSTRUMENTS, DEREGULATION AND REGULATORY REFORM AND EUROPEAN SCRUTINY**), which report to the House on individual items of legislation; the domestic committees (on matters such as accommodation and works and catering); the **SELECT COMMITTEE ON THE MODERNISATION OF THE HOUSE OF COMMONS**; and the **COMMITTEE OF SELECTION**, which appoints Members to standing committees, and some other committees.

Select committee chairmen meet as the **LIAISON COMMITTEE**, which considers general matters relating to the work of select committees.

Members sometimes sit jointly with Lords in a **JOINT COMMITTEE**, with a remit such as examining a draft Bill or monitoring Delegated Legislation or the operation of the Human Rights Act.

GRAND COMMITTEES

The **SCOTTISH, WELSH** and **NORTHERN IRELAND GRAND COMMITTEES** debate motions and put questions to Ministers relating to the area concerned. They consist of all the Members for that area and in some cases additional Members.

Chronology

294

1957	**HAROLD MACMILLAN (C)**	1990	**JOHN MAJOR (C)**
1958	Life Peerages Act	*1991*	*Gulf War*
1963	Peerage Act	1997	**TONY BLAIR (L)**
1963	**ALEC DOUGLAS-HOME (C)**	*1997*	*return of Hong Kong to China*
1964	**HAROLD WILSON (L)**	1998	Scotland Act
1965	Churchill lies in state in		Government of Wales Act
	Westminster Hall		Northern Ireland Act
1969	*first manned landing on the Moon*	1999	House of Lords Act
1970	**EDWARD HEATH (C)**	*2001*	*Sept 11th attacks on World Trade Center*
1973	*United Kingdom joins the European*		*and Pentagon, USA*
	Economic Community		
1974	**HAROLD WILSON (L)**		
1976	**JAMES CALLAGHAN (L)**		
1978–9	*Winter of Discontent*		
1979	**MARGARET THATCHER (C)**		
	first woman Prime Minister		
1982	*Falklands War*		
1989	*fall of the Berlin Wall*		

Parties of government and coalition
since the beginning of the 20th century:

(C)	**CONSERVATIVE**
(L)	**LABOUR**
(LIB)	**LIBERAL**
(N)	**NATIONAL COALITION**

Bibliography

GENERAL

Cooke, R. *The Palace of Westminster* (Burton Skira, 1987)

Cormack, P. *Westminster: Palace and Parliament* (Warne, 1981)

Johnson, P. (ed.) *Political Anecdotes* (Oxford University Press, 1989)

Jones, C. *The Great Palace* (BBC, 1983)

Jones, C. (ed.) *A Pillar of the Constitution* (Hambledon, 1989)

Laundy, P. *The Office of Speaker* (Cassell, 1964)

Longford, Lord. *A History of the House of Lords* (Sutton, 1999)

Macmillan, H. *The Past Masters* (Macmillan, 1978)

Silvester, C. (ed.) *The Pimlico Companion to Parliament* (Pimlico, 1997)

Smith's Peerage, The House of Lords

Smith's Peerage, The House of Commons

Wild, H. and Pope-Hennessy, J. *The Houses of Parliament* (Batsford, 1953)

Wilson, H. *A Prime Minister on Prime Ministers* (Weidenfeld and Nicolson. Joseph, 1977)

Wright, A. and Smith, P. *Parliament Past and Present,* Vol. 2 (Hutchinson & Co. 1902)

House of Commons Library Documents

Dod's History of Parliament (Hurst Green, 1991)

THE MIDDLE AGES

Besant, W. *Early London; Medieval London*

Brayley and Britton, *The Ancient Palace of Westminster* (John Weale, 1836)

Butt, R. *History of Parliament: The Middle Ages* (Constable, 1989)

Colvin H. M. *History of the King's Works,* Vol. 5 (HMSO, 1975)

Fabyan, *Chronicles* (John Kyngston, 1559)

Gerhold, D. *Westminster Hall* (James & James, 1999)

Hall, H. *Court Life Under the Plantagenets* (Swan Sonnenschein & Co, 1890)

Harvey, J. H. *Henry Yevele* (B. T. Batsford, 1946)

Hastings, M. *Parliament House* (Architectural Press, 1950)

Hastings, M. St. *Stephen's Chapel* (Cambridge University Press, 1955)

Holinshed, *Chronicles*

Lethaby, W. *The Palace of Westminster in the Eleventh and Twelfth Centuries*

Pendrill, C. *London Life in the Fourteenth Century* (Allen & Unwin, 1925)

Powell, J. E. and Wallis, K. *The House of Lords in the Middle Ages* (Weidenfeld & Nicolson, 1968)

Riley, H. T. *Memorials of London Life: Thirteenth–Fifteenth Centuries* (Longmans & Co., 1868)

Saunders, H. St G. *Westminster Hall* (Michael Joseph, 1951)

Sayles, G. O. *The King's Parliament of England* (Edward Arnold, 1975)

Stow, *Chronicles*

Douglas, D. C. (ed.) *English Historical Documents*, Vol. 2, 1042–1189 (Eyre Methuen, 1981)

Chronicle of London 1089–1543

TUDORS AND STUARTS

Ashley, M. *England in the Seventeenth Century* (Penguin, 1977)

Ashley, M. *The Glorious Revolution of 1688* (Panther Books, 1968)

Aylmer, G. E. (ed.) *The Interregnum* (Macmillan, 1972)

Davies, *The Early Stuarts* (Clarendon Press, 1959)

Elton, *Reform and Reformation* (Edward Arnold, 1977)

Elton, *The Tudor Constitution* (Cambridge University Press, 1982)

Fraser, *The Gunpowder Plot* (Weidenfeld & Nicolson, 1996)

Graves, M. A. R. *The Tudor Parliaments* (Longman, 1985)

Hill, C. *God's Englishman* (Weidenfeld & Nicolson, 1970)

Kenyon, J. P. *The Stuart Constitution* (Cambridge University Press, 1986)

Kirk, N. *Parliament and the Glorious Revolution* (HMSO, 1988)

Kishlansky, M. *A Monarchy Transformed* (Allen Lane, 1996)

Neale, J. E. *The Elizabethan House of Commons* (Fontana, 1976)

Neale, J. E. *Elizabeth I and Her Parliaments* (Jonathan Cape, 1957)

Paul, R. S. *The Lord Protector* (Butterworth Press, 1955)

Russell, C. 'Parliamentary History in Perspective 1604–1629' included in Cust, R. and Hughes, (eds.) A. *The English Civil War* (Arnold, 1997)

Sharpe, K. *Faction and Parliament* (Clarendon Press, 1985)

Tomlinson, H. *Before the English Civil War* (Macmillan, 1983)

Wedgwood, C. V. *The King's War* (Penguin, 1983)

Worden, B. *The Rump Parliament* (Cambridge University Press, 1974)

1689–1832

Bentley, M. *Politics Without Democracy* (Fontana, 1984)

Cannon, J. *Parliamentary Reform 1640–1832* (Gregg Revivals, 1994)

Derry, J. *English Politics and the American Revolution* (Dent, 1976)

Gash, N. *Aristocracy and People* (Edward Arnold, 1979)

Halevy, E. *The Liberal Awakening* (Ark, 1987)

Holmes, G. and Szechi, D. *The Age of Oligarchy, 1722–83* (Longman, 1993)

Lenman, B. *The Jacobite Risings in Britain 1689–1746* (Scottish Cultural Press, 1995)

Smout, T. C. *A History of the Scottish People 1560–1830* (Fontana/Collins, 1977)

Speck, W. A. *Stability and Strife* (Edward Arnold, 1977)

Thomas, P. D. G. *The House of Commons in the Eighteenth Century* (Clarendon Press, 1971)

1832–1906

Bond, M. (ed.) *Works of Art in the House of Lords* (HMSO, 1980)

Briggs, A. *Victorian People* (Penguin, 1965; University of Chicago Press, 1970)

Briggs, A. *The Age of Improvement* (Longman, 1979)

Briggs, A. 'The Political Scene' (essay)

Clark, K. *The Gothic Revival* (John Murray, 1974)

Cocks, B. *Mid-Victorian Masterpiece* (Hutchinson, 1977)

Hay, M. and Riding, J. *Art in Parliament* (Palace of Westminster and Jarrold Publishing, 1996)

Hibbert, C. *Disraeli and His World* (Thames and Hudson, 1978)

McCord, N. *British History 1815–1906* (Oxford University Press, 1991)

Thomson, D. *England in the Nineteenth Century* (Penguin, 1978)

1906–2000

Benn, T. *Years of Hope: Diaries 1940–62* (Hutchinson, 1994)

Boardman, H. *The Glory of Parliament* (George Allen & Unwin, 1960)

Clark, A. *Diaries* (Weidenfeld and Nicolson, 1993)

Cole, J. *As It Seemed to Me* (Phoenix, 1996)

Critchley, J. *The Palace of Varieties* (Faber, 1990)

Davis, D. *A Guide to Parliament* (Penguin BBC Books, 1997)

McDougall, L. *Westminster Women* (Vintage, 1998)

Mackintosh, A. *Echoes of Big Ben* (Jarrolds, 1945)

Morgan, K. *The People's Peace: British History 1945–1990* (Oxford University Press, 1990)

Nicolson, H. *Diaries and Letters* (Penguin, 1984)

Sansom, W. *Westminster in War* (Faber & Faber, 1947)

Scott, C. P. *Political Diaries* (Collins, 1970)

Silk and Walters, *How Parliament Works* (Longman, 1995)

Tanfield, J. *In Parliament 1939–50* (HMSO, 1991)

Taylor, A. J. P. *English History 1914–45* (Penguin, 1981)

Glossary

Adjournment Debate: a debate on the question 'That this House do now adjourn', providing an opportunity for a general discussion without a substantive question on which the House has to come to a decision; they often provide backbenchers with an opportunity to raise constituency matters.

Bar of the House: Point within each Chamber beyond which unauthorised people may not go.

Business Statement: an announcement of forthcoming business in the House (usually made on Thursday).

Closure: (C) a motion to end the debate and proceed immediately to a decision even though there are members still wishing to speak; a way of getting the business through and preventing filibusters; needs both a majority and 100 Members in favour to be successful.

Commons Privilege: since the 17th century Bills to raise taxes or authorise expenditure always start in the Commons and cannot be amended by the Lords.

Cross Benches: (L) benches in the House of Lords where Members without Party affiliation sit.

Delegated Legislation: legislative provision made under the authority of a parent Act (which has specified that provision may be made) rather than needing to be set out in an Act of its own; subject to much less parliamentary scrutiny than an Act.

Division: a vote, for and against, registered respectively as Aye and No in the Commons and Content and Not Content in the Lords.

Guillotine: (C) a motion setting out a timetable for debate on a Bill, with 'choppers' to end discussion at certain times; sometimes called programme motions.

Hansard: the word-by-word record of debates in the House and certain Committees (properly the 'Official Report').

Notices and Orders of the Day: (L) future business.

Oath: sworn by new Members before they are able to take their seats.

Opposition Days: (C) the 20 days set aside in each annual Session when Opposition parties can choose the subject for debate.

Order Paper: the document setting out the House's business for the day.

Point of Order: attempts by Members to draw the Speaker's attention to breaches of the House's rules (but often used to make a point).

Private Bills: Bills put forward by organisations outside the House, such as local authorities or companies, seeking legislation for their own benefit rather than changing the general law (and thereby distinct from public Bills).

Private Notice Questions (PNQs): questions tabled after the normal notice period which the Speaker accepts relate to matters which are urgent and of public importance and which he therefore allows to be answered on the day they are tabled; taken after Question Time. In the Lords they are raised after starred questions.

Prorogation: the period (usually a few days in November) between the end of one Session and the start of the next; puts an end to virtually all business, including Bills which have not completed their passage.

Public Bills: Bills put forward by Members of one of the two Houses (whether government ministers or backbenchers) to change the general law.

Private Members' Bills: Bills put forward by backbencher Members; unlike government Bills few of these become law.

Recesses: periods when the House is adjourned and does not sit.

Salisbury Convention: arrangement between the Lords and Commons which ensures that major Government Bills can proceed when the government of the day has no majority in the Lords.

Sessions: the period for which a Parliament lasts (up to five years) is divided into Sessions, which are usually from November to November.

Standing Orders: Each House has its own set of rules (which 'stand' from one Session to another).

Statement: Government statement on important or urgent business.

Statutory Instrument: legislative provision made under the authority of a parent Act rather than set out in an Act of its own.

Steps of the Throne: (L) Place where Members and certain other specified people may sit.

Ten-minute Rule Bill: (C) twice a week after Question Time, a Member may make a short speech seeking the House's permission to introduce a Bill; the Bills rarely make any progress, but members have an opportunity to make a speech on a subject of their own choosing in prime time.

Vote Bundle: (C) the bundle containing the Commons' papers for the day, including the Order Paper.

Whips: Members appointed to indicate to fellow Party members when support will be required; from *Whipper-in*, a hunt official who uses a whip to manage hounds.

Woolsack: (L) the seat of the Lord Chancellor.

Except where indicated, (L): Lords and (C): Commons, terms are used by both Houses.

Index

Page numbers in *italics* refer to illustrations.